Ireland and the Politics of Change

Ireland and the Politics of Change

Edited by
William Crotty and David E. Schmitt

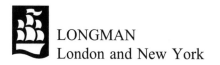
LONGMAN
London and New York

Addison Wesley Longman Limited
Edinburgh Gate
Harlow
Essex CM20 2JE
England
and Associated Companies throughout the world

Published in the United States of America
by Addison Wesley Longman Inc., New York

Visit Addison Wesley Longman on the World Wide Web at:
http://www.awl-he.com

First published 1998

ISBN 0 582 32894 2

British Library Cataloguing-in-Publication Data
A catalogue record for this book is
available from the British Library

Library of Congress Cataloging-in-Publication Data
Ireland and the politics of change / edited by William Crotty and
    David E. Schmitt.
        p.   cm.
    Includes bibliographical references (p.   ) and index.
    ISBN 0–582–32894–2 (ppr)
    1. Social change—Ireland.   2. Ireland—Social conditions—20th
century.   3. Ireland—Politics and government—20th century.
4. Social change—Northern Ireland.   5. Northern Ireland—Social
conditions.   6. Northern Ireland—Politics and government.
I. Crotty, William J.   II. Schmitt, David E.
HN400.3.A8I745   1998
303.4′09415—dc21   98–35479
                                                                             CIP

Set by 35 in 10/12 pt Times
Printed in Malaysia, PP

To Mary and Joan

Contents

Contributors

John Coakley, BA, MA (National University of Ireland) College Lecturer, Department of Politics, University College, Dublin. Secretary General, International Political Science Association; formerly lecturer in politics, University of Limerick. Research interests include Irish politics, comparative politics and ethnic conflict. Select publications: *The Social Origins of Nationalist Movements* (contributing editor; Sage 1992); *The Territorial Management of Ethnic Conflict* (contributing editor; Frank Cass 1993); *Politics in Republic of Ireland* (contributing co-editor; PSAI Press and Folens 1992; second edition 1993).

William Crotty, PhD (University of North Carolina, Chapel Hill) Thomas P. O'Neill Chair in Public Life, Director of the Center for Comparative Democracy and Professor of Political Science at Northeastern University. Research interests include political representation, political parties' democratisation, electoral change and comparative election procedures and policy. He is the author and editor of a number of books, has served as president of several professional organisations and was the recipient of the Lifetime Achievement Award of the political parties' section of the American Political Science Association and the Hubert H. Humphrey Award of the Policy Studies Association.

Tony Fahey, MA (Maynooth College), **PhD** (University of Illinois, Urbana) is a Senior Research Officer at the Economic and Social Research Institute in Dublin. His research interests include religion, the family, family law and demography in Ireland. His most recent book, co-authored with John FitzGerald is entitled *Welfare Implications of Demographic Trends* (Oak Tree Press 1997).

Yvonne Galligan, BA, MA (National University of Ireland), **PhD** (University of Dublin, Trinity College) Lecturer in Political Science, Trinity College, Dublin. Her research interests include public policy, interest groups and women in politics. She has written numerous articles, reports, book chapters and conference papers on the role of women in Irish politics. She is author of *Women in Contemporary Irish Politics* (Pinter 1998) and contributing co-editor of *Contesting Politics: Women in Ireland, North and South* (Westview Press 1998).

Tom Garvin, BA, MA (National University of Ireland), **PhD** (Georgia) Professor of Politics; Head of Department of Politics, University College, Dublin. Alumnus, Wilson Center, Washington, DC; Fulbright Scholar. Research interests include nationalism as an international phenomenon, Irish political history and development. Select publications include *The Irish Senate* (Institute of Public Administration 1969); *The Evolution of Irish Nationalist Politics* (Gill and Macmillan 1981; second edition 1983); *Nationalist Revolutionaries in Ireland* (Clarendon 1987); *1922: The Birth of Irish Democracy* (Gill and Macmillan 1996).

Adrian Guelke, MA (Cape Town), **PhD** (London). Professor of Comparative Politics and Director of the Centre for the Study of Ethnic Conflict, Queens University, Belfast. Formerly Jan Smuts Professor of International Relations at the University of Witwaterstrand, Johannesburg. Research interests include international relations and the politics of deeply divided societies (particularly South Africa and Northern Ireland). Select publications include *The Age of Terrorism and the International Political System* (1995), *Northern Ireland: The International Perspective*. Editor of *The South African Journal of International Affairs*.

Niamh Hardiman, BA, MA (National University of Ireland), **D. Phil.** (Oxon). College lecturer, Department of Politics, University College, Dublin. Formerly Fellow and Tutor in Politics at Somerville College, Oxford. Research interests include the political economy of labour movements, economic policy, and welfare states. Select publications include *Pay, Politics and Economic Performance* (Clarendon Press 1988); and papers in J. H. Goldthorpe and C. T. Whelan (eds) *The Development of Industrial Society in Ireland* (Oxford University Press and the British Academy 1993), C. Whelan (ed) *Values and Social Change in Ireland* (Gill and Macmillan 1994), D. Nevin (ed) *Trade Union Century* (Mercier Press 1994).

Jonathan Haughton, PhD (Harvard University) is an Assistant Professor of Economics at Suffolk University and Faculty Associate at the Harvard Institute for International Development. He has taught at Harvard University, Wellesley College and Northeastern University. His publications include 'Historical Overview' in John O'Hagan (ed) *The Economy of Ireland* (Macmillan 1995) and numerous articles in scholarly journals. He has taught, lectured or undertaken research in almost 20 countries. His most recent work deals with ways to speed the economic recovery of countries emerging from civil war.

Brigid Laffan, BCS (Limerick), **PhD** (Dublin) Jean Monnet Professor of European Politics, Department of Politics, University College, Dublin. Visiting Professor, College of Europe, Brugge; Director European Studies MA; Council Member, Institute of European Affairs, Dublin; advisor in European Union enlargement to Foreign Affairs Committee, Oireachtas. Research interests include governance in the EU, constitution building in the EU, finances and the EU and Ireland and European integration. Select publications include *Integration and Co-operation in Europe* (Routledge 1992); 'The Politics of Identity and Political Order in Europe',

Journal of Common Market Studies (1996); *The Finances of the European Union* (Macmillan 1997); *Constitution-Building in the European Union* (contributing editor, Institute of European Affairs 1996).

Rory O'Donnell, BA, MA, PhD, Jean Monnet Associate Professor of European Business Studies at University College Dublin. His research interests include European integration and social partnership. His recent publications include *A Framework for Partnership* (for the National Economic and Social Forum) and *Negotiated Governance and European Integration* (co-editor, with Joe Larragy; Routledge 1999).

Joseph Ruane, **BA** and **MA** in economics (University College, Dublin), **MA** in anthropology (Cornell University). Lecturer in Sociology and Anthropology, University College Cork. He has published extensively on Irish development and on the Northern Ireland conflict. He is co-author (with Jennifer Todd) of *The Dynamics of Conflict in Northern Ireland: Power, Conflict and Emancipation* (Cambridge University Press 1996).

David Schmitt, PhD (University of Texas, Austin), Edward W. Brooke Chair and Professor of Political Science at Northeastern University. Research interests include the political systems of the Republic of Ireland, Northern Ireland and Canada. Author, editor and co-author of numerous articles and books dealing with political development, ethnic conflict and public administration as well as Northern Ireland and the Republic, including *The Irony of Irish Democracy* (D. C. Heath 1973).

Jennifer Todd, BA (University of Kent at Canterbury), **MA** (Boston University), **PhD** (Boston University), Lecturer in Politics, University College Dublin. Research interests include Northern Ireland conflict, contemporary political theory and political ideologies. She has published extensively on political theory and on the Northern Ireland conflict, including 'Two Traditions in Unionist Political Culture,' *Irish Political Studies* (1987); and *The Dynamics of Conflict in Northern Ireland: Power, Conflict and Emancipation* (co-author with Joseph Ruane; Cambridge University Press 1996).

Christopher T. Whelan, PhD (London University), Research Professor at the Economic and Social Research Institute in Dublin. Research interests include the causes and consequences of social stratification. A leading Irish social scientist, Professor Whelan has published numerous books and articles, including *Social Mobility and Social Class in Ireland* (co-author with Richard Breen; Gill & Macmillan 1996) and *Values and Social Change in Ireland* (editor, Gill and Macmillan 1994).

Preface

This book assesses the fundamental changes in Irish society over the last several decades, changes that have led to a more prosperous, more economically self-sufficient and more outward-looking nation. The areas addressed include: a social profile of Irish citizens over time; the restructuring of the Irish economy and its consequences for the modern Irish state; the evolution of social and religious values and their political ramifications; the role of the Catholic Church and its changing relationship to Irish society and governmental power; political decision-making in Ireland and the quality and representativeness of Irish political institutions; policy formation and impact in areas ranging from social welfare, industrial finance and economic policy to education and religion; the evolving international role of Ireland and in particular its relationship to the European Union; the efforts to promote a lasting peace with Northern Ireland and the changing conception and potential resolution of the divisions present; and the relevance of these developments for appreciating the current Irish state and its contribution to democratic development and economic modernisation.

Our assumption is that considerable social, economic, demographic and international change has taken place within Ireland (and Northern Ireland) and without in relation to the rest of the world, and particularly in response to association with the European Union, that has had a marked influence on politics. We look at institutional developments, economic forces, demographic and attitudinal profiles and group-based (religious, gender, class) concerns as they have evolved and assess their significance for policy enactment and political representation. The focus is on change, where it has occurred (or not occurred), mapping it and evaluating its political implications. We are concerned with the leadership role of government and other political institutions in stimulating, managing and responding to the changes taking place that are of fundamental importance to understanding contemporary politics and today's Ireland in the world community.

The editors would like to thank for their assistance at various points in the development of this volume: Chris Harrison, Publishing Director, Higher Education Division, Addison Wesley Longman; Lynette Miller, Martin Klopstock and Ursula Springham, all of Addison Wesley Longman; Mary Hauch Crotty; Joan Morse;

Molly Crotty; George E. Monroe; Janet-Louise Joseph; Frances Ricker; Marie Arnberg; Joseph McMeekin; James O'Brien; Thomas P. O'Neill, III; Michael Marsh; Jerry Hickey; John Fitzsimons; P. J. Mara; Brian Farrell; Garrett Fitzgerald; Jimmy Smith; Maurice Manning; Eunan O'Halpin; Gary Murphy; Jim Miley; Bridget Simmons; Angie Mulroy; Ruairi Quinn; Kieran O'Mara; Dermott Lacey; James Wrynn; Philip Hannon; Sean Field; Ray Cavenaugh; Mary Ann Burke; Maureen Allen; Tom Simpson; Mary Bowers; Mary Rowley; Brendan Walsh; Michael Doyle; Jim Williams; Jean Brennan; Arthur Guiness; Tom, Helen and Maisie Crotty; Kitty, Paudy, Eimear and Úna Daly; Suzanne Crotty; Marian and Neal Flavin.

To all, we say thank you.

Chapter 1

Democratisation and political development in Ireland

William Crotty

Introduction

Substantial, even radical, change has occurred in the Republic of Ireland. Few if any, a few short decades ago, would have envisioned how far-ranging the changes underway would take the nation; internally in terms of its social attitudes and economic revitalisation and externally in its relations with others in the world community. The distinctive Irish culture and the nation's unique history remain, providing a context and background for the transformation in progress. They also provide a marking point for measuring the extent of what has taken place. In some areas, the evolution has been transformative; in others, more subtle and constrained. Overall, the process, while making substantial gains, has been uneven. Its ramifications and, in particular, its political implications are the focal point for the assessments in this book.

In the economic sphere, Ireland is moving from being one of Europe's 'poor cousins' to a position of equality and, should it continue (and there is little reason to expect otherwise) economic leadership, even relative affluence, in comparison to its European neighbours. Such a prospect after Independence in a rural, resource-poor and farm-based, non-industrial economy would have seemed unimaginable. Economic development along the scale experienced within the time frame realised and with the consequences for individual lifestyles and the nation's psyche sets the Irish experience apart among established democracies in the western world.[1]

The ramifications of the changes underway vary for different sectors of the society. Social attitudes and the corresponding societal structure – the family, views on religion and the proper role of the Church (Whyte 1980; Kenny 1997; Fahey 1994; Hornsby-Smith 1994), a recognition of the full partnership of women in the nation's life – more often than not have undergone a slow, uncertain and frequently painful reassessment. A few key referenda over the years serve to mark the changes underway. Domestically, there have been the successful efforts in 1972 to amend the Constitution to remove reference to the 'special position' of the Roman Catholic Church in the nation's political and cultural affairs (84 per cent approving), the legalisation of divorce in 1995 by the slimmest of margins 50.3 per cent in favour to

49.7 per cent against (after another referendum on the issue had been convincingly defeated in 1986, 68 per cent disapproving) (Girvin 1996). A referendum in 1992 to restrict abortion failed (65 per cent against). Related issues growing out of an abortion controversy that split the nation, guaranteeing a right to travel (a court had denied a raped woman travel to England for an abortion) and a right to information (on contraception and abortions) passed by respective majorities of 62 and 60 per cent, introducing a new era in Ireland in an area of particular contentiousness. Less than a decade earlier (1983), 67 per cent had voted in favour of a resolution to prohibit abortion's legalisation.[2]

In international affairs, the nation had voted overwhelmingly in 1972 to join the European Community (83 per cent), a rejection of Ireland's traditional insularity and a key to its future economic growth; in 1987 to endorse the signing of the Single European Act (70 per cent); and in 1992 to favour ratification of the Maastricht Treaty (69 per cent). These votes, reflecting a more cohesive national will than in domestic areas, helped recast Ireland's role in the European market and the world economy.

Ireland, while aggressively entering the global marketplace, has continued to demonstrate a sensitivity to the concerns of the Third World and a willingness to actively participate in international peacekeeping and relief efforts on a scale matched on a per capita basis by few if any other nations. It has done this while keeping its own military forces small (approximately 12,000). And it has evidenced a new sense of equality and self-confidence in dealing with its neighbour and old adversary, Great Britain, and it has replaced its economic dependence on Britain with trade with its European partners.

The Republic has entered a new phase of cooperation with Britain, symbolised by the Anglo-Irish Agreement of 1985, in dealing with the issue of Northern Ireland. Actively supported by the United States, the two governments have shown a resolve to settle the Northern Ireland problem, instituting processes for the peaceful resolution of the conflict. All sides of the dispute willing to forego violence have been incorporated into the deliberations. A more open and conciliatory relationship built on mutual trust with its once dominant neighbour and oppressor for centuries would have, as in many other areas, seemed most unlikely a few short decades ago. Equally so, the prospect of an acceptable resolution to the Northern Ireland question as well as an end to 'some of the most serious and sustained intercommunal violence experienced anywhere in the industrialised world' (Hayes and McAllister 1996: 61), violence that has claimed over 3,200 lives since 1969. While this has yet to be realised, it would have appeared equally unattainable a generation ago.

Less obvious have been changes in, and pressures on, the structuring and representational capacities of Ireland's political institutions. As examined by David Schmitt in his conclusion and by others in this volume, Ireland's governing machinery and its delivery of services have been challenged by pressures generated from, in particular, associations with the European Union and the demands this has made on the organisational capacity of the Irish government. Basically, it has required a degree of restructuring in the government's ability to deliver services, administer an increasing volume of domestic and cross-national programmes and manage the social transformations underway. The institutions of government are much the same as they have been, not significantly expanded beyond the forms of an earlier age. Governing structures as a consequence are experiencing something of a performance overload, one that calls for attention.

The extent to which a restructuring of the society's institutions has taken place, moving these in the directions of a more rationalised delivery of services, is difficult to measure. In some areas, there are few indications of institutional modernisation – especially in relation to many of the formal agencies of the government – to better meet the demands of a changing society. In others, there is evidence that such a process is underway. These appear to be particularly significant in the development of what could be called the organisation of the civil society, the intermediate agencies of representation within the society, those non-governmental groups and associations positioned between the mass public and the nation's official institutions of policy making, and in the articulation of its political agenda. Such intermediate agencies of group representation are taken to be an indication of the sophistication and continued maturation of a society's democratic impulses.

The least change may be evident in the political parties and the party system, built on issues that divided the nation at its founding (Garvin 1996). Political parties in democratic societies pride themselves on their flexibility and survival instincts, their ability to adapt to changing social conditions and political demands. The major Irish parties (Fianna Fáil and Fine Gael) have demonstrated impressive survival skills; less impressive has been their ability to represent competing class and economic interests or to organise the politics of a newly evolving social order, defining the major issues confronting the nation and providing the leadership needed to address these. Rather, the principal parties have tended to coalesce near the centre of the political spectrum and to compete on the basis of personalism and traditional loyalties. Flexibility, pragmatism, parochialism and patronage have characterised the politics of the parties. Whether this represents a suitable response to more recent domestic and international challenges is an open question.

Democratisation: assessing the evolution of democratic impulses

In the beginning there was the Irish nation as envisioned by its founders, most notably Eamon de Valera, architect of the Constitution and a force in developing Ireland and its political institutions from the birth of the Republic until his retirement in 1959. Addressing the nation by radio on St Patrick's Day 1943, de Valera gave his vision of an the 'ideal Ireland':

> That Ireland which we dreamed of would be the home of a people who valued material
> wealth only as the basis of right living, of a people who were satisfied with frugal
> comfort and devoted their leisure to the things of the spirit – a land whose countryside
> would be bright with cosy homesteads, whose fields and villages would be joyous with
> the sounds of industry, with the romping of sturdy children, the contests of athletic
> youth and the laughter of comely maidens, whose firesides would be forums for the
> wisdom of serene old age. It would, in a word, be the home of a people living the life
> that God desires that man should live. (McLoughlin 1996: 206)

Such a vision may have related to Ireland in the past. However, it appears well removed from contemporary realities; in fact, today's Ireland may well be a virtual reversal of what de Valera intended. Still, the Ireland de Valera struggled to realise gives insight into the country's culture and early goals and provides a background for assessing current developments.

There are many ways of examining processes of political and social change in the Irish Republic and their domestic and international implications, as the chapters in this book make clear. One possibility is to approach Ireland as a case study in democratisation, albeit an unusual and even unique one. The continued maturation of democratic institutions and in the evolution of a more open and modernised democratic culture within the nation are attractive points of focus for such an analysis.[3]

Clearly, the Irish Republic is a democracy of long standing, with established democratic structures, free elections, majority rule, open and inclusive political competition and public discourse, individual rights, government accountability, the rule of law and an equity in resource distribution that would meet any criteria of democratic performance. In effect, this is one reason that Ireland is of such unusual interest. All democracies (all governments for that matter) are in a state of evolution; change (or degrees of change) is a constant. Among the established democracies in the world, Ireland may well have experienced the most accelerated evolution in the shortest time period. The point is arguable given developments in Eastern Europe, the former Soviet Union and in relation to German unification, all fundamentally affected by World War II and the Cold War. This is not the case with the Republic. The evolution, while rapid, was simulated by internal forces in an independent democracy freed of external pressures or control and responding to its own developmental needs. The insular, sectarian, peasant nation once overshadowed and economically dependent on its powerful neighbour and colonial oppressor has emerged in a matter of decades to become an open, prosperous and self-confident world citizen.

> Irish society has changed more in the two decades leading up to the 1990s than in the whole of the previous one hundred years, going back to the Great Famine of the mid nineteenth century. An inward-looking, rural, deeply conservative, nearly 100 per cent Roman Catholic and impoverished country has become urbanized, industrialized, and Europeanized. (Hussey 1995: 1; see also Coakley 1993)

Compare this depiction of Ireland with de Valera's vision. This development constitutes the processes and outcomes we wish to explore, and to do so employing standards familiar to the broader study of democratic development. Among such criteria of democratisation, four have been chosen for analysis in the Irish context. These are:

1 *Economic self-sufficiency and well-being.* A stable economic base in line with a productive economy and a reasonably equitable distribution of wealth is considered by many as critical to democratic longevity. The relationship between economic development/liberalisation (associated in the literature with a free-market, capitalistic economy and the evolution of increasingly democratic form of political representation) has received more

attention than any other in the literature as well as from governments and international lending agencies promoting democratic ends. The contrast evoked is between free-market capitalism and a centrally controlled, state-centred economy, the first argued as being crucial in maintaining a democratic state, the second as inimical to democratic freedoms. The point can be argued, but the debate clearly favours free-market economic emphases.[4]

2   *A strong civil society*. The concept of civil society consists of 'areas of social life – the domestic world, social activities, economic interchange and political interaction – which are organised by private or voluntary arrangements between individuals and groups outside of the direct control of the state' (Held 1995: 181; see also Putnam 1993; Almond and Verba 1965, 1989). Basically, these would include intermediate groups and structures (between the mass public and government decision-makers) that coalesce and focus demands for political representation: trade unions, professional and economic associations, social clubs, women's groups, grassroots and community organisations, among others, would all qualify. Civil society adds a layer of complexity and sophistication to democratic politics and in the process distributes power among a variety of social actors.

3   *Pluralism/tolerance/religious freedom*. Pluralism has its roots in the recognition of diversity within society – including economic, religious, ethnic and racial dimensions. It promotes an acceptance of the differences in beliefs and values within the society and emphasises support for the rights of all individuals to equal political representation and equality before the law. The point may appear fundamental, but an inability to achieve a broad acceptance of the legitimacy of diversity within a state can prove a formidable barrier to full democratic participation.

Tolerance is closely associated with pluralism and 'is valued in liberal democracy, both on moral grounds, as a recognition of equal rights for all citizens, and on pragmatic grounds that the free market of ideas is the best means toward the discovery of "truth" . . . liberal democracy assumes that tolerance will increase as education and the opportunities for widespread, meaningful participation in the political process increase' (Sullivan, Piereson, and Marcus 1982: 24).

One aspect of pluralism and tolerance and a central one in Ireland (and Northern Ireland) is the acceptance of views and behaviour patterns not in line with the dominant religious orthodoxy or ethnic or political objectives.

4   *National autonomy/territorial integrity/political independence*. The argument has been made that to be a fully functioning democratic state, a country must be independent – politically, militarily and economically – of interference from, or undue reliance on, other nations. The relevance for the Irish Republic is in its longstanding, and often tortured, relationship to Great Britain and, more relevant to the present, its efforts (in collaboration with others) to resolve the long-standing controversy over Northern Ireland, a key concern for the nation since its Independence.

To repeat, in exploring these broad issues of democratic representation and development in relation to present-day Ireland, two assumptions bear restating. First, there is no one form or model for a successful democracy; each nation evolves its own version within the context of its history and culture and in line with broad principles of democratic representation. Secondly, political and social change is inherent in society; it is the direction such change takes and its ramifications for a democratic state that are of interest and provide the focal point for examining the political and structural implications such processes have for the Irish nation.

Economic self-sufficiency and well-being

The debate over the proper relationship between economic modernisation – liberalisation as it is frequently referred to – and political development is one of the longest running, most ideologically charged and most exhaustingly argued in the literature on the capacity of individual states to fulfil democratic ambitions. The focus traditionally concerns such issues as: national economic self-sufficiency, seen as the dependency, or independence, of economic development from international control; the concentration of wealth and economic power and the equality of distribution and dispersion of economic resources within the population; the avoidance of excessive polarisation of wealth within a society and the presence of a substantial middle class and the qualities and interests it represents within a democratic forum; the diversification of economic sources of power and wealth; and the nature of the processes for economic decision-making and development, with the polar extremes being state-dominated centralised planning and a capitalistic free-market regime, the latter very much in vogue with international lending agencies representing the world's dominant economies.

For Ireland, economics has proven a spur to greater social equality and international influence. The Republic has evolved a social-democratic model of state expenditures within a broad programme of targeted economic investments in selected industries. The approach has been sustained by governments of both the major parties for almost half a century. It has been coupled with an early recognition of the opportunities offered by both new markets within the European Union, and the investment monies, agricultural subsidies and transfer payments for infrastructure development from the EU that has enabled Ireland to upgrade and compete more effectively with its European partners (see Chapter 9). The consequence is that the nation has experienced an 'economic miracle' comparable to the 'tigers' of Asia ('the Celtic tiger') without the corresponding economic retrenchment and potential collapse recently suffered by economies in Southeast Asia. The evolution from a rural and near-poverty level existence to its current robustness is one of Ireland's, and the world's, economic success stories (see Chapter 2).

Economic development did not happen by chance. It was carefully planned, subsidised and nurtured by a variety of governments. It self-consciously built on the strengths of a strong educational system, an intelligent and hard-working population and an English-speaking nation with access to European markets. Membership in the European Economic Community/European Union magnified its advantages while providing funding aid and, to a degree, guidance for the transformation required.

The policy programmes favoured were neo-Keynesian, an approach now in disfavour among the world's banks and other powerful lenders. Basically this meant aggressive if selective government investment in productive industries, the positioning of the Central Bank to direct investment by commercial banks and substantial (and often controversial) inducements to attract foreign capital.

The results have been impressive. The first (of a succession) of economic plans during the period 1958–63 envisioned a growth rate for the economy of 2 per cent/ year. In fact, this projected rate was doubled, with corresponding increases in other economic indicators (gross national product (GNP), employment opportunities, imports and personal expenditures). One sign of the economic transformation in progress, during the 1960s an estimated 350 foreign companies located in Ireland as the nation enjoyed its most substantial economic growth to that point in its history.

If anything, and despite a degree of unevenness and uncertainty in its development, matters have only improved over time. An analysis published by the Department of Finance of the Irish Government, the focal point for the planned economic development, reported economic growth combined with the GDP up from an average of 5.3 per cent for the years 1991–96 to 7.9 per cent for 1996, the last full year for which data were available (and projected to continue at the same level for 1997). GNP increased from an average of 4.9 per cent for the same period to 6.9 per cent for the year 1996 (and again projected to remain at the same level for 1997). In addition, private consumption and exports were up while consumer prices, the balance of payments, government deficits and unemployment were down, as compared with averages for the years 1991–96. Trends were projected to continue in the same direction for the immediate future. The dominance of information and computer technologies and service occupations over the former economic mainstay, agriculture, was underscored in the government statistics.

The government could report:

> The National Accounts for 1996 show another very strong performance by the Irish economy. GNP growth at almost 7 per cent was once again the highest in the OECD. Despite very strong growth, inflation remained moderate at 1.6 per cent, while the balance of payments remained in comfortable surplus. Strong domestic demand boosted tax receipts so that the General Government Deficit was reduced to less than 1 per cent of GDP . . . the indications are that 1997 is turning out to be another very good year, with GNP likely to grow by about 6.5 per cent. Inflation has been lower than expected – averaging about 1.5 per cent so far . . . With strong economic and employment growth boosting tax revenues, the budget deficit is likely to be well below that projected at the beginning of the year. (Department of Finance 1997: 7)

In short, the government saw a continued growth in GDP and the GNP; a further decline in unemployment, politically the most sensitive economic problem facing the nation; increased consumer spending; a growth in fixed investments; a balance of payments surplus and a strong export market, especially for high-technology industries, a staple of the new economy; low to moderate inflation (2 per cent); and a budgetary deficit of only 0.7 per cent of the GDP. Overall, it is a strong record of performance with projections of a continuity in trends well into the next century. Ireland's rate of growth may well continue to outperform that of its European Union partners.

There are problems, of course. As indicated, unemployment may represent a more pernicious and intractable problem over the long run than the government chooses to admit. There is a clear class dimension to the unemployment. While unemployment was 11.3 per cent for 1996 (and expected by the Department of Finance to drop to 10.3 over the next year or so), it is particularly severe among the less skilled, less highly educated and less well-off sectors of the workforce. Given the nation's emphasis on hi-tech, service-industry development, there is no apparent or easy solution to the problem confronting the more vulnerable groups in society, those least equipped to handle the economic restructuring underway.

Tony Fahey and John FitzGerald conclude:

> The incidence of unemployment in Ireland is exceptionally high and is dominated by long-term unemployment among older men. Their employment prospects are poorer than for other groups partly because they have been unemployed so long (employers are often reluctant to hire those who have been out of work for a long time) and partly because they find it difficult to compete in the labour market with the flood of younger, better educated workers coming into the labour market . . . The difficulty in absorbing this group into employment partly accounts for the expectation that unemployment will remain relatively high in the foreseeable future despite the undoubted growth in labour demand. (Fahey and FitzGerald 1997: 76)

Like many economically successful economies today, Ireland is experiencing a growing gap in income, and associated social values and lifestyles, between the younger, better educated, middle- to upper-middle-class professionals who benefit directly from the economic modernisation and those less well-off, socially and financially. This constitutes a new, and unwelcome, experience for a country that did not previously have significant concentrations of wealth and one that prided itself, for historical and cultural reasons, on the equality (political, economic, social) of its citizenry.

Additionally, there are questions as to the social welfare commitments of the state in the newly emerging economic alignment and the extent to which it is willing to commit resources to health, educational and welfare programmes many once took for granted (see Chapter 7). The international experience has seen an emphasis on government downsizing and a contraction in social welfare expenditures in economies dominated by free-market thinking.

There are no clear or universally accepted solutions to the problems indicated. What can be said is that the government and the political parties in their appeals to voters recognise them and indicate an intention to address them, although in what manner and with what broader goals or long-run programmes remains unclear.

Civil society

'Civil society' refers to the strength of intermediate group associations not connected to the government and intended to represent a variety of interests in a society. A viable, sophisticated and assertive civil society is seen as a precondition for a functioning democracy. The strength of the civil society can be taken as a barometer of the democracy's vitality and long-term stability. The less differentiated in structural terms the social groupings in a nation, the weaker are their collective voices and the more dependent they are on government support and protection, resulting in an increased susceptibility to control. In this situation, the more likely the political system is likely to struggle with its democratic identity and the less likely it is to fully mature. A healthy civil society helps a nation to realise distinctive institutional structure and to establish the boundaries of its governing institutions, thus better achieving the full measure of its democratic development.

Civil society, then, is those non-governmental groups and institutions within a society that focus and direct into politically accessible channels the interests of their constituents. Their key features are their independence from political control; the political space allowed these institutions to evolve and prosper; and the capacity of such agencies to direct member needs into political channels. Organisation translates into power in any society. The independence and vitality of these groups and their ability to frame social issues for political action promotes a pluralism of voices, competition among interests and additional nuance to political representation that strengthens democratic responsiveness and accountability. Professional, economic, trade, labor and civic associations; organised religions; multiple and single-issue groups; fraternal and social organisations; social movements; agrarian collectives and representational associations, environmental movements, as well as other types of organised interests all qualify as components of the civil society under this definition of the concept. Such 'associational autonomy' helps protect civil and political rights, foundations of the liberal democratic state.

Civil society is not, and has not been, a problem in Ireland. If anything, the assumption is that Irish civil society, building on a traditional and more restructured base, has expanded and strengthened considerably in recent decades, coterminous with the nation's economic development and the evolution of associational developments in a more differentiated, complex and stratified social ordering. The difficulty has been in providing the evidence of such change. The impressions are primarily anecdotal and non-measurable, qualitative rather than quantifiable. Nonetheless, the limited evidence available as well as impressions reinforce the picture of a substantial increase in non-governmental associations with representational roles. These appear more diversified in kind and structure, sophisticated and articulate in advocating member interests and politically assertive than at any time previously (see Chapters 6 and 7). If they were not, an unusual contradiction would exist between where Irish society has been historically and where it is now. The assumption is that civil society in contemporary Ireland is one of the strongest elements in the nation's political culture.

All of this is a 'good' in the broad assessment of the quality of the Irish democratic experience. There are, however, cautions. The type of development Ireland has experienced can lead to a corporatist mentality; a strong, mutual interdependence between the state and selected industries in establishing the nation's economic agenda and policies and in prioritizing the groups that benefit the most, a type of decision-making effectively beyond the public's control. And, of course, there is the broader question of the acceptability of political institutions doing business outside of public scrutiny or direct accountability. There is potential for concern in such styles of decision-making that moves beyond an economy of operation and the potential economic gains.

There is the related concern as to who is represented in such decisions allocating preferences and channelling public resources. In what has become the standard for understanding Irish politics, Basil Chubb makes the point:

> Close relationships between government and pressure groups are handy and are becoming more and more essential; but 'to put the matter crudely, a close relationship tends to become a closed one'. Moreover, many of the processes and persons traditionally and commonly associated in the public mind with democratic government and the representation of public opinion – elections, parties, the Oireachtas [Parliament] itself – in truth play a comparatively small part in shaping policy. Much of the activity of policy-making and administration is carried on far from electoral politics . . . much interest-group activity, including that which is most effective, is concentrated where the Oireachtas and the public do not and cannot see it. The increase in the volume and importance of such activity and in particular the development of 'concentration' in corporate structures and processes contribute to a growing isolation of electoral and parliamentary politics from public policy decision-making. (Chubb 1993: 128–9)

It is a situation that has a potential for undermining democratic institutions of consent and the electorate's primacy over policy directions. Such issues have not been deeply explored; they may well hold relevance for a future Ireland. Power, status and wealth can be reinforced through contact with government; alternatively, policy decisions can be made on a redistributive calculus: both are signs – although in differing directions – of the health and impact of civil society.

Pluralism/tolerance/social attitudes and religious values

Pluralism and tolerance are intimately associated: pluralism represents the diversity within a modern democratic state, in effect the dispersal of power among a variety of social and political actors; tolerance is the acceptance of that diversity and of the civil and political rights of all individuals within the society. Both are key components of representative democracy.

John L. Sullivan, James Piereson and George E. Marcus develop the association:

> The liberals . . . saw toleration as a desirable protection of individual autonomy. They also believed toleration, encouraging the open competition among ideas, would allow the 'truth' to emerge . . . The modern liberal . . . believes that a free market of ideas will compel wrong opinion to yield to the power of fact and argument. Suppressed opinions may ultimately be true, whereas the authority claiming infallibility may assert false ideas. Tolerance is to be valued, therefore, on both moral (individual rights) and pragmatic (truth will emerge) grounds . . .
>
> In modern times, the major liberal concern has been to protect the rights of unpopular political groups, since in most modern democracies the right of religious liberty has not been threatened. So although the precise concerns of modern liberalism

differ . . . the grounds for tolerance are essentially unchanged. Tolerance is central in liberal democratic theory, and although it may be legitimately limited, it must be broadly protected in order to preserve the liberal character of society. (Sullivan, Piereson and Marcus 1982: 11–12)

The concept of tolerance as it relates to a democratic state began with the efforts to promote an acceptance of religious toleration and end the repression and persecution of alternative forms of religious worship and thought. From here, it has evolved into a broader emphasis on the freedom, equality and rights accorded all individuals and groups within society.

Religion and society in Ireland

A discussion of social values and movement towards a more open, pluralistic and tolerant society in Ireland must begin with religion and the influence of the Catholic Church historically on government actions and the national conscience. Equally relevant would be the traditional commitment to the Protestant religious associations and related religious and civic practices and the consequences these have had for social developments in Northern Ireland and for North–South relations (see below). Here we begin with the Republic and the once official acknowledgement of the primacy of the Catholic Church, a reflection of Ireland's distinctive, and still significant, religious orientation.

By any comparative measure, Ireland is a religious nation. It is also a Catholic nation, 'the most orthodox Catholic country in the world' (Hussey 1995: 373).

The most visible, and contentious, symbol of this association was Article 44 in de Valera's 1937 Constitution which acknowledged 'the special position' of the Catholic Church and recognized it 'as the guardian of the Faith professed by the great majority of the citizens'. The same article went on to state: 'Freedom of conscience and the free profession and practice of religion are, subject to public order and morality, guaranteed to every citizen.' It was not enough. For many, inside Ireland and out, the Constitution served to reinforce the political as well as religious primacy of the 'one, true Church' and to re-emphasise the strong traditional association between 'Irishness' and Catholicism (see Chapters 5 and 8). The provision was removed from the Constitution by referendum in 1972, with 84 per cent of those voting favouring the change.

Dermot Keogh identifies the factors that 'enabled the Catholic Church to mould a strong influence over the shaping of the dominant philosophy of the Irish state and over the legislation of that state' (Keogh 1996: 94). These included:

- the early and close association between the Catholic Church and the nationalist movement under British rule
- the role the Church played at the centre of Irish life and as the conservator of Irish culture prior to independence
- the influence of the Church in establishing the early Irish State and legitimising its existence

- the impact of the Church in educating generations of Irish people, including the nation's leaders
- the development of a 'populist Catholicism' in rural areas, close to the people and their concerns and often opposed to higher authorities and outside influences
- the development of a national corporate structure and identity by the Catholic Church provided it with an increased force, cohesiveness and authority in national life
- a shared vision between Church and national leaders in Ireland's formative years – 'the building of a State based on the philosophy of Catholic nationalism.' (Keogh 1996: 4)

In addition to these factors, over 90 per cent of the population in the Republic identify as Catholics. The ties between Church and government and the Church and the Irish people have been unusually strong and, for generations, resilient. More recently, and beginning generally in the 1960s, the perception of the proper role of the Church in society and in its relation to political authorities has moved from being questioned to, at times, coming under assault. The reasons are many and basically relate to the changing nature of Irish society. They also relate to media reports and official investigations into revelations of abuses among the clergy (sexual misconduct, corporal abuses of children and patients in Church-run institutions, such as orphanages, hospitals and schools). Vatican II provided an impetus for a redefinition and reassessment of the Church's place in Irish society, as has the opening of Ireland to broader influences from Europe and elsewhere. One measure of the change is the significant decrease in vocations; the Catholic Church is not recruiting clergy in anywhere near the numbers it once did: 'The Irish people are emerging from centuries of unquestioning loyalty to the Catholic Church to face a world full of uncertainties. Their dominant Church struggles to come to terms itself with a changing country and its changing people' (Hussey 1995: 395).

While the role of the Catholic Church is changing, the religious commitments of the Irish people remains strong. The 1990 European Values Survey compared the Irish State with Catholic practices in Northern Ireland and other European nations (Hornsby-Smith and Whelan 1994; Chapter 4 in this volume). Some findings: Irish Catholic religiosity is substantially more pronounced than that of Catholics in other European nations; Irish Catholics attend religious services with significant regularity; and they are more likely to accept the traditional teachings of the Church, from a belief in heaven and hell to the resurrection of the dead and life after death. The Catholic population of the other European nations do not approach the Irish in the intensity of these beliefs.

In relation to the areas considered appropriate for the Catholic Church to exercise its influence, there is less conflict in the views that emerge as they relate to moral, family and spiritual concerns, but the Irish (even more so than other European Catholics) draw the line on social problems. In a related question, an average of 75 per cent of the Catholics in the Republic feel it proper for the Church to speak out on issues ranging from Third World conditions and social and other forms of discrimination to homosexuality, but only 36 per cent would extend this tolerance to government policy.

If anything, the Catholic community in Northern Ireland, while attending mass with less regularity, is more traditional and conservative in its support for such Church teachings as the presence of the devil and hell; they are therefore more out of line than Catholics in the Irish State are with Catholics in other European nations. They are also more accepting of Church guidance on a range of problems, with particular emphasis on family life and social concerns than are either Catholics in the Republic or the rest of Europe. The conservatism of their positions and the general absence of movement towards a greater openness and flexibility appears consistent with a broad range of social attitudes held by Protestants and Catholics in Northern Ireland more generally (Dowds, Devine and Breen 1997).

What to make of such findings? In a survey (1988–1989) that explored issues related to those discussed above by Christopher T. Whelan and associates (see also Chapters 3, 5 and 8 in this volume), Micheál MacGréil (*Prejudice in Ireland Revisited*, 1996) found that the common identity between Catholics and Protestants in relation to other citizens was much the same as it had been in an earlier survey (1972–73); that most attitudes remain basically consistent with the earlier study; that there had been a minor strengthening of cross-border religious identification; and there was a small increase in the North among Protestants who saw themselves as more Irish than British (while the majority of Northern Protestants still saw themselves as closer to the British).

Religious toleration and the acceptance of a diversity of positions, beliefs and practices of worship is not widespread. It does, however, appear to be evolving. Religious views are affected by demographic variables such as age, social class, occupation, education, gender and urban-rural residency with generally the younger, better educated and those of higher social status indicating a greater distancing from conventional Catholic teachings. Still, by these indices, the secularisation of Irish society, while slow, is apparent among certain social groupings. Michael P. Hornsby-Smith and Christopher T. Whelan, in summarizing these forces, write:

> Church attendance in Ireland, adherence to traditional religious values and levels of religiosity remain remarkably high by western European standards . . . the Catholic Church can take satisfaction from the extent to which Irish society has remained insulated from secularisation influences. It does, however, face problems, if of rather different kinds, at both ends of the class hierarchy and among the younger cohorts. It also has to confront the fact that confidence in its ability to provide solutions to problems in a variety of areas is relatively low and has declined over the past decade. At the same time there is clear majority support for the view that it is appropriate for the church to speak out on a wide range of social and moral issues. The evidence relating to the younger cohorts does suggest the possibility that, after a time lag of some decades, Irish Catholics will be seen to come significantly closer to western European norms. (1994: 43)

The process, as the authors caution, is not inevitable. It does however appear to be under way.

Social attitudes in Ireland

The Irish tend to be more conservative and authoritarian, on average, than their European cousins. They also take a greater pride in their country and their social institutions than people in other European countries. As examples, and calling on data from the 1990 European Values Survey as reported by Whelan and associates, 78 per cent of the Irish are 'very proud' of their nationality compared with a European average of 38 per cent. They also have more confidence in their political and social institutions (excepting the legal system and the media) than the average European. An extraordinary 85 per cent take pride in their police (as against a European average of 65 per cent).

Political and social views reinforce the picture of a more conservative, traditional and less cosmopolitan citizenry. The Irish are more conservative-to-moderate and significantly less leftish politically than their neighbours. In relation to ideological self-placement, a questioning of institutions of authority and sexual permissiveness, they score as substantially more conservative than other Europeans. Only on measures of economic liberalism do they approach the European norm. They give less support to free speech protections, have considerably greater respect for authority in general and favour clear and absolute guidelines as to good and evil. And they are more likely to believe that political change is moving too rapidly, again all in comparison with the averages for European countries as a whole.

Various aspects of authoritarianism and its role in Irish society have been assessed by David E. Schmitt (see Chapter 12) and by others. Whatever its less democratically useful aspects, by reinforcing authority through the institution of the Church can be said to have had a positive impact in underpinning an early acceptance of, and continued support for, the state. The Church also reinforced the early state by fulfilling many of its educational and social-welfare responsibilities. In general, authoritarian attitudes do appear stronger in Ireland than in most other Western democracies. As with the other measures and indicators of social values, there is a substantial difference in acceptance and support by social grouping, with age (younger cohorts) and education (those with more formal schooling) in particular predictors of less rigid attitudes.

The family and the role of women

An emphasis on the primacy of the family and the role of women within a traditional family structure as nurturer, mother and wife have been dominating themes in Irish cultural life. The Constitution of 1937 (Article 41) leaves little doubt about the mother's role: '. . . the State recognizes that by her life within the home, woman gives to the State a support without which the common good cannot be achieved' and 'The State shall . . . endeavour to ensure that mothers shall not be obligated by economic necessity to engage in labour to the neglect of their duties in the home.'

A series of laws and church decrees discouraged or banned outright everything from divorce and contraception to recruiting married women for the public service, provocative dress and close dancing. The picture could be grim:

> For almost thirty years after the Constitution was adopted, the position of women in Irish society hardly changed at all. The litany of deprivation is long and almost incredible today. Laws based on the premise that women's rights were inferior to those of men stayed on the statute books. Women were kept in the home by various means . . . It was virtually impossible for the battered wife to get her husband out of the home, while if she fled, her husband had a right to damages from anyone who enticed her away, harboured her, or committed adultery with her (she was considered his property). Women with real crisis pregnancies died, suffered mental and physical ill-health, were ostracized from society, or resorted to the dangerous and criminal activity of backstreet abortions . . . until 1965, a wife could be disinherited totally by her husband. Women were not entitled to unemployment assistance. The social-welfare system treated women only as dependents of males, even giving children's allowances to the father and not the mother. (Hussey 1995: 420)

Clearly, the situation has begun to change, although progress in many areas has been slow (Galligan 1993). Most dramatically, the election as President of the outspoken feminist and humanitarian, Mary Robinson, in 1992 and her successor, Mary McAleese, a professor of law from Northern Ireland (in itself, an example of changing times) and feminist as President of the Republic in 1997 provides a broad gauge of the changes in attitudes. Both the beginning of the women's movement and the entrance into the European Union has meant a conformity to laws equalising employment opportunities and pay and an emphasis on greater protection for the women's status in society. The feminist movement begun in the 1960s has drawn attention to issues long neglected or ignored of concern to women and, along with the more general trends in the secularisation of the society, has resulted in advances (see Chapter 3). Still, as Yvonne Galligan points out in Chapter 6, the gains have been uneven, with the number of women elected to public office one indicator of the work yet to be done.

Social attitudes relevant to women and the family are, in themselves, perhaps as good a gauge as is available to the pull of traditional views, the pressure to adapt to a modernising society and the contradictions that exist. These concerns go to the heart of a traditional society in Ireland and its struggle to transform itself (Hornsby-Smith and Whelan, 1994; Whelan *et al.* 1994; Chapters 3, 4 and 6 in this volume). Despite the recent referendums on the subjects, Irish acceptance of divorce and abortion are well below levels for other European nations (ratios of one-half to one-third the support levels in the other countries). The Irish are much less sympathetic in allowing for conditions under which abortions can be performed, averaging a little over a 25-point difference between themselves and other Europeans in the scenarios presented. On the other hand, European and Irish attitudes are generally comparable in relation to women's employment, with the highest discrepancies resulting over the effect a working mother has on children and the belief that being a housewife is as satisfying as participating in the workforce. On both issues, the Irish support the more traditional position (by an average 15 percentage points).

Christopher T. Whelan and Tony Fahey, who conducted this particular analysis of data from the European Values Study, report that overall '. . . while Irish attitudes are not significantly more traditional than European views, the pattern of results does point to the continuing influence of values that underpin sex role differentiation' (Whelan and Fahey 1996: 51–2).

Social characteristics again indicate different levels of support for the traditional perspective of the family. Gender – males of all ages tend to be more conservative on these issues, women more supportive – women's employment, age (the younger are more in favour) and education (those with more formal education are more in favour) influence views. The polar extremes are represented by less educated males, over 60 years of age and unemployed as against younger, highly educated, professional women, who strongly favour women's equality. The views held by the younger and better educated can be taken as an indication of the direction the society is heading in.

To conclude, social change is taking place in Ireland and it has proceeded faster over recent decades than many would have thought possible. The change in social attitudes has been uneven, impacting social groupings and traditional commitments differently. The role of the Catholic Church is in transition, its once formidable influence weakened. The Republic of Ireland remains heavily Catholic; it is a country with a long history of support for the Church, and one that continues to show a strong sense of religious commitment. The role of women is also in flux. In broad perspective, social attitudes are supportive of a more tolerant, less rigid and more open society. This appears to be an indication of the future direction of the society, given the views of younger, more affluent and professional groups in comparison to those of the oldest cohorts in the society. Ireland, as in the economic sphere, is in the process of moving closer to the European norm on most issues, giving evidence of an increasingly secularised and pluralistic society. Micheál MacGréil sees the country as moving towards 'the creation of a [more] peaceful and just Irish society based on [an] integrated pluralism' (1996: 289). It is a worthy goal and the direction the Irish state appears to be embracing.

National autonomy/territorial integrity/political independence

Democratic development assumes a nation independent of foreign influences, free to make its own political and economic decisions and develop its own governing institutions. Initially, this often meant freedom from rule imposed by other nations and an end to colonialism, concerns particularly relevant to the Irish situation in its struggle for independence. It also means a level of economic independence and the ability of a country to function as a stable, self-sufficient and vital member of the world community.

None of these concerns are problems of consequence for present-day Ireland. In effect, these issues were resolved generations ago. What is of concern, a by-product of Irish history, its long struggle against rule by Great Britain and its peculiarly Roman Catholic culture, is its relations with Northern Ireland. The division between North and South, for some, symbolises the unfinished fight for Irish freedom and represents a nation still not geographically or politically whole. For others, it is a matter of religious and cultural differences, economic well-being and a long and beneficial association with Great Britain, the nation many in the North see themselves as part of (see Chapter 11).

The broader consequence is that the Irish state is placed in an unusual position, effectively pulled in two directions simultaneously. In many respects, Ireland is the prototype of a country that has benefited enormously from the new world economic order, the globalisation of trade and markets and the supra-national regional development of economic and political blocs – in this case the European Union. Ireland has prospered under these conditions, fully exploiting the economic opportunities offered. This is in stark contrast to its more hesitant and suspicious neighbour, Great Britain.

Ireland, as indicated earlier, voted to join the European Economic Community (as it was then known) in 1972. Since that decision, it has aggressively sought the resources needed to modernise its infrastructure and streamline its economy, and it has subsequently positioned itself well to compete effectively in the information age. Between 1994 and 1999, Ireland has been scheduled to receive 6 billion Irish pounds in transfer funds from the European Union for structural improvements (roads, schools, harbour facilities), job creation and training programmes, transportation improvements and related programmes and in agricultural subsidies to improve productivity and encourage exports, as well as funds to safeguard and rebuild its environment. By the end of 1995, the total net transfers to Ireland since joining the EEC/European Union amounted to 18.45 billion Irish pounds. One side-effect of this association with the European Union has been a decreased emphasis on trade and a lessened economic dependence on Great Britain, until recently Ireland's principal economic partner (see Chapter 2).

The entrance into the European Union has had psychological as well as economic advantages for Ireland, seriously affecting its sense of identity. A White Paper published by the Department of Foreign Affairs in reviewing the association commented that EU membership allowed the Irish state to 'best pursue its economic and social development' and it offered Ireland 'the best prospect for the protection and promotion of [its] living standards'. A second rationale was that it allowed the country 'to participate with other democratic and like-minded countries in the movement towards European unity'. The consequences, in addition to the economic gains, fundamentally affected Ireland's conception of herself: The 'Irish people increasingly see the European Union not simply as an organisation to which Ireland belongs, but as an integral part of the future. *We see ourselves, increasingly, as Europeans*' (Department of Foreign Affairs 1996: 58–9, italics added).

This is the new Ireland, prosperous, self-confident and forging new links in an emerging world economy: Ireland the success story (Keatinge and Laffan 1993: also see Chapter 9).

On the other hand, there is the backward pull of history; the Irish nation remains caught up in the question of Northern Ireland. In effect, its time as a focal point for national anxiety and self-identity has come and gone. The issue, while still contentious and emotionally charged for some and in need of peaceful resolution, no longer dominates national debate. The mechanisms are in place for a resolution of the problem – one unlikely to fully satisfy any group – and the prospects for an end to the controversy, while always uncertain, are stronger now than at any previous point in time. Clearly, both the Irish and English governments would like to broker some type of agreement and the vast majority of people in both North and South would welcome an end to the violence. Whether these conditions will prove enough to bring about a permanent settlement to the conflict can only be considered problematical.

The question of Northern Ireland

The outlines of the conflict are well known. The underlying strains have festered for centuries, reinforced and kept alive by tribal rituals in an ethnically segregated society.[5] The tensions are periodically reinvigorated by historical events: the Irish struggle for independence and the birth of the Irish State in the 1920s legally recognising the division; the adoption of a new Irish Constitution in 1937 and with the primacy given the Catholic Church; the civil rights disturbances and the beginning of the 'Troubles' in the North and the introduction of British troops in the late 1960s; the violence of 'Bloody Sunday' in Derry (1972) and the repression of the 1970s; the hunger strikes in Long Kesh in the 1980s; and the continued violence, sporadic killings and retaliations of the 1990s.[6] All these serve to rekindle old hatreds and to subvert the persistent efforts at reconciliation (Ruane and Todd 1996: see also Chapters 10 and 11).

John Whyte, in his influential study *Interpreting Northern Ireland* (1996), identifies the forces contributing to a community divide in Northern Ireland. These include:

1   A society largely segregated along religious lines.
2   Religion which provides a basis for social and religious conflict.
3   A majority Protestant community more fragmented than the minority Catholic community, divisions that foster increased Protestant insecurity.
4   Different levels of economic opportunity and prosperity for Catholics and Protestants. Catholics see this as a result of discrimination, an explanation Protestants refuse to accept.
5   Conflicting national identities: most Catholics see themselves as Irish, most Protestants (although less certain about their identity) British.
6   Contrasting political agendas and agencies of representation. Most Protestants oppose a united Ireland, most Catholics favour it (but with less degree of certainty). The opposing groups have their own distinctive political parties and political representatives.
7   Perceptions of the security forces and legal system are polar extremes, a division stronger even than that over constitutional issues such as affiliation with Britain or Ireland.

8 While a range of opinions are present in both countries, the moderate are held hostage to the minority extremists.

9 Psychological factors reinforce other divisions, moving the intensity of feelings beyond that justified by real-world assessments. This factor operates with particular force in the concern over national identification and is more of a problem for Protestants, whose identities are weaker.

10 A 'double-minority' model helps explain the intensity and intractability of divisions. Both communities see themselves as the minority, fearful of oppression by the other.

If this were not enough, and to add to the complexity of the situation, there are the research findings of political scientist Richard Rose. Rose undertook a massive series of over 12,000 interviews in Northern Ireland in the late 1960s, concluding these immediately prior to the explosion of the 'Troubles' and the ensuing violence that further polarised the Catholic and Protestant communities. Published in 1971, the results continue to have relevance for understanding the depths of the conflict. Ironically perhaps, Rose concluded that generally the two communities disagreed little on the vast majority of issues they confronted in everyday life – family, economic and community concerns. However, they could not agree on fundamental political questions relating to the nature of the state.

In addition, a confusion as to approach existed within the communities and among even the most committed ideologues on both sides, adding another level of complexity:

> The fragmentation of Unionists when confronted with civil rights challenges, and the fragmentation of Catholics when confronted with Protestant resistance jointly emphasize that polarization on matters concerning the regime does not mean that those at each extremity are united. Instead, they are dispersed . . . this fragmentation carries autonomy to the point of confusion. It characterizes armed political groups as well as non-violent parties. As Ultra [Protestant Unionist extremists] and IRA [Irish Republican Army] groups have demonstrated, fragmentation is no obstacle to sporadic, localized and intense expression of anti-regime views. (1971: 325)

Further, and disconcertingly, Rose believed that bringing the two communities together in ordinary and non-political ways 'will *not* lead to a reduction in political discord' due to the basic nature of the political values in dispute (Rose 1971: 325).

John Hume, the moderate mainstream leader of Northern Ireland's Social Democratic and Labour Party (SDLP) and possibly the North's and the Catholic community's most respected international spokesman, in referring to what he calls 'this bitter land' adds another dimension. As he sees it:

> . . . the British government had no policy on Northern Ireland. There had been an abject failure to face up to the causes of the problem, to engage the principal parties to the conflict in realistic negotiation about the future, to identify British interests, or to develop a purposeful government strategy for solving the problem . . . This failure had led to the deadly impasse which paralysed us for so long, the net result being to embroil Britain in a long-term military commitment in which she had no vital interest commensurate with the expenditure of money and lives involved. (1996: 105–6)

Hume's solution is to offer 'patient political negotiation'. The approach is 'undramatic, unspectacular' but it appears to be the reasonable way out of the endless cycles of violence and conflict (Cunningham 1997). It appears also to be the approach being taken at present (Bew and Gillespie 1996).

The most recent negotiations over Northern Ireland's status were given impetus by the Anglo-Irish Agreement of 1985, acknowledging that the Irish state had a legitimate interest in the affairs of Northern Ireland and stipulating, on behalf of both governments, that any institutional changes would be implemented only if approved by a majority vote of the electorate of Northern Ireland (Crotty 1997; Schultze 1997). The negotiations have been chaired by George J. Mitchell, former US Senator from Maine and the Democratic Party's Majority Leader in the Senate, and backed by the governments of Ireland, Britain and the United States. They have involved the balance of interests in the North (the Reverend Ian Paisley and his Democratic Unionist Party are among the holdouts), including David Trimble of the Ulster Unionist Party and their polar opposites, Gerry Adams, president of Sinn Féin, the political wing of the Irish Republican Army (Cochrane 1997; Cooke 1996; and Adams 1995, 1997).

The outline of the basis for a long-term settlement has emerged. Essentially, these call for a variety of collective arrangements for North–South cooperation and for collaboration among the governments of Ireland, Northern Ireland and Britain on a variety of issues. These include a regional legislature to govern the province (replacing direct British rule); a council of ministers from Northern Ireland, the Republic of Ireland and Britain to manage across-border concerns (tourism and agriculture are examples); and an intergovernmental body of officials from Britain and the Irish Republic to consult on governing issues relating to the North. The agreement that has emerged from the five-year peace effort was ratified by voters in both the North and South and is now in the process, to a degree in itself experimental, of being implemented.

Accommodation, cooperation, reasoned argument, compromised goals, all call for a sense of commitment and a degree of restraint – as well as a rethinking of cultural issues, political lines of authority and national identities – that will test the determination of the governments and parties involved to end once and for all a conflict with deep historical roots and, it would appear, a never-ending series of present-day challenges.

Political parties and the party system in Ireland

The structured cleavages that gave birth to the Irish party system – the pro-(Fine Gael) and anti-(Fianna Fáil) Treaty positions of the 1920s – are the same ones that serve as the basis for the party divisions today. The result is a traditional party system built on issues from another era that are no longer compelling. It is a system identified with and legitimised by its contributions to associations with the nation's founding, historically rich in association and surviving on personalism (in candidate appeal and positioning within the electorate) and patronage rewards as incentives for continuing loyalty and support. In many respects, it is a curious situation and represents an apparent disconnection for a nation that has burst on the international scene as the embodiment of a future-oriented, carefully managed model for the coming age of cross-national economic and political interdependence.

It is a party system conspicuous for its flexibility and pragmatism in its approach to positioning itself on policy matters – especially evidenced in the major parties and their coalition partners in elections – and localised and even parochial in its outlook and appeals. By themselves, these features are not necessarily bad. Combined with the forces that framed its birth and its failure to adapt to anything corresponding to the cleavages dividing the modern democratic parties, it may be a party system increasingly out of touch with the social changes in progress and the demands of the new global order that has engaged the country.

These qualities – deficiencies, perhaps – were present in the 1996 election. Differences in party positions, from economic development to addressing social inequities, can be difficult to detect (see below), with both parties drifting towards the middle ground on most major issues and leaving the voters' decision to the pull of ancient loyalties and the perception of the candidates' personal appeal. The one issue that did draw clear differences in approach (although not necessarily in ultimate objectives) was the manner in which the Northern Ireland question was addressed. Incumbent Taoiseach John Bruton and Fine Gael favoured a more moderate emphasis on full cooperation with the Conservative British government of the day. Bertie Ahern, the Fianna Fáil party leader and its candidate for Taoiseach, took a more direct and implicitly nationalistic tone towards the deliberations over Northern Ireland. The positions taken reflect, of course, the historical concerns of the two parties. Even then, the differences were more in tone and emphasis than in policy direction; to an extent they served as a substitute for basic discussions of approaches to contemporary social issues.

Within this context also, the third and minor parties that evidence a firmer commitment to policy goals in their manifestos – Labour, the Greens, the Progressive Democrats, the Democratic Left and the Workers' Party – have shown a marked tendency in recent elections to deemphasize, or modify, their issue commitments when opportunities arose to enter governing coalitions with Fine Gael or Fianna Fáil. Equally of concern, the negotiations over collaboration – the issues to receive attention, the ministerial posts to be awarded – take place, out of necessity, beyond public scrutiny and with little obvious acknowledgement of the interests of the voters who supported (or who are projected to endorse) the coalitional parties' agreements. The decisions are made in personal negotiations between party representatives based on a calculus as to what is needed to win. The process, in itself, is not unusual. When operating within a party system less credentialled in representing the current needs of an electorate, it could be a matter of concern, one that delays the readjustments in patterns of support and issue appeals that may be needed to reconstitute the system along lines more relevant to the contemporary political context.

It is, in short, a party system that has lost its *raison d'être*; one that has moved well beyond the concerns that historically defined its mission. As the generations

Table 1.1 Major Party Competition: Fianna Fáil and Fine Gael, 1922–92

	Popular vote (per cent)		Seats in dail (number)	
Period	Fianna Fáil	Fine Gael	Fianna Fáil	Fine Gael
Pre-1932	27.6	35.9	45	58
Post-1932	45.8	30.5	74	48

pass, the stimulus that produced the original structural cleavages fades in memory and intensity. It may be a party system undergoing a process of deinstitutionalisation, one less in touch with the changes taking place in an electorate in transition. In general, there is a lag in institutional development between the social demands pushing for attention and a stasis built on responding to the pressures that created the initial organisation and best explain its structure and operations. The Irish party system may presently be in just such a developmental stage.

Party competition

As the foregoing would suggest, two political parties have dominated the nation since its inception: Fianna Fáil, the party of Eamon de Valera, Charles Haughey and Bertie Ahern, the current Taoiseach, and the party born of opposition to the Treaty of 1922, and Fine Gael, the pro-Treaty party of William T. Cosgrave, Garrett FitzGerald and the former Taoiseach, John Bruton (Maye 1993) historically are the major contenders for public office. In point of fact, the dominant party electorally in the nation since 1932 (and a reversal of outcomes from the period 1922–32) has been Fianna Fáil, averaging 46 per cent of the vote and 74 per cent of the seats in the Dáil to Fine Gael's 31 per cent of the vote and 48 per cent of the seats in the Dáil (Table 1.1).

Party ideology

In terms of ideology, while there are relevant differences, Fianna Fáil and Fine Gael tend to group towards the centre of the political spectrum. Labour and the minor parties (most more political factions than political parties) such as the Democratic Left, the Green Party and the Workers' Party are to Fianna Fáil's left, with the most liberal party in this context being Sinn Féin. On the conservative side, the small Progressive Democrats are to the right of Fine Gael. Richard Sinnott has provided a spatial analysis of the competing party positions, concentrating on such policy commitments as tax cuts versus social services, views on Northern Ireland and social issues such as homosexuality and abortion. An approximation of his analysis would show the parties scaled on a left–right continuum as follows:

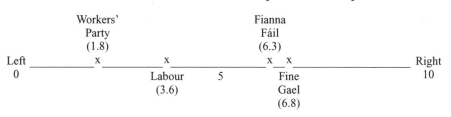

Figure 1.1

Sinnott examined the manifestoes of the various parties and concluded:

> The picture of Irish party competition that emerges from this analysis is notable first of all for the considerable overlap between the appeals of the parties . . . it emerges that seven of the ten most frequent themes in Fianna Fáil and Fine Gael election manifestoes were common to both parties. The seven themes were social group interests, productivity, expansion of social services, government authority, governmental efficiency, enterprise and national effort. Furthermore, five of the above themes also occurred in Labour Party manifestoes. (Sinnott 1995: 70)

Sinnott asks the question of immediate concern: 'Does this mean that Irish political parties are all identical?' His answer:

> No, but it does mean that the differences are differences of degree and of emphasis rather than outright conflict. The differences arise both because the parties put a different order of priority on the themes they share, and because there are themes that are specific to each party. The themes emphasised by Fianna Fáil and not by Fine Gael were defence of the Irish way of life, law and order and Irish unity. In their place Fine Gael emphasised social justice, economic orthodoxy and a controlled economy. The two Labour themes were not shared by either of the other two parties were freedom and democracy and quality of life. (1995: 70–1)

One indicator of the pragmatism, flexibility or shapelessness, each depending on your perspective, of the party alliances is the election of 1996. Recalling Sinnott's spatial placing of the parties on an ideological continuum, the coalitions that evolved challenge explanation except in terms of the party leaders' judgements as to short-run electoral advantage. One party coalition united Fianna Fáil with the Progressive Democrats (not on Sinnott's scale), a newer minor party with a limited appeal built along the policy lines of Margaret Thatcher's Conservative Party of the 1980s in Britain. It was the most conservative party of those running. This coalition proved to be the winner. The losing coalition, the 'Rainbow Coalition' as it was called, matched the slightly more conservative other major party, Fine Gael, with the liberal Labour Party and the even more liberal minor party (or faction), the Democratic Left, an offshoot of the old Workers' Party. It is difficult to explain such alignments on the grounds of compatible ideologies, complementary policy programmes or coalitional cohesion. They do serve to symbolise the state of the modern party system.

Table 1.2 Social basis of party support, 1996 (per cent)

		Fianna Fáil	Fine Gael	Labour
I.	Gender			
	Male	37	22	9
	Female	40	18	8
II.	Age			
	18–24	38	16	13
	25–34	42	18	4
	35–49	40	18	7
	50–64	30	25	13
	65+	41	26	7
III.	Education Level			
	I (ABC1) least	34	21	7
	II (C2DE)	40	14	10
	III (F1)	39	41	4
	IV (F2) most	40	30	9
IV.	Residence			
	Urban	36	17	7
	Rural	41	25	7
V.	All	38	20	8

Note: In the poll, a total of 22 per cent indicated they did not know, would not vote, would vote for another party or refused to answer.
Source: Sections I–IV are based on a poll of December, 1996 by Market Research Bureau of Ireland / *Irish Times* as appearing in Simon King and Rick Wilford, 'Irish Political Data 1996', *Irish Political Studies*, Volume 12, 1997, pp. 164–5.

Group support

In relation to the pattern of political party group support within the electorate (Table 1.2), Fianna Fáil does well among all sectors, the most impressive finding, while demonstrating its greatest strength among those with the least formal education, less skilled workers and farmers, large and small. While there is some evidence of a class-based profile to party support, the general characterisation of a party system that depresses class and economic status distinctions is also evident, an unusual situation for a western democracy (Main 1993).[7]

Finally, in terms of party affiliations and party organisation, Fianna Fáil claims a base party membership of 65,000 with 3,000 branch offices, which if accurate gives it an enormous edge over its nearest rival, Fine Gael (with a claim of 21,000 members and 2,000 branches) or, of course, any other of its other potential competitors.

Both major parties' hold on the electorate has weakened over time, a development of concern for the normally dominant Fianna Fáil, in particular. Coalitional alliances between a major and third (Labour) or minor party now characterise governing coalitions, a relationship Fianna Fáil once refused to consider.

In assessing stability and change within the Irish party system, Peter Mair notes that 'it was primarily ensured by the paramount need to choose between Fianna Fáil and its opponents'. Times have changed and 'this is no longer the case . . . Fianna Fáil . . . is no longer such a credible alternative. In the future, as now, it is likely to require partners in government . . . it is also no longer distinct from its traditional opponents, nor they from it . . . It is in this sense that all the options are now open, with both the electors and the parties being no longer constrained and hence no longer so predictable' (1996: 102).

Much like the society, the party system is undergoing change. How fundamental is the change is arguable. A more volatile electorate, less attached to individual parties, can make for an adventuresome politics. Less clear, and more fundamental, is whether the individual parties, or the party system itself, will reposition itself (that is, realign) to incorporate groups of growing importance and contrasting issue agendas of greater relevance to a modern Ireland. There already are indications of a less stable, less predictable electorate. At the same time, though, there is little evidence to date of the beginnings of any realignment of the party system.

Conclusion

Ireland is a nation in transition. Everything from social attitudes and religious concerns to economic priorities and international relationships are being reassessed. The consequences of these changes and their political implications, the impressive accomplishments to date and the formidable problems yet to be satisfactorily addressed form the basis for the chapters that follow. Each of the authors share the belief that significant change has occurred and more is on the way and that an understanding of both the transformative processes in progress and their outcomes contributes to a better appreciation of where Ireland as a nation has been, where it might be heading and, importantly, what constitutes today's Ireland.

Endnotes

1 In relation to the economic development of Ireland, see: Goldthorpe and Whelan (eds) 1994; O'Hagan 1995; Jacobsen 1994; Munck 1993; Ó Gráda 1995; Breen et al. 1990; Girvin 1997; Hardiman 1994; and Whelan, Breen and Whelan 1994.

2 On social and cultural development, see: Lee 1989, 1995; Brown 1985; and Coakley 1993.

3 The literature on democratic development and its components is extremely varied. As examples, see: Dahl 1971; Held (ed) 1995, 1993; DiPalma 1990; Inkeles (ed) 1991; Elster and Slagstad (eds) 1993; Diamond and Plattner (eds) 1996; and Hadenius (ed) 1997.

4 On the relationship between economic development and democratisation, see: Przeworski 1993, 1991 and (ed) 1995; Diamond and Plattner (ed) 1993; and Haggard and Kaufman 1995.

5 There is a large number of books on issues relating to the conflict in Northern Ireland, not surprising given its duration and

intensity. These include: O'Malley 1997; McGarry and O'Leary 1996; Darby (ed) 1983; Keogh and Haltzel (eds) 1994; Bew, Gibbon and Patterson 1996; Teague (ed) 1993; Boyce 1996; Harkness 1996; Boyle and Hadden 1994; Wilson 1995; Wichert 1991; Dowd, Devine and Breen, 1997 (one study in a continuing series); and O'Clery 1997.

6 On these issues, see: Beresford 1994; Coogan 1987, 1995, 1997a and 1997b; Jarman and Bryan 1996; Jennings (ed) 1990; Peace Watch Ireland 1997; and Sutton 1994.

7 For a different point of view, one emphasising the weak representation of the left, a not unfamiliar situation in some European countries, see: Laver 1994.

Chapter 2

The dynamics of economic change

Jonathan Haughton

Introduction

Since 1960, economic change in Ireland has occurred faster than in any other country in western Europe. In this chapter, we first document the extent and nature of this change. Two relevant questions then arise: What was the role of government in bringing about the economic revival of Ireland? And what has been the effect of economic change on electoral outcomes and government policy?

Most of the chapter deals with the economy of the Irish Republic, because it constitutes the major part of the economy of all Ireland, and because it has been more thoroughly documented. Where possible the discussion has been expanded to cover Northern Ireland, as well as to put Irish economic performance into an international context.

The economic facts

Economic growth in the South

In per capita terms and using constant prices, the 1997 gross domestic product (GDP) of the South was 3.6 times that of 1960. The evolution of per capita GDP over this period is shown in Figure 2.1, which clearly indicates the period of slow growth in the early 1980s and the very rapid increase in the 1990s.

The rise in real per capita GDP between 1960 and 1997 was greater in the Irish Republic than in any other country of the European Union, giving rise to talk of the 'Celtic tiger'. Mainly as a result of a spectacular growth spurt since 1992, the country's per capita GDP, which was 60 per cent of the EU average in 1960, has now risen to 85 per cent of the EU average; it overtook the UK level in 1996. Ireland in the twentieth century has never been poor by world standards, always ranking among the two dozen richest countries in the world, but it has seemed to be poor compared with its European neighbours. The perception of a poor nation on the fringe of Europe is giving way to a new picture of an affluent and dynamic

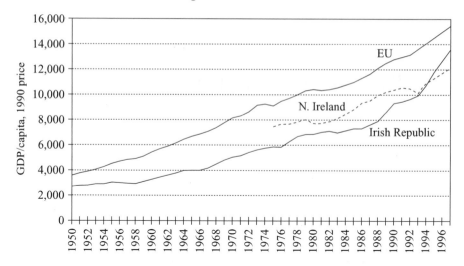

Figure 2.1 Real GDP/capita, Ireland and the European Union, 1960–1997
Note: Figures show GDP/capita in 1985 international prices, which correctly
reflects purchasing power parity. Figures since 1992 were spliced to continue
the Summers and Heston data series.
Sources: Summers and Heston (1995) through 1992; OECD, *Main Economic
Indicators: Northern Ireland: Annual Abstract of Statistics* (various issues
through 1997); Ireland: Department of Finance, *Economic Review and Outlook*
1997.

Table 2.1 Irish economic growth in comparative perspective

	1950–1960	**1960–1973**	**1973–1988**	**1988–1994**
	(% increase in per capita GDP per year)			
Irish Republic	2.2	3.7	2.1	4.7
Northern Ireland			1.7	1.6
UK	2.3	2.6	1.9	0.4
Western Europe*	3.7	4.2	1.9	1.0

Note: 'Western Europe' includes Austria, Belgium, Denmark, Finland, France,
West Germany, Greece, Italy, The Netherlands, Norway, Portugal, Sweden,
Spain and Switzerland.
Source: Ó Gráda and O'Rourke 1995: 212; for Northern Ireland, based on
Northern Ireland: Annual Abstract of Statistics, various issues.

society. With new-found confidence, the Irish penchant for begrudgery, decried so
eloquently by Lee (1989), is fading fast with the realisation that it is possible for
everyone to get rich together.

The numbers in Table 2.1 are designed to put Irish economic growth in international perspective. They show that since 1960 Irish per capita GDP has risen faster
than in the UK; since 1973 it has grown faster than in western Europe as a whole.
A survey published in June 1997 found Irish workers to be the happiest, healthiest

Table 2.2 Alternative measures of Irish economic growth

	1960–1973	1973–1979	1979–1986	1986–1994	1995–1997
	(% increase in per capita GDP per year)				
Real GDP	4.4	4.1	1.5	4.3	8.3
Real GNP	4.3	3.4	−0.3	4.3	7.1
Gross National Disposable Income	4.9	2.8	0.3	3.2	4.6*
GNDI/capita	4.2	1.2	−0.4	3.1	3.3

Note: *1995/96
Sources: GNDI from OECD (1997: 18). Other figures from World Bank, *World Tables*, and Department of Finance, *Economic Review and Outlook*, various issues.

and hardest-working in Europe (McArt 1997: 12), even though they were certainly not the richest.

GDP measures the value of final output produced within the boundaries of the country, but in recent years this overstates the increase in incomes accruing to residents of the country. This point may be made most clearly with the help of Table 2.2, which shows that GNP (Gross National Product), which is the final output attributable to Irish workers, firms and government, has consistently grown less quickly than GDP. This is because an increasing proportion of production within the country accrues to foreigners, mainly in the form of the profits going to foreign investors and as interest on the foreign debt; together these now account for about 12 per cent of GDP.

It is also possible that GDP itself is overstated, because of transfer pricing by multinational corporations. Ireland is a low-tax jurisdiction for most corporations (10 per cent on the profits of manufacturing firms), so they have an interest in making their profits appear in Ireland. This can be achieved by underpricing the inputs which Irish subsidiaries buy from affiliates abroad, or by overvaluing the exports which the Irish subsidiaries sell to foreign affiliates; both boost measured GDP. A possible illustration is the case of Powerscreen, which reported pre-tax profits in 1990–91 of £5.8 million on a turnover of £6 million (Ó Gráda and O'Rourke 1995: 214). In 1995, US companies operating in Ireland posted a remarkable 23 per cent post-tax rate of return on capital, which surely is due in significant measure to transfer pricing. The extent of transfer pricing is almost impossible to measure when the goods and services which flow from one part of a multinational firm to another – such as Coca-Cola concentrate, or specialised micro-chips, or management consultant services – do not have arm's-length world prices which are generally agreed upon.

When the concern is to measure the increase in prosperity, which is presumably of most interest when looking at the links between economic activity and politics, two further adjustments to GNP are needed in order to arrive at a measure of *gross national disposable income* (GNDI). First one needs to correct for changes in the terms of trade, i.e. in the price of exports relative to imports. In recent years, the volume of Irish exports, particularly such items as computer equipment and software, has grown very rapidly (and GNP picks this up), but the value has risen less quickly because the price of these products has been falling over time. Under such conditions, GNP overstates the rise in the purchasing power of Irish incomes. The second adjustment is to take account of foreign transfers, such as Structural Fund subsidies from the European Union, which raised GDP by 2.5 per cent in the period prior to 1993 (European Commission 1996: 14). Between 1979 and 1986 real GNP actually fell, but transfers from the EU rose, so incomes in fact increased; conversely in the 1990s, when GNP rose rapidly, transfers from the EU fell, mitigating the rise in incomes.

These adjustments make a big difference, particularly in recent years. For the period 1995–97, real GDP rose by a remarkable 8.3 per cent annually, one of the highest rates in the world; rising outflows of profits to foreign investors meant that real GNP rose by 7.1 per cent per year; because of falling terms of trade and a slowdown in transfers from the European Union, GNDI increased by just 4.6 per cent p.a.; and the immigration which was sparked by this recent rise in prosperity ensured that the rise in GNDI per capita was just 3.3 per cent per year. This last measure is the best indicator of the rise in living standards; although the increase is substantial, it is slower than the growth in living standards that Ireland experienced in the 1960s.

Economic growth in the North

Sometime in the early 1990s per capita GDP in the South rose above the level in Northern Ireland, as Figure 2.1 shows clearly. Other measures suggest that Northern Ireland may still be marginally more affluent than the Republic. For instance, there were 32 cars per 100 people in the North in 1994, but only 27 in the South. Northern Ireland had the best housing stock of any region of the UK, with just 2.8 persons living in a unit (house or apartment), compared with 3.5 in the South. To an outsider the similarities are probably more striking than the differences: life expectancy at birth in 1990–92 (72 years for men, 78 for women) was the same in both parts of the island, as was the infant mortality rate (6 per thousand births in 1994, one of the lowest rates in the world).

One measure of the success of an economy is the extent to which it forces its people to emigrate. By this standard the Irish Republic was far less successful than Northern Ireland during the 1950s, and significantly more successful in the 1970s (and possibly the 1990s), as Table 2.3 shows.

The economy of Northern Ireland is highly dependent on subsidies from Britain, which amounted to 24 per cent of GDP in 1993–94, a level comparable to the 1980s, but up from 10 per cent in 1970. If the Irish Republic were to provide this subsidy, it would require the South to transfer about a tenth of its GDP to the North every year, a clear impossibility.

Where 25 per cent of total employment in the North was in the public sector in 1970, by 1992 the proportion had risen to 39 per cent (see Chapter 10). While per

Table 2.3 Migration into (+) and out of (–) Ireland, 1956–1996

	1956–61	1961–66	1966–71	1971–79	1979–81	1981–86	1986–91	1991–96
	(Number of migrants per 1,000 population per year)							
South	–14.8	–5.7	–3.7	+4.3	–0.7	–4.1	–7.6	+0.0
North	–6.7	–5.3	–3.3	–7.3		–4.5		n/a

Source: Ireland: Statistical Abstract 1995.

Table 2.4 Proximate sources of Irish economic growth

	1960–1973	1973–1979	1979–1986	1986–1996
	(% increase per year)			
Real GDP	4.4	4.1	1.8	5.6
	(percentages)			
% of GDP growth due to:				
– larger labour force	5	22	–33	21
– more capital	25	39	67	13
– shift out of agriculture	9	10	17	4
– other sources ('residual')	60	30	52	62
	(% increase per year)			
Memo:				
Total Factor Productivity	2.6	1.2	0.9	3.5

Note: Calculations by author, based on same sources as Tables 2.1 and 2.2. For a discussion of the methodology, see text.

capita GDP in Northern Ireland was 83 per cent of the UK level in 1994, the sub-vention enabled personal income per head to reach 93 per cent of the UK level in the same year and probably pushed it above the level in the South. With the onset of peace, albeit fragile, in the mid-1990s, foreign firms that had invested successfully in the South began seriously to consider comparable investments in the North as well.

The proximate causes of growth

National output will typically rise when there is an increase in the inputs, and especially the amounts of labour, capital and technology that are available. For instance, if 30 per cent of output is attributable to capital, and the stock of capital rises by 4 per cent, then this alone should raise total output by 1.2 per cent. It is instructive to use this approach to account for the immediate causes of economic growth, with the help of Table 2.4.

With more workers, output rises. Of the four time periods indicated in Table 2.3, the number of people employed rose significantly both in the 1970s, and between 1986 and the present, accounting for about a fifth of total growth in each case. On the other hand, the growth of the 1960s occurred even though employment did not rise, and in the early 1980s employment actually fell.

A substantial part of Irish growth is attributable to increases in the stock of capital – more machines, shops, roads, factories and houses. In the 1960s the proportion of GDP devoted to investment rose to about 20 per cent, and climbed even higher in the 1970s, before easing back to somewhat below 20 per cent in recent years. During the 1979–86 period, fully two-thirds of the (anemic) growth was attributable to the fact that the capital stock became larger; this is an unduly high proportion, and suggests that investment during this period was not used very efficiently. By way of contrast the contribution of capital to economic growth over the past decade has been surprisingly small, and the stock of capital has actually fallen relative to GDP.

To a more minor extent, Irish economic growth is a reflection of the shift out of low-productivity agriculture and into high-productivity industry and services. This shift alone accounted for about a tenth of economic growth until the mid-1980s, but has become comparatively unimportant now that the agricultural sector accounts for just 10 per cent of employment and 7 per cent of GDP, down from 36 per cent of employment and 25 per cent of GDP in 1960.

The increases in labour and capital, and the shift out of agriculture, are only sufficient to account for about half of Ireland's economic growth. The remaining residual is a measure of the impact of unknown influences, a 'coefficient of ignorance' which is typically interpreted as *total factor productivity*. Put another way, the part of economic growth that cannot be explained directly by applying more inputs such as labour may be thought of as a measure of how much more productive the inputs into the economy have become.

There are good explanations for the growth in (total factor) productivity in the Irish case. In part it reflects improvements in education, as the effects of universal secondary education (introduced only in 1968) and expanded higher education improve the productiveness of the labour force – a factor emphasised in Chapter 3. In part, productivity gains are due to greater economies of scale; these occur when firms are able to cut their unit costs of production by serving a larger market, and in the Irish case have occurred as firms located in the country have increasingly served a European and even world marketplace rather than just the narrow local market. The largest single reason for productivity increases is probably improvements in technology, interpreted widely to include advances in management techniques as well as more narrow scientific breakthroughs.

Over the period 1986–96, productivity growth alone raised Irish GDP by 3.5 per cent per year. This is an exceptionally high rate of improvement by world standards. Even if one takes the longer time period since 1960, Irish productivity growth is high, broadly comparable to the levels found in Hong Kong, South Korea and Taiwan during about the same period; the relevant numbers are shown in Table 2.5.

Table 2.5 Total factor productivity growth compared internationally

	Time period	Growth rate of total factor productivity (% p.a.)	Source
Ireland	1960–1996	2.3 [1.8]	As in Table 2.4
Ireland	1974–1994	2.8	European Commission (1996: 681)
European Union	1974–1994	1.1	European Commission (1996: 681)
Hong Kong	1966–1991	2.3	Young (1995: 673)
Singapore	1966–1990	0.2	Young (1995: 673)
South Korea	1966–1990	1.7	Young (1995: 673)
Taiwan	1966–1990	2.1	Young (1995: 673)
United Kingdom	1960–1989	1.3	Dougherty (1991)
United States	1960–1989	0.4	Dougherty (1991)

Note: The Irish figures have not been adjusted for improvements in the educational level of the labour force; this adjustment reduced the measure of TFP by 0.2 in Taiwan and 0.7 in South Korea. An intermediate figure of 0.5 is reasonable in the Irish context. This would give a measure of TFP growth for Ireland of 1.8 per cent p.a., which may be compared more accurately with the figures for the other countries reported here. The precise methods used differ somewhat; the European Commission figures have not been adjusted downward for the effects of structural change in the economy or for education.

Employment

Until recently the greatest failure of the Irish economy – North and South – was its inability to create jobs. Figure 2.2 tells the story in a simple and eloquent way: the number of jobs in 1990 was approximately the same as in 1960, which in turn was lower than in 1950. Ireland was thus typical of the European Union, where there are no more jobs now than 25 years ago; by way of contrast, the number of jobs in the United States increased by two-thirds over the same period.

What is surprising is that in the 1990s the number of jobs in the Irish Republic rose by a total of 18 per cent (up to 1997), reflecting the boom in economic activity during this time. One consequence has been a change in attitudes, because getting a job is no longer like playing a zero-sum game. Instead of reasoning 'If I get a job, it's because someone else does not', one can now say 'I have a job and so I am adding to employment', which is psychologically more satisfying, and has ended talk of job-sharing and other alleged fixes to the unemployment problem. One result has been a rise in the proportion of the adult population (aged 15–64) that is in the labour force – to 62 per cent by 1995, although it is still somewhat below the EU average of 66 per cent. While about a tenth of the jobs in the South are part-time, the figure for the North is much higher, at about 30 per cent.

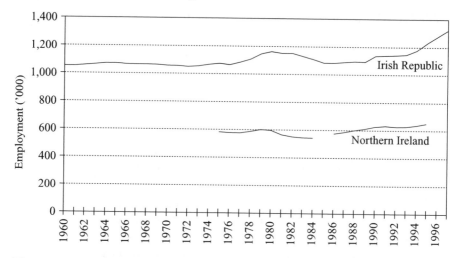

Figure 2.2a Employment in Ireland

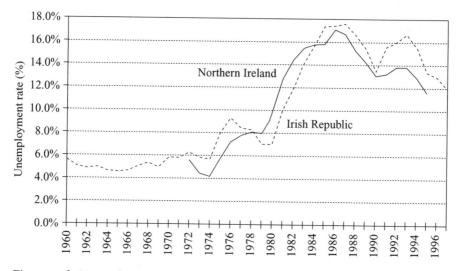

Figure 2.2b Unemployment rates in Ireland
Sources: For Ireland, World Bank, *World Tables* and Ireland: Department of Finance, *Economic Review and Outlook*, various issues. For Northern Ireland, *Northern Ireland: Annual Abstract of Statistics*, various issues.

Unemployment

During the 1980s Ireland had the dubious distinction of one of the highest unemployment rates in Europe. In the South, unemployment rates of about 5 per cent in the 1960s gave way to an average rate of 7 per cent in the 1970s and 13 per cent in the 1980s, with a very comparable pattern in Northern Ireland (as Figure 2.2b shows). The recent rapid economic growth has lowered the rate in the South from

16.7 per cent in 1993 to 11.9 per cent in 1997; this latter rate is in line with the EU norm, but is high by world standards. However if the long-term unemployed (i.e. anyone unemployed for a year or more) are excluded, the short-term unemployment rate is just 4.7 per cent, or below the OECD average; this indicates that the labour market is in fact relatively tight. Skilled workers face low unemployment rates – just 4 per cent among university graduates in 1995, compared with 19 per cent for those with no more than a primary education.

In the South, the unemployment rate for men (19 per cent in 1993, for instance) is typically somewhat higher than the rate for women (13 per cent in the same year). Women in the South enjoyed just 37 per cent of the jobs, up from 33 per cent in 1989, which is a low proportion by world standards. Over time the proportion of adult women who are in the labour force has been rising, from 34 per cent in 1973 to 48 per cent by 1995, while the proportion of men working has been falling (to 78 per cent in 1995) as more men stay longer in school and retire earlier. There appears to be a large pool of people, particularly women and Irish working abroad, who would be willing to work in Ireland if the appropriate job opportunities were to arise. This helps explain why, when the number of jobs in Ireland rose by 192,000 between 1992 and 1997, the number of people unemployed fell by just 37,000. In other words, five jobs needed to be created in order to reduce unemployment by one job.

The situation in Northern Ireland is quite different. Not only did women make up fully 46 per cent of the labour force in 1995, but the unemployment rate is much lower for women (7 per cent in 1994) than for men (18 per cent). The relatively large pool of unemployed and indeed marginalised men in the North, a phenomenon which is especially pronounced in the Catholic population, has historically proved to be a fertile recruiting ground for the IRA.

Ireland has relatively limited control over its unemployment rate, which tends to move in tandem with the UK rate, albeit consistently a few percentage points higher. This is because the Irish labour market is effectively an extension of the British labour market. During the period 1991–96 there was no net migration into the Irish Republic, but every year about 35,000 working-age people left, and entered, the country, or the equivalent of roughly 3 per cent of the total labour force. If jobs are harder to find in the UK, then more people will stay in Ireland, raising the unemployment rate there.

Despite the closeness of the Irish and British labour markets, three elements of government policy play some role in explaining the very high long-term unemployment rates in the Irish Republic. First, it is easy to obtain unemployment benefits. In 1995, the number of people receiving unemployment benefits and assistance was estimated at 149 per cent of the total number of people truly unemployed! This was the highest figure among the OECD countries, and contrasts with the rate of 36 per cent in the United States (OECD 1997: 69). One reason is that unemployment assistance continues indefinitely, whereas in seven of the OECD countries it terminates within three years, and in most others it at least diminishes over time.

The second explanation for Ireland's unusually high unemployment rate is that for some groups the replacement ratio – i.e. the amount of net income one receives when unemployed, as a fraction of net income when employed – is high; in 1991–92 it was 82 per cent for a married worker with two children earning the average wage. The typical unemployment payment in the Irish Republic is now about a third higher than in the UK and Northern Ireland, so some unemployed Irish residents in the UK have probably returned to the South to be unemployed there instead (OECD 1997: 84).

The third problem is the poverty trap, which keeps some unskilled workers in part-time or low-paying positions or even out of employment. In 1995–96 a married worker with four children and a gross annual income of £9,000 (about US $14,400) would have had a net disposable income of £9,687; if the gross income were to rise to £14,000 (about US $22,400) the net disposable income would actually fall to £9,468 (European Commission 1996: 85, based on Dáil debates of November 28 1995). This anomaly occurs because with higher income the household loses a number of state-provided benefits and also faces high marginal tax rates.

Wages

Another corollary of the fact that the Irish and UK labour markets are closely related is that wages in Ireland are very similar to wages in the UK. During the second half of the nineteenth century the two labour markets gradually became more closely integrated, and Irish workers moved from (low-wage) Ireland to (high-wage) Britain, pulling up Irish wages so that by the time of Irish independence the wage rates in each country were essentially comparable for workers with similar skills. The link remains strong, although the adjustment is not instantaneous; between 1987 and 1996 an index of hourly wages in Ireland rose by 39 per cent, or very similar to the 42 per cent increase in the UK but markedly different from the 26 per cent rise in the US and the 50 per cent jump in Japan (Department of Finance 1997: 42).

The logical implication is clear: Irish governments have very restricted ability to influence the real wage rates paid to workers with a given set of skills. What they can influence to some degree is the number of people who will earn these wages in Ireland rather than elsewhere, and also the mix of skills which the Irish population achieves.

The limited room for manoeuvre in setting wage rates has not deterred the government from trying. Since 1987 the Irish Republic has used a system of centralised wage bargaining, 'very firmly based on a social consensus involving the government, employers and trade unions' (European Commission 1996: 88). Over time the number of participants in these talks has widened, as has the number of topics on the agenda, which now include tax and welfare reform, and active labour market measures, in addition to wage determination. The recent agreements, poetically named, include:

1987–1990   Programme for National Recovery
1991–1993   Programme for Economic and Social Progress
1994–1996   Programme for Competitiveness and Work
1996–2000   Partnership 2000 for Inclusion, Employment and Competitiveness.

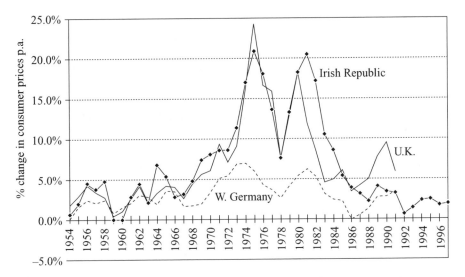

Figure 2.3 Inflation in Ireland, UK and Germany, 1954–1997
Source: IMF, *International Financial Statistics*, various issues.

It is fortunate indeed that the wage agreements have coincided with rapid economic growth, because the agreements create considerable rigidity in the labour market. They tend to favour 'insiders' – especially those who are already employed – and so have a bias in favour of agreeing to higher wage increases than might be justified given the extent of unemployment. The 1991–93 agreement hurt the indigenous industrial sector, which had difficulty meeting the wage increases stipulated in the programme.

The Second National Understanding of 1977–1981 agreed to wage increases which were well in excess of productivity increases, and so contributed to higher unemployment and inflation, as well as widening the budget deficit. It was during the subsequent six years of free wage bargaining that the market pushed labour costs back into line and laid the foundation for a return to macroeconomic stability.

Inflation

Between 1826 and 1979 the Irish pound was linked, one to one, with the pound sterling. Sterling banknotes and coins circulated in Ireland, and shopkeepers in some parts of Britain, such as Liverpool, accepted Irish banknotes. This fixed exchange rate could only be maintained if inflation in Ireland were the same as in Britain. For instance, if Irish inflation were high, then Irish exports would fall and imports rise, leading to a leakage of banknotes out of the country, a credit shortage and monetary contraction, and in due course, a reduction in inflation. The closeness of the two inflation rates prior to 1979 is evident in Figure 2.3. The link with sterling made sense when three-quarters or more of Irish trade was with the UK.

British (and therefore Irish) inflation rose dramatically after the oil price shock of 1973, peaking at over 20 per cent in 1975. Just as the inflation rate seemed to be under control again, falling to 7 per cent in 1978, the second oil price shock led to a second bout of inflation. Germany had not experienced such severe inflation, and so in 1979 Ireland broke the link with sterling and joined the Exchange Rate Mechanism of the European Community, hoping to jump from British to German inflation rates immediately (because in practice, the ERM was anchored by the deutschmark and reflected the German rate of inflation). The adjustment did occur, but it took nearly a decade, since when Irish inflation has been very close to the rate experienced by the core member countries of the ERM. After 1985, when the rate fell below 5 per cent, inflation ceased to be an issue of political importance.

Ireland has qualified to be a charter member of the group of EU countries that will begin to use the euro from 1999 onwards. The net benefits of the shift to the euro will be small; on the one hand, traders will save the expense and risk of exchange rate transactions in currencies such as the franc, deutschmark and guilder, but they will still be exposed to fluctuations in the exchange rate between the euro and sterling, which is significant because 30 per cent of Irish trade is still with the UK (EIU 1997: 38). When sterling dropped out of the European Monetary System in 1992, the Irish pound was forced to follow shortly thereafter in order to maintain its competitiveness in the UK market. Some of the conditions accompanying the use of the euro, particularly the limits on government deficits, will also reduce the country's ability to respond in periods of recession. On the other hand, there is enthusiastic support for participating in the euro, with an estimated 75 per cent of the electorate favouring it in 1996 (EIU 1997: 15).

Trade

As recently as 1966 Irish industry faced an effective rate of protection, from competitors abroad, of 60 per cent. Since then Ireland has transformed itself into one of the most open economies in the world, with exports of goods and services rising from 32 per cent of GDP in 1960 to 80 per cent by 1996 (CSO 1996; Department of Finance 1997). It is sensible for small countries such as Ireland to trade a lot, because the domestic market is too small to support the efficient production of the wide range of goods demanded in an affluent society. Of the EU countries, only Luxembourg is more open. The gradual opening of the economy has been important in the country's efforts to attract foreign investors, who need to be sure that they can import the inputs they require, and repatriate their profits.

One of the most basic propositions in trade theory is that when a small and a large country open to trade with one another, it is the smaller country that stands to gain most. A substantial proportion of Irish economic growth since 1960 is certainly due to this effect, as the country has widened the range of goods in which it has a comparative advantage, and used its export earnings to buy what it cannot produce efficiently at home. In the 1960s the revealed comparative advantage of the

Table 2.6 Grubel-Lloyd Indices of revealed comparative advantage of Irish Republic

	1959–70	1987–93
	(average value of index)	
Food	0.40	0.47
Beverages and tobacco	0.03	0.36
Crude materials	−0.30	0.23
Fuel products	−0.81	−0.77
Oils, fats, waxes	−0.48	−0.55
Chemicals	−0.76	0.20
Manufactures	−0.48	−0.23
Machinery and equipment	−0.77	0.02
Miscellaneous manufactures	−0.14	0.10

Note: Index varies from −1 (comparative disadvantage) to 1 (comparative advantage), and is calculated as (exports − imports)/(exports + imports) within each of the 9 SITC categories.
Source: As reported in European Commission (1996: 71).

Irish Republic was confined to food and beverages, as Table 2.6 shows. By about 1990 it had also developed export strength in chemicals (mainly pharmaceuticals) and exported about as much machinery and equipment (mainly computers and parts) as it imported (mainly cars).

The rapid industrial development of Northern Ireland dates from the mid-nineteenth century, with the establishment of shipbuilding and ancillary industries, and the concentration of linen spinning and then weaving into factories. By about 1920, 35 per cent of the labour force in the North worked in industry, making the region one of the most industrialised anywhere; the comparable figure for the South was 14 per cent. The North's industries were almost completely reliant on sales in Britain and elsewhere. It was thus in the interest of the industrial north-east of the island to remain part of the UK in 1922, in order to maintain an assured access to its key markets; the economic risk involved in joining an independent and potentially protectionist state, dominated by agricultural interests in the relatively underdeveloped South, was too great.

Economically the choice to stay within the UK paid off, for the first half century anyway, as Northern Ireland continued to have access to the UK market throughout the protectionist 1930s, the economic war, and World War II. In the 1950s and 1960s, economic growth was higher in the North than in the South, widening the gap between the two. This was followed by two decades of industrial stagnation and increasing dependence on British subsidies, so that now per capita GDP is significantly higher in the South than in the North. Where enterprising and dynamic Northerners had looked with disdain at their sleepy and rural Southern neighbours in the 1960s, by the 1990s the reversal in attitudes was almost complete, with enterprising and well-educated Southerners looking down at the parochialism and rigidity of their Northern co-habitants.

Table 2.7 Poverty in the European Community

	National average equivalent expenditure, 1985	% in poverty in 1985 (poverty line taken as 40% of Community mean equivalent expenditure in 1980)		
		Persons	Children	Elderly
Belgium	6,200	0.5	0.6	1.0
Denmark	6,700	1.1	1.3	2.9
Germany	5,500	2.8	3.9	3.9
Greece	4,700	10.9	11.0	17.9
Spain	3,800	19.7	21.0	24.7
France	5,500	6.2	7.7	9.5
Ireland	**4,500**	**14.4**	**21.6**	**9.8**
Italy	5,200	8.5	8.3	11.9
Netherlands	6,000	1.3	2.0	0.6
Portugal	2,600	58.2	61.3	70.4
U.K.	5,300	8.4	11.7	11.3
Total	**5,000**	**9.3**	**11.6**	**11.9**

Note: Adult Equivalent Expenditure calculated as total household expenditure divided by number of adult equivalents; first adult in household counted as 1.0, subsequent adults as 0.7, children as 0.5.
Source: Eurostat (1990), Tables 3.5 and 3.6 and Figure 3.1.

Income distribution and poverty

A 1973 survey found that 7 per cent of GNP accrued to the poorest 20 per cent of the population, compared with 39 per cent to the most affluent 20 per cent. This pattern of distribution is in line with the experience of the UK and somewhat more even than in the United States. It also represents much greater equality than at the time of independence.

In 1990 Eurostat published a comparative study of poverty in the European Community, based on household survey information from the early and mid-1980s (ISSAS 1990). A sampling of the results is shown in Table 2.7. A common poverty line was used for all EC countries, equivalent to 40 per cent of the average level of expenditure per adult equivalent in the Community. By this measure, 9.3 per cent of all persons in the EC were in poverty in 1985. In Ireland the poverty rate was 14.4 per cent, higher mainly because Ireland at the time was substantially poorer than the average for the EC.

The structure of Irish poverty differed from the European norm. Unusually, the poverty rate was lower for elderly people than for the population as a whole, reflecting improvements that were introduced in the system of pensions in the early 1980s. The rate of poverty among children was unusually high in Ireland. This is because in Ireland poor households have tended to have significantly more children. A similar trait is found in most other countries, but not to as strong an extent.

There is a widespread belief that income distribution worsened in the decade after 1985, much as it did in the United States during the same period; Chapter 7 makes the same point. It appears that the wages of those at the bottom of the earnings distribution have stagnated. In 1987, a man working full-time and in the top 10 per cent earnings bracket made 3.5 times as much as a man working full-time but in the lowest 10 per cent bracket; by 1994 the ratio had widened to 5.0 (Nolan and Hughes 1997). These numbers need to be treated with care however, since most Irish households in poverty are there because no one is earning at all.

The type of economic growth which Ireland has experienced favours the employment of those with skills, in such areas as computing and professional services. As in the United States, this type of growth has left behind those workers who have few skills, including the long-term unemployed whose job skills have atrophied. Ireland has put in place a plethora of schemes for training such individuals, in the hope of preparing them to (re-)enter the ranks of the employed. The government spent 1.8 per cent of GDP in 1995 – twice the OECD average – on active labour market policies such as training, and on subsidies to help the unemployed get back to work and those with low skills to upgrade. The effectiveness of much of this spending has been questioned (see, for example, OECD 1997, chapter III).

The role of government in economic management

How government policy has sought to promote growth

An enumeration of the immediate causes of economic growth is as helpful as listing the ingredients in a cake – useful, but does not get to the heart of what makes the cake rise. What fundamentally explains Ireland's recent growth record, and what role did government play in the process?

Since independence Ireland has experimented with a number of growth strategies. In the 1920s the Cumann na nGaedheal government followed an agriculture-first policy, with free trade, low taxes, parity with sterling, and modest government intervention. Economic growth was significant during this period and exports hit a peak in 1929 which was not surpassed until 1960. The policy became harder to sustain in the 1930s, as other countries erected stiff protectionist barriers and the world went into depression (Haughton 1995).

The Fianna Fáil government which came to power in 1932 quickly raised tariffs on imports, from 9 per cent in 1931 to 45 per cent by 1936. When the new government refused to pay land annuities, Britain retaliated by imposing special duties on its imports of Irish livestock, dairy products and meat. The 'Economic War' continued until the Anglo-Irish Trade Agreement of 1937. Heavily protected, the industrial sector boomed initially, with its output rising 40 per cent between 1931 and 1936, while agriculture stagnated. As is usual with a strategy of import-substitution, the initial burst of growth is not sustained, and the Irish case was no exception. After the difficult period of World War II, and the subsequent boom, the protected industrial sector found itself unable to compete successfully in the 1950s, and Irish per capita GDP slipped sharply relative to the fast-growing economies of western Europe. Emigration picked up again during the 1950s, as four-fifths of all those born in Ireland in the 1930s left the country (Lee 1989).

The period of gloom and self-doubt began to end with the publication of *Economic Development*. Written by T. K. Whitaker, then secretary of the Department of Finance, the report called for tariffs to be dismantled, for incentives to stimulate private industrial investment, for government spending to be directed more towards economically productive ends, and for expanded spending on agriculture. The report sounded a note of hope in despondent times. And, as the 1960s progressed, the Irish version of export-led growth took root. The strategy had three inter-related parts: trade liberalisation, an active policy of seeking foreign investors, and (subsequently) improvements in the system of education and training.

Trade liberalisation began with unilateral cuts in import tariffs in 1963 and 1964 and was followed by the Anglo-Irish Free Trade Area Agreement in 1965 and subscription to the General Agreement on Tariffs and Trade in 1967. Trade barriers fell further once Ireland joined the European Economic Community in 1973, culminating in the single market which was ushered in from 1993.

To attract foreign investors, the powers of the Industrial Development Authority (IDA), which had been set up in 1949, were broadened in 1958. Tax relief on profits from exporting had been introduced in 1956. The Shannon Free Airport Development Company was established in 1959. The IDA actively pursued investors, at considerable expense; by 1983–86 subsidies to industry amounted to 3 per cent of GDP and were equivalent to almost an eighth of industrial valued added, a level of support only exceeded by Italy and Greece among EU countries. The 10 per cent tax on the profits of manufacturing firms, good through 2010, is also a major attraction.

The strategy has succeeded in attracting investors. By the end of 1994, 45 per cent of manufacturing jobs were in foreign-owned enterprises, which produced almost entirely for export. In 1995, 23 per cent of new US manufacturing investment in Europe was in Ireland. In the same year, 14 per cent of all new manufacturing startups in the European Community were in Ireland, a country with less than 2 per cent of the EU population. An important, if recent, spin-off from the foreign investment has been the increasing number of local entrepreneurs who are setting up businesses in the high-technology area.

The strategy of basing economic development on attracting foreign investors has been criticised. It is now recognised that the system of incentives favoured capital over employment, and foreign over domestic firms. This has led to some changes in the way subsidies are provided. The Culliton Report of 1992 (Culliton *et al.* 1992) argued convincingly that Ireland needed a wider set of reforms to maintain and enhance its competitiveness (or at least its ability to create more well-paying jobs), including changes to the system of taxation and the structure of education and training. Chapter 9 discusses these issues in further detail.

In retrospect, it is now clear that a third important piece of Irish economic strategy was an emphasis on education. Only in 1968 was secondary education made compulsory, and since then the system of secondary and higher education has seen rapid growth in size, diversity and probably quality. In a recent international comparison of 'human capital', which measures the depth of education and training of the labour force, Ireland was ranked number seven in the world (Mankiw *et al.* 1992). A higher proportion of young Irish workers have science or engineering degrees than in any other country. The proportion of 17-year-olds at school is now 83 per cent, or significantly above the OECD average of 78 per cent and higher than in Northern Ireland (73 per cent) and England (65 per cent). In 1994–95 a greater proportion of 18-year-olds went on to higher education in the South (40 per cent) and North (36 per cent) than in Britain (30 per cent). A higher proportion of school leavers finish upper secondary school than in any other OECD country.

In a 1996 survey of businessmen, Ireland was ranked second among European countries in the availability of skilled labour, and first in the relevance of the education it provides (OECD 1997: 14–16). It is clear that the old stereotype of the poorly educated Irishman has been replaced by a new stereotype, of the young, talented and well-educated Irish worker.

Irish governments have on occasion tried to sustain economic growth by expansionary fiscal policy. The first attempt was in 1974, after the quadrupling of the price of oil which occurred as a result of the first oil shock. The higher price of oil diverted spending from domestic to foreign goods, and the coalition government responded by boosting spending sharply, raising the current budget deficit from 0.4 per cent of GDP in 1973 to 6.8 per cent by 1975. This countercyclical policy moderated the rise in unemployment, but did not prevent it from increasing from 5.7 per cent in 1973 to 9 per cent by 1977. In 1978, the new Fianna Fáil government believed it could lower the unemployment rate by raising spending. This boost in demand was pro-cyclical, coinciding with a worldwide surge in economic growth, and unemployment did fall to 7.2 per cent by 1979. But continued high government deficits carried a price, as the national debt jumped from 52 per cent of GDP in 1973 to 129 per cent by 1987, then the highest level in the European Union. By 1986, the cost of servicing the debt took up 94 per cent of all revenue from the personal income tax, the economy had not grown for five years, inflation had fallen only slowly, the Irish pound had been devalued on two occasions within the European Monetary System, and it was clear that the policy was a failure.

All the political parties learned a lesson in economics from the failed fiscal experiment, and there remains 'a strong consensus that fiscally induced expansion is not feasible in a small open economy' (European Commission 1996: 7). As with exchange-rate policy, macroeconomic policy is no longer a subject of political debate, because Ireland's room for manoeuvre in this area is so limited.

How government policy has sought to use the fruits of growth

In 1960, government expenditure amounted to 25 per cent of GDP. By 1981 the proportion had risen to 55 per cent, one of the highest rates in the world. Since 1990, the government has consistently spent about 37–40 per cent of GDP, which is somewhat lower than the spending level of most EU countries, comparable to the rate in the UK, and higher than in the US or Japan. The pattern shows up clearly in Figure 2.4a.

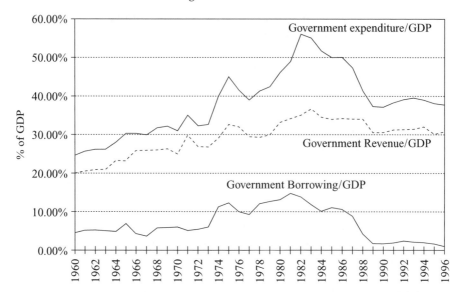

Figure 2.4a Government Expenditure and Borrowing in the Irish Republic, 1960–1996

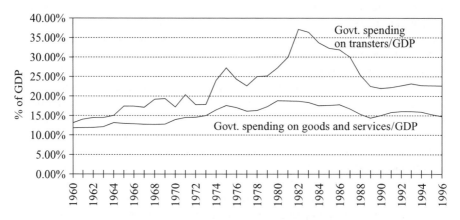

Figure 2.4b Composition of Government Spending in the Irish Republic, 1960–1996
Sources: Department of Finance, *Economic Review and Outlook* (various issues) for 1982 onwards. World Bank, World Tables for borrowing, and spending on goods and services, up to 1981. IMF, International Financial Statistics for other services up to 1981.

Government spending on goods and services, which includes such items as education, health, the armed forces and police, and new investments in ports and roads, has been relatively stable at 12–15 per cent of GDP for most of the past four decades. Much less stable has been spending on transfer payments, which includes interest on the national debt, pensions, unemployment assistance and benefits, and other income support programs. This instability is evident in Figure 2.4b.

The rise in government spending during the 1960s, both on transfers and goods and services, is similar to the increases seen in most other industrial countries at the time, with the consolidation of the welfare state. Spending increased dramatically after 1973, when the Fine Gael/Labour coalition government sought to deliver on their spending promises, largely by borrowing. By 1977, government spending had been trimmed, but then it surged again, as the new Fianna Fáil government tried to reduce the unemployment rate by borrowing for a spending binge. This Keynesian remedy was the wrong solution; in a small open economy, additional government spending mainly goes to buy imports, and so the effect on unemployment was modest and temporary.

Throughout the early 1980s, government borrowing exceeded 10 per cent of GDP. This was widely recognised as unsustainable, but a series of weak governments was unable to do what was so evidently needed, which was reduce spending sharply. The problem came to a head in 1986 when foreign investment almost collapsed and over £2 billion (about 7 per cent of GDP) fled the country.

The new Fianna Fáil government, with Charles Haughey as Taoiseach, dramatically reduced spending, particularly on transfer programmes and on the salaries of civil servants. The result was that government spending fell from 50 per cent of GDP in 1986 to 37 per cent by 1988, and has not exceeded 40 per cent since. This is one of the few cases anywhere of a significant shrinkage in the size of government, much more dramatic than anything achieved in Britain during the Thatcher era. With less expenditure, and almost as much revenue as before, the government's borrowing requirement fell to about 2 per cent of GDP, where it has remained since. As a result of the modest borrowing, the country's foreign debt rose far more slowly than GDP, and by 1997 the debt-to-GDP ratio had fallen to about 70 per cent, one of the lower levels in the EU.

The rectification of government finances in 1987 ushered in a period of robust growth. The policy changes were sufficiently credible for foreign investment to surge; most of the money that had left the country returned. The Irish pound's position within the European Monetary System was now secure, and so Irish inflation converged to the German rate (see Figure 2.3), as did interest rates.

The effect of economic change on government

Has economic change influenced economic institutions?

Economic institutions evolve over time. Economic change renders some obsolete, but also creates a demand for new institutions. An interesting case is the rise and fall of economic planning in Ireland. The five-year *First Programme for Economic Expansion* was published in November 1958, embodying the ideas that T. K. Whitaker had set out earlier in the year in the now-celebrated *Economic Development*. The report called for a reorientation of government investment towards more 'productive' uses, a lowering of tariffs, the eradication of bovine TB, the maintenance of low taxes, and incentives to stimulate private industry. It hoped that such measures would permit GNP to grow by 2 per cent annually.

As it turned out, GNP grew by 4 per cent per year during the first plan period (1958–63), and much of the increase was attributed to the plan itself. So the *Second Programme* was drawn up, to run from 1963 to 1970, with ambitious growth targets for GNP, industry and exports. When it was clear that the targets would not be met, the plan was allowed to lapse. A *Third Programme* followed, but got little respect, and Ireland has not undertaken any large-scale indicative economic planning since.

A more durable institution has been the state-owned enterprise or, in Irish parlance, the semi-state body (SSB). The first of these was the Electricity Supply Board which was established in 1927, followed by the Agricultural Credit Corporation, the Sugar Company, and a growing number of bodies running airports and air transport, shipping, trains and buses, writing insurance, operating peat bogs, running radio and television, manufacturing fertilisers, managing forestry, importing petroleum and exploiting gas fields. The SSBs were not the product of an ideology of nationalisation, but rather were established pragmatically as 'individual responses to specific situations', frequently filling lacunae left by the unenterprising private sector. In the 1960s SSBs employed 50,000 people, accounting for 7 per cent of the labour force.

If anything, SSBs are more important now, with about 100 of them employing nearly 75,000 people. This is surprising, because the weight of academic thinking about SSBs has changed, and state-owned enterprises are now generally viewed as inefficient and wasteful. Irish governments have been slow to embrace this view, although in the 1980s, an effort was made to force most SSBs to operate on commercial lines, and a few of them have been privatised (most notably Irish Life) or allowed to go bankrupt (Irish Shipping). One possible explanation is that Irish SSBs have, for the most part, been run with minimal amounts of interference from government, and so have in fact operated relatively efficiently. Most of the remaining commercial SSBs are in markets where they are the monopoly suppliers (such as electricity or gas), and Ireland is simply following the European model of state-owned monopolies rather than the American (and now UK) version of private providers subject to government regulation.

Some semi-state bodies are non-commercial. One of the more interesting is the Industrial Development Authority (IDA), which was founded in 1949 to promote industry, and strengthened in 1958. It actively sought foreign investors, offering a generous package of subsidies and tax concessions. The IDA's apparent success in attracting investors has spawned imitators in other countries. But two problems have needed to be rectified: the IDA's penchant for subsidising machinery rather than workers, which meant that the new industry did not create many jobs; and its bias in favour of foreign over domestic investors. Although economists have recognised these problems since the 1970s, the institution was slow to change, although now the IDA pays more attention to the employment consequences of its actions, and a separate body (Forbairt) has been established to support indigenous industry. Here, too, the institutions have evolved, but not particularly quickly.

Has the state of the economy significantly influenced electoral outcomes?

There is clear evidence that the outcomes of the presidential elections in the United States depend in part on the state of the economy in the year or two prior to the election (Kramer 1971; Stigler 1973). Fair (1978) argued that US presidential elections are essentially referenda on the party in power, and so the track record of the opposition is less important than the performance of the incumbent government. He found that the most important determinant of the outcome was the growth rate of per capita income during the election year. Similar results were found in an updated version of the model (Fair 1996), with estimates based on election results stretching back to 1916. Fair's model also showed that an incumbent president has a slight advantage when running again, but that higher inflation in an election year is likely to hurt the chances of the candidate of the incumbent party.

We have applied these ideas to the Irish context, by testing whether the state of the economy affected the results of general elections since 1960. There are two versions of the model. The first version of the model takes the form

$$VFF = \alpha_0 + \alpha_1(\%\Delta C \times FF) + \alpha_2(UE \times FF) + \alpha_3(\pi \times FF) + \alpha_4(FF) + \alpha_5(year) + u$$

where

VFF is the share of the vote in general elections going to Fianna Fáil
$\%\Delta C$ is the percentage change in real consumption per capita in the year prior to the election
UE is the unemployment rate
π is the rate of consumer price inflation
FF is a dummy variable which is set equal to 1 if Fianna Fáil is the incumbent party and to -1 otherwise
year is the year of the election
u is an error term

This first model seeks to identify the factors which explain the share of the vote going to Fianna Fáil. Since the 1930s, Fianna Fáil has been the only political party large enough to form a government alone, and the key question in most general elections is 'Will Fianna Fáil win enough seats to be able to form a government?'

In the second model the variable we try to explain is the percentage change in the vote going to the party (or parties) in power. For instance, a Fine Gael/Labour coalition government was in power when the 1977 election was called. The vote for Fine Gael plus Labour was 48.8 per cent in the previous (1973) election, and it fell to 42.2 per cent, a reduction of 6.6 per cent. In this case, the dependent variable takes on the value of -6.6 per cent. By using this variable, we are considering the general election as a referendum on the incumbents; it is reasonable to suppose that if economic performance were strong during the period of the government, then their share of the vote might rise (or not fall much), while poor economic performance would probably sink their chances of being reelected.

Table 2.8 Results of estimating models explaining the outcomes of general elections, 1960–1997

Dependent variable:	Model 1: Fianna Fáil share of general election vote		Model 2: Change in vote going to incumbent parties	
	Coefficient	t-statistic	Coefficient	t-statistic
Independent variables:				
Constant (α_0)	9.689	3.51	3.739	0.64
% change in consumption/head × FF (α_1)	0.337	1.10	0.312	0.48
Unemployment rate × FF (α_2)	0.704	2.16	0.348	0.50
Inflation rate × FF (α_3)	0.342	1.65	−0.020	−0.05
Fianna Fáil incumbent (α_4)	−0.141	−2.33	−0.028	−0.22
Year (α_5)	−0.005	−3.34	−0.002	−0.65
Memo items:				
Adjusted R^2	0.45		−0.09	
Number of observations	12		12	
F-statistic	2.77		0.82	
(significance)	(0.12)		(0.57)	

Source: Based on data given in appendix 1.

The results of estimating the models, applied to the 12 elections since 1960, are shown in Table 2.8. Model 1 is moderately successful at explaining Fianna Fáil's share of the vote in general elections. The estimated equation is significant at the 12 per cent level, which is just about good enough to believe in. An estimated 45 per cent of the variation in the Fianna Fáil vote is 'explained' by the variables in the equation.

The estimates show that Fianna Fáil's vote is declining over time, by about half of a percentage point per year (coefficient α_5). This is consistent with the observation by Hardiman and Whelan (1994) that Fianna Fáil's strongest support is among demographic groups (small farmers, older less-educated men and women) whose share of the population is shrinking, pulling the party's vote down.

The vote for the incumbent falls by about nine percentage points in the subsequent election, holding other influences constant. It is not surprising that when real consumption per capita is rising quickly, the government in power will receive more votes (α_1), but this effect is not statistically significant (the t-statistic is well below the benchmark value of about 2).

It is surprising that a higher unemployment rate, or a higher inflation rate, favours the incumbent party. Neither finding is highly significant, but the effect is too strong to be dismissed as a fluke. Perhaps this reflects the economic conservatism of the electorate, in difficult times preferring the devil it knows to the one it does not.

The estimate of the second model is not statistically significant, as the low F-statistic shows. In other words, we are unable to explain whether the vote of an incumbent government will rise or fall in the subsequent election. And more importantly for our present purposes, economic variables do not appear to influence the electoral outcome. This conclusion is robust; we did a modest amount of experimenting with other equations (for example, using per capita GDP instead of per capita consumption, and measuring unemployment, consumption growth and inflation as deviations from trends), but had no greater success at finding a significant relationship between economic factors and election results. We deliberately did not undertake very many experiments, because of the risk of overfitting, in other words, stumbling on a significant equation whose significance is largely attributable to chance and so does a poor job at prediction.

In contrast with studies of Presidential voting patterns in the US, we have found that economic influences on voting patterns in Ireland are negligible to non-existant. This need not be surprising. The major Irish political parties, and particularly Fianna Fáil and Fine Gael, differ little in their economic policies, and so the choice of which party to vote for is more likely to rest on other factors. Even if they did differ, the scope for economic policies to make much difference is highly constrained in such a small open economy. This observation holds with even more force in Northern Ireland, where most of the important economic decisions are made in London or Brussels (since there is no local parliament, although one has been proposed in the recent peace talks), leaving local politicians to turn their energies to other issues. The situation in the US is markedly different: the economic positions staked out by the Democrats and Republicans in the US differ quite clearly, and the US is large enough to be able to make more meaningful choices about the direction of economic policy.

Concluding themes

A few themes are worth emphasising. The first is that the scope for economic policy is highly restricted in a small open economy such as Ireland. This limitation is widely recognised in Ireland, although it has been learned the hard way, through trial and error. As a result, political debate on economic issues focuses on a narrow range of issues. It is accepted that Ireland should join the euro, which rules out independent monetary policy and constrains fiscal policy. The close link with the British labour market limits the scope for wages to diverge, a fact of life which is less well accepted as Ireland continues to try to set wage policy through a series of centrally bargained, and potentially rigid, agreements.

The consequence is that economic debate centres on the microeconomic issues, the more mundane details of how to improve the educational system, changing the incentives to look for a job, training the unskilled, continuing to attract foreign investment, encouraging local entrepreneurs. There is not a lot of disagreement about what should be tried, but rather a certain pragmatism in looking for solutions which work. One result is that it is difficult to distinguish between the main political parties on the basis of differences in economic policy. Given that all the actual or potential leaders have the same view of economics, it should come as no surprise that we were unable to find any discernible link between economic performance and the outcomes of general elections.

After slipping behind the rest of Europe in the 1950s, Ireland's economy began to catch up when the country turned outwards. First it turned to free trade with the UK, and then with the rest of the European Union. It welcomed foreign investors, and so was open to new ideas and technology. As in any small country, residents tend to be well-informed about the outside world, and the increasingly well-educated populace has acquired a sophistication about world events, and about how other countries handle their economic and political problems, that would have been un-dreamed of in 1960. Despite the new-found affluence, which puts living standards in the South almost on a par with those of the North, the economy of the South is too small to be able to afford subsidies to the North on the scale currently provided by Britain. For the foreseeable future, Northern Ireland's economic interest lies firmly with a continued link with the rest of the United Kingdom.

The political tensions of Northern Ireland are somewhat easier to understand when one recognises that the province is economically bipolar. Well housed, and almost as affluent as the rest of the UK, in significant measure due to large sub-sidies from Britain, it sends a higher proportion of its young people to higher education than the rest of Britain. At the same time, there is a significant group of poorly educated unemployed men whose economic prospects are not good. A last-ing peace in the North requires a politics of inclusion that will embrace this group, and that calls for local politicians who, for the first time in a generation, will turn their attention to economic policy once again.

Chapter 3

Progress or decline? Demographic change in political context

Tony Fahey

Introduction

On many demographic indicators, Ireland is no longer the outlier among western countries that it once was. Population is no longer falling, the massive emigration of the past has ended, marriage and fertility rates have converged toward the European norm and new social patterns such as unmarried parenthood and marital breakdown have become commonplace. This convergence of Irish demography towards European patterns has had two quite different sets of repercussions in the political sphere. On the one hand, it has lent substance to the image of Ireland as a modernising, developing nation. Where demographic decline up to the 1960s had been a sign of national backwardness and stagnation, the demographic recovery since then and its consolidation in the 1990s has signalled a new vibrancy and has helped justify the positive rhetoric which now dominates political discourse about Ireland's socio-economic performance and prospects. Furthermore, the more marked pace of Ireland's demographic upswing in the 1990s coincides with an incipient sluggishness in the demography of other western countries (as reflected especially in rapid population ageing, a trend which is virtually absent in Ireland). This particular international conjuncture accentuates the gloss on Ireland's recent demographic performance.

While these aspects of the 'normalisation' of Irish population patterns have been read as unambiguously positive in political circles, other aspects have led to controversy and conflict. What has connoted advance and modernisation from one perspective has connoted threat and crisis from another and has given rise to concerns in some quarters about fundamental social decline. The dark perspective on recent demographic change has focused on changes in sexual and family mores, as reflected in growing sexual permissiveness, soaring rates of unmarried parenthood, abortion, the rise of marital breakdown and the threats to children's well-being which all these entail. In the political sphere, these changes have generated a conservative reaction, much of which has been played out as a struggle against the 'liberal agenda' in social policy. The high points of this political struggle were the 'moral' referenda on the constitution – abortion in 1983, divorce in 1986, abortion again in 1992 and divorce again in 1995. More generally, party political differences over these and related issues – usually between what is portrayed as the social conservatism of Fianna Fáil on the one side and the liberalism of Labour, sometimes of Fine Gael and more latterly of the Progressive Democrats on the other – served as important axes of differentiation in Irish electoral politics for much of the last three decades.

The purpose of the present chapter is to review these contrasting 'progress' and 'decline' aspects of Ireland's recent demographic and social history. The aim is less to provide a general overview of demographic and social change than to pick out those changes which have aroused the greatest interest in the political sphere and outline what they have entailed. The chapter thus uses political prominence as a rough criterion by which to identify the topics to focus on, but there is no attempt to examine the political significance of those topics in any detail.

The focus is almost entirely on the Republic of Ireland, with little more than passing references to Northern Ireland. Demographic developments in the North have differed from those in the South and have had different political connotations, so that they would be difficult to link to the concerns of the present chapter. Overall population totals in the North have followed a slow but almost constant upward movement since partition (Kennedy 1994). In consequence, the fall and rise in population numbers which have been a focus of so much interest in the Republic have been largely absent in the North. The 'moral politics' of abortion, contraception and divorce have also been much less prominent in the North, in spite of moral conservatism on both sides of the community divide (Cairns 1991). Quite a different concern has been central in the North as far as population is concerned – the question of similarities and differences between Catholics and Protestants. This question has been a concern both from a political point of view, where the main issue is the prospect that Catholics (because of higher fertility and lower emigration) may soon come to outnumber Protestants, and from an academic point of view, where the main issue is the influence of religious culture on demographic behaviour (Jardine 1993/94; Coleman, forthcoming).

Recovery and progress

A half-century ago, as the worldwide population boom was seriously taking off, Ireland seemed stricken by an inability to keep up, much less increase, its population numbers. Crippling waves of emigration and an extraordinary reluctance among Irish people to marry and form families had given Ireland's population trends a pathological quality, the only country in modern times to have sustained more than 100 years of population decline. As a balance sheet of national performance, the census of population in 1961 was a dismal document, as it showed that Ireland's demographic malaise had deepened rather than eased during what for most other countries were the golden years of the 1950s.

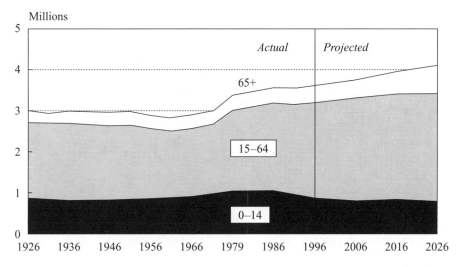

Figure 3.1 Population by Broad Age-Group, 1926–2026 (actual and projected) *Sources*: Population Censuses and CSO (1995).

Growth in numbers

The demographic recovery since the 1960s has been halting, incomplete and uneven. Population growth rates over the whole period have been modest, at an annual average of 0.7 per cent from 1960 to the mid-1990s. Net emigration persisted over much of the period, albeit at lower levels than in the past. A brief recurrence of high emigration in the late 1980s carried echoes of the massive population haemorrhage of the 1950s. However, in the light of Ireland's long history of demographic decline, the post-1960s turnaround was significant and was enough to halt the erosion of national self-confidence. The 1996 census showed that total population had increased by 28 per cent since 1961 (from 2.8 million to 3.6 million). A marriage surge in the 1960s and 1970s had given rise to a baby boom in the 1970s and early 1980s. The baby boom of that time is now translating into a fast-growing young-adult population. Rapid employment growth in the 1990s means that young people can now be absorbed into the economy to an unprecedented extent. Net migration is now inwards by a substantial margin (15,000 in the year to April 1997, CSO 1997) and Ireland has a reasonably strong demographic foundation for future development (Fahey and FitzGerald 1997).

Figure 3.1 shows the general shape of demographic developments since 1926 and traces the implications of present trends for demographic performance up to 2026. As this figure shows, demographic decline prior to the 1960s had a particularly damaging character, in that it consisted mainly in a contraction of population in the active age-ranges (due to emigration). The demographic recovery in the 1970s turned that pattern around, in that the active-age ranges showed the greatest growth, fuelled in part by a net inward migration of almost 50,000 35–54 year olds

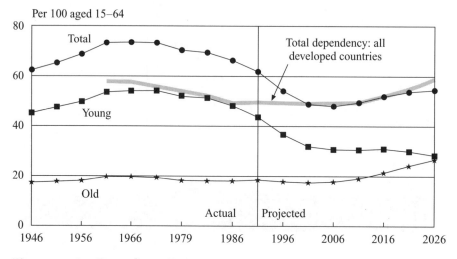

Figure 3.2 Age–Dependency Ratios, 1946–2026
Sources: Figure 1 and United Nations (1995).

between 1971 and 1981. Those in-migrating adults also brought some 50,000 children with them and that, combined with a marriage surge and a consequent fertility surge, raised the population of children from 877,000 in 1961 to above the million mark from the mid-1970s to the mid-1980s. The record since the mid-1980s and projections for the coming decades suggest that growth in the numbers of active-age adults will continue to dominate Ireland's demographic performance, to a degree which is unprecedented in Ireland's modern history. It is also unique among present-day western countries, where relative (if not absolute) decline in the size of the active age group is the norm.

Dependency trends

These population trends translate into favourable movement in dependency ratios (Figure 3.2). As a result of the heavy emigration losses in the active-age ranges in the 1950s and early 1960s, age-dependency rose in the 1960s to levels that were exceptionally high both by Irish standards of earlier decades and by comparison with contemporary patterns in other developed countries. Despite growth in the child population in the 1970s, these levels began to decline slowly at that time because of simultaneous recovery in the size of the active population. After 1986, continued growth in the active population, coupled with decline in the child population and an elderly population that grew only slowly, set age-dependency trends on a more sharply downward slope. This downward movement is projected to continue until the middle of the first decade of the next century. After that time, it will be driven upwards again by growth in the numbers of older people. However, the slowness in the increase in age-dependency from then on, coupled with the low base from which it will then start out, means that in 2026 it will be far below the peaks which were reached in the 1960s and somewhat below present levels. In short, age-dependency levels will be lighter over the next three decades than they have been over the last three decades, and they will become especially favourable in the early years of the next century.

Ireland's demographic structure is thus now reaping the benefits of the juvenation of its population which has occurred since the early 1970s and those benefits are likely to continue over the coming decades. One important policy implication which arises from this situation concerns the overall affordability of the welfare state, an issue which has come to the forefront in a number of countries on account of the worsening ratio between dependents and workers. In Ireland, exceptionally among western countries, there will be considerably *fewer* dependents per worker in the future than there have been in the past (in the mid-1980s, there were 220 dependents per 100 workers; recent projections have forecast that that ratio will have fallen to 133 dependents per 100 workers by 2010 – Forfás 1996, Tables S3.1, S4.1). The welfare state should thus become more affordable in Ireland over coming decades than it has been at any time in the past three decades (see Fahey and FitzGerald 1997, where these implications are explored in more detail). In the political realm, this means that distributional conflicts are likely to be less intense than they might otherwise be, thus providing a basis for the continuation of the consensus approach to distributional issues which has been in place since 1987 (see Chapters 2 and 7).

Fertility decline and population replacement

It is a paradox of Ireland's present improved demographic outlook that it has been accompanied by a sudden and sharp decline in fertility. Following the marriage boom of the 1970s, fertility rose rapidly up to the end of that decade and then plummeted. The number of births rose to 74,000 in 1980 (a high for the century) but fell below 48,000 in 1994 (a low for the century). A slight rise has occurred since then, to just above 50,000 in 1996, but the fertility rate is likely to remain at present below-replacement levels for the foreseeable future.

The arrival of below-replacement fertility does not necessarily herald a new era of declining population. In fact, changed migration patterns mean that the low fertility rates of today could well yield a higher population growth performance than the high fertility rates of the past. Of those born in Ireland in 1932–35 (295,000 in total), less than half were still in Ireland by their early 30s (in the 1966 census, the age-group 30–34 numbered only 146,600). Death in childhood and early adulthood had accounted for a certain portion of the loss, but the bulk of it was accounted for by emigration. In 1996, by contrast, the 30–34-year-old age group, at 260,929, was 77 per cent larger than it had been in 1966, even though the birth cohort from which it was drawn was only 7 per cent larger (315,000). Even so, retention to age 30–34 in 1996 amounted to only 79 per cent of the birth cohort, an improvement over earlier decades but still less than complete. In the future, if the retention rate were to rise to 100 per cent (or even exceed it by means of net inward migration), the 50,000 births per year now being produced would yield as large a cohort of mid-life adults as any experienced in the present century.

In summary, population recovery since 1960 represents not just a reversal of the long previous history of falling population totals but also a transition from the high-fertility, high-emigration patterns of the past to the low-fertility, low-emigration patterns of today and the years to come. This is a movement from inefficient reproduction, where the extensive resources used in bearing and rearing children yield a relatively small total of adults, to a more efficient system where the results of reproductive effort are preserved and carried forward more completely into the adult population living in Ireland. The benefits of this reduction in wastage of reproductive effort are hard to calculate but it is reasonable to assume that they are substantial, not only in economic terms but also in terms of their subtle effects on national self-confidence.

Growth in human capital

Quantitative recovery in population since 1960 has been accompanied by qualitative population development as a result of the sustained increase in human capital investment which has occurred over the same period. The expansion of the education system which was the means of this increase has been remarkable. The numbers in second-level education grew from 132,000 in 1965 to almost 370,000 in 1993–94 and the rate of retention of pupils to second-level completion stage (Leaving Certificate standard) has risen from 20 per cent in 1960 to over 85 per cent today. The present government target is to raise the completion rate of second-level education among 16- to 18-year-olds above 90 per cent by the year 2000. Third-level student numbers increased from 18,500 in 1965 to almost 91,000 in 1993–94 and now 40 per cent of the age-cohort of school-leaving age progresses to third level (Department of Education 1995).

While the growth in educational participation represented by these figures has been impressive, it still carries the consequences of the lowness in the educational base from which expansion started in the 1960s. Figure 3.3 shows that the educational profile among those aged over 25 worsens dramatically as age increases and is quite low among the older age groups. For example, less than a third of men aged 55–59 have complete secondary education or better. It is worth recalling that the first beneficiaries of free second-level education (introduced in 1966) are still only in their early forties, while the surge of graduates which emerged from the rapid expansion of third-level education in the 1980s are still aged under 30. Unemployment, and especially long-term unemployment, among older adults is high in part because of their poor education levels and that in turn arises because their formal schooling took place too long ago to benefit from the educational expansion of recent decades.

Poor educational attainment is by no means only a matter of the past or of older people. It is still present among a significant minority of young adults, and

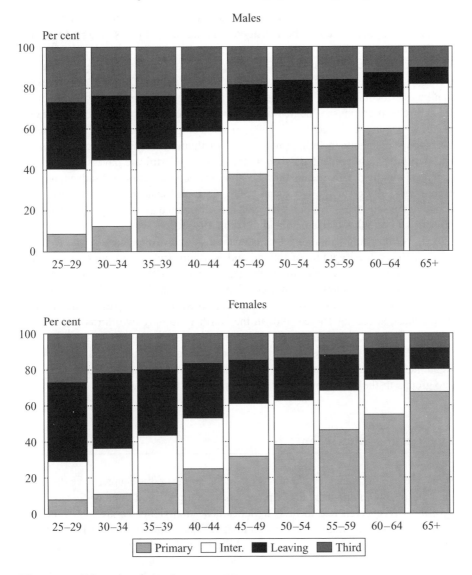

Figure 3.3 Educational Attainment, 1994
Source: Labour Force Survey microdata, 1994.

especially among young men. Among the youngest age-group in Figure 3.3 – those aged 25–29 – 40 per cent of males and 30 per cent of females have progressed past the mid-point of second-level education (Intermediate Certificate or less). Over 8 per cent of both males and females in that age group have primary education only. Using a notion of educational disadvantage based on a combination of reading difficulties among 14-year-olds, early school leaving, low incomes and material deprivation, Kellaghan *et al.* (1995) conclude that about 16 per cent of the present school population could be considered as suffering from serious educational disadvantage.

The persistence of a substantial degree of educational disadvantage is the key weakness in the education record since 1960. While educational inequality exists in all western countries, it has a particular significance in Ireland since employers in Ireland rely to an unusual degree on educational credentials as a screening device in hiring employees (Breen *et al.* 1995). This is so partly because of the extensive oversupply of labour in Ireland makes rule-of-thumb screening devices necessary and partly because credentials such as the Leaving Certificate have such a widely accepted standing. This means that the link between educational disadvantage and employment disadvantage is exceptionally close and exacerbates the many other negative consequences of poor educational performance as young people make the transition to adulthood (Hannan and Ó Riain 1993).

It is worth noting in passing that education is one of those areas where differences between the Republic of Ireland and Northern Ireland are quite marked and are heavily in favour of the Republic. As far back as the 1960s, the South had higher participation rates in post-compulsory education than the North. The 1966 *Investment in Education* report, for example, noted that participation rates in full-time education among 16-year-olds in the North were only two-thirds those of the Republic (22.6 per cent in the North compared to 36.7 per cent in the Republic, OECD 1966: 20). A differential of this order has persisted since and, as a result, the Republic now has a substantial human-capital advantage over the North across all age-groups in the adult population (Breen *et al.*, forthcoming).

The 'decline' dimension

While the demographic developments looked at so far in this chapter have dispelled the kind of gloom about Ireland's prospects which prevailed three or four decades ago, they have given rise to new anxieties. These anxieties centre very much on developments in the family and related matters. The family is a central mechanism of population reproduction and so might have been thought to deserve some of the credit for the overall improvement in reproductive performance already outlined. In fact, much of the public discussion of family life in Ireland today is dominated by the themes of crisis and decline and has led to intense political controversies surrounding questions of family and sexual morality. These controversies have reverberated noisily through the political system, particularly in connection with divorce and abortion. They have spread out beyond the political sphere to touch on basic aspects of Irish culture, with reference especially to role of religion and the Catholic Church in Irish life. Here we look at some the main demographic developments which have underlain these controversies. We will focus on three topics in particular – non-marital parenthood, marital breakdown and abortion – and comment briefly on their political and cultural significance at the end.

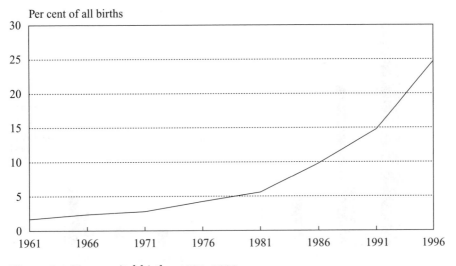

Figure 3.4 Non-marital births, 1961–1996
Source: Vital Statistics, various years.

Non-marital births

The growth in non-marital births has been one of the most striking changes in family behaviour in recent decades, though in comparison to the controversies which have arisen over marital breakdown and abortion, public debate about it has been relatively muted. As Figure 3.4 shows, recorded non-marital births accounted for less than 3 per cent of all births in the early 1960s. By 1996, one in four births (24.7 per cent) took place outside of marriage. In 1992 (the most recent year for which relevant data are available), 34.6 per cent of *first* births (that is, of new family formations) took place outside of marriage.

The significance of this pattern differs greatly according to the age-group of mothers – women aged under 25 behave differently regarding fertility outside of marriage than do women aged over 25. For teenage mothers, the great majority of births in 1996 (95 per cent) took place outside of marriage, while the same was true of almost 70 per cent of births to mothers aged 20–24 (Figure 3.5). For mothers aged over 25, however, fertility outside of marriage was much rarer, falling below 9 per cent for mothers aged 30–34. Non-marital fertility also has social-class associations: it is concentrated among young working-class women who leave school early, have poor employment prospects and have sexual relationships with young men who are in a similar socio-economic position (Hannan and Ó Riain 1993).

Little information is available on the long-term development of families that are started outside of marriage. However, the indications are that large proportions subsequently enter marriage (the only systematic study is O'Grady 1992, which suggests that over half of the unmarried women giving birth in the mid-1980s had married within five years). While marriage thus has lost much of its previous

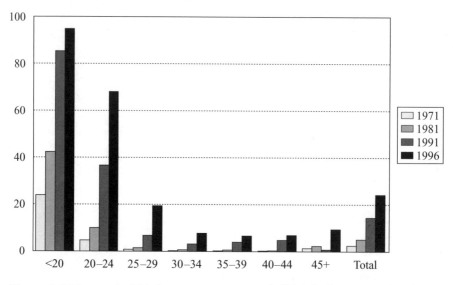

Figure 3.5 Non-marital births as a percentage of all births by age-group of mother, 1971–1996
Source: Vital Statistics, various years.

dominance as a gateway to sex and reproduction, it is far from having lost its role completely even among those who bypass it in the early years of family formation.

Marital breakdown

Apart from developments in the role of marriage in the initial formation of families, trends in marital breakdown also indicate that it has also lost some of its former stability. There are no comprehensive, reliable data on the rate of marital breakdown (partly because, since divorce became available only in 1997, there has been nothing like the comprehensive registration of divorces found in other countries). Census of Population data on marital status provide the best indicator (Table 3.1), though these data do not take account of those who have entered second unions following a marriage breakdown, nor do they make clear why the number of separated women (52,131 in 1996) should be so much higher than the number of separated men (35,661 in 1996).

In 1996, according to Census data, separated women accounted for 6.6 per cent of ever-married women, in comparison to 3.3 per cent 10 years earlier. However, the average annual increase in the numbers of separated women did not seem to rise very much over the 10-year period – it was not greatly higher in the years 1991–96 than it was in the years 1986–91. This would seem to suggest that the stock of separated women is growing but the net rate of inflow into that state is relatively stable. However, one would need to know more about the rate of outflow from the separated state (that is, through entry into subsequent unions) before one could

Table 3.1 Marital Status among the Ever-married, 1986–96

Marital status	Women			Men		
	1986	1991	1996	1986	1991	1996
Ever-married (excl. widowed)	676,193	700,844	733,789	700,844	683,727	710,616
Separated	22,607	33,793	52,131	14,638	21,350	35,661
Deserted	9,038	16,904	16,785	2,584	6,781	6,363
Marriage annulled	540	722	1,287	443	499	920
Legally separated	3,888	5,974	14,616	3,299	5,178	11,863
Other separated	6,792	7,195	14,430	6,090	5,787	11,741
Divorced in another country	2,169	2,998	5,013	2,222	3,105	4,774
Separated as % of total	3.3	4.8	6.4	2.2	3.1	4.3
Inter-censal increase in numbers separated	—	11,186	13,325	—	6,712	9,537
Annual average increase	—	2,237	2,665	—	1,342	1,970

Sources: Census of Population, Vol. II, 1986, 1991; Census 96 Principal Demographic Results.

draw any conclusions about underlying trends in the marital breakdown rate from these numbers.

Apart from the limited amount they tell us about the incidence of marital breakdown, these data are also interesting for what they tell us about the apparently low recourse to legal separation among those whose marriages broke down. In 1996, for example, less than one-third of women who were *de facto* separated reported themselves as *legally* separated, while a further one-tenth had a foreign divorce. This leaves about six out of ten *de facto* separated women whose formal legal status is unclear. They classify themselves under the headings 'deserted' and 'other separated' on the census forms but since these terms have no precise definition, it is not clear how they were understood by those who classified themselves in that way. There is some indication that, prior to the introduction of divorce, demand for the then available formal legal remedies to marital breakdown was limited, especially among lower-class couples (Fahey and Lyons 1995). Preliminary indications from the Department of Justice, Equality and Law Reform on the take-up of divorce since it became generally available in March 1997 suggest that this pattern may still hold. As yet unpublished data suggest that there were approximately 1,300 divorce applications in the nine months to the end of 1997, which is far from the flood which many had expected to break loose once the divorce option had become available in courts. It thus seems that the introduction of divorce has not altered the pre-existing reluctance of Irish couples to approach the courts for a fully fledged legal remedy for a marital breakdown. While the reasons for this reluctance are not fully clear, they seem to rest mainly on the cumbersomeness and slowness of the Circuit Court in processing family law cases rather than on any cultural resistance to the idea of using court remedies for marital breakdown (Fahey and Lyons 1995).

Given the incomplete nature of the Irish data on marital breakdown, comparisons with other countries are difficult. However, the rough estimates of Irish marital breakdown rates made by Fahey and Lyons (1995: 109), which relate both to legal and informal separations, suggest that Irish rates are of a similar order of magnitude to divorce rates in the low-divorce countries of southern Europe (such as Italy, Portugal and Spain) and are much lower than those of countries such as Britain and the United States which have high divorce rates.

Non-marital births and marital breakdown have together caused an increase in lone parenthood in families with dependent children (though widowhood also plays a role in this area). In 1996, 13.8 per cent of family units with children aged under 15 were headed by a lone parent (of these, 85 per cent were headed by lone mothers and 15 per cent by lone fathers) (CSO, *Census 96*, Vol. 3, Table 34). The rise of lone parenthood implies increasing burdens on state income supports for the families involved, the growth of a new category of families at risk of poverty and possible knock-on effects for the social integration of children in those families (as reflected, for example, in vandalism and crime rates). However, these implications should be seen in context. State supports for families with children are low, so that any increases which arise from the growth of lone parenthood in the future are starting from a low base – and, as we have seen above, are doing so in the context of sharply declining overall dependency levels. Furthermore, the principal 'problem family' in Ireland as far as poverty is concerned is still the large two-parent family rather than the lone-parent family. In 1994, two-parent families with four or more children had a higher poverty risk than lone-parent families, and 85 per cent of children in poverty were in families with at least two adults present (Callan *et al.* 1996: 89, 92). A similar pattern holds in the case of crime risk: O'Mahony's (1997) study of prisoners in Mountjoy showed that the stereotypical family background of the Mountjoy prisoner is the large inner-city family (of 5–6 siblings) with two parents present, rather than the lone-parent family.

Abortion

Following the famous 'X' case judgement by the Supreme Court in 1992, despite the anti-abortion clause inserted into the Constitution in 1983, abortion is legal in Ireland in circumstances which could in theory be interpreted widely (such as where the mother has suicidal feelings as a result of her pregnancy). In practice, because of strong anti-abortion provisions in the code of medical ethics in Ireland, no acknowledged abortions are carried out and Irish women who require abortions still obtain them abroad, typically in Britain.

Abortions in Britain to women who give Irish addresses have numbered 72,000 since 1970. In 1991, the number of such abortions was 4,154 and this had risen 4,590 in 1994 (see Mahon and Conlon 1996, from which the present data on abortion are drawn). The number in 1994 represented an abortion rate per 1,000 women aged 15–44 of 5.8, which compares with the British rate of 14.79 in the same year and a rate of 6.0 in The Netherlands (which has the lowest rate in Europe among countries with legalised abortion).

In 1993, 79 per cent of abortions to Irish women in Britain were to single women and 14 per cent to married women. The age-distribution of abortions by age among Irish women, compared to the age-distribution of births, suggests that abortions are somewhat over-represented in the 25–29 age-group (38 per cent of abortions are in that age-group, compared to 27 per cent of births). Abortions to those aged under 20 account for only 0.8 per cent of the total, compared to 5.3 per cent of total births. While little is yet known of the social characteristics of those who have abortions, it appears from the limited information available that it is most common among middle-class women and relatively rare among working-class women and the unemployed (Mahon and Conlon 1996: 604). The concentration of abortions among single middle-class women in their late twenties or early thirties contrasts with the earlier noted concentration of non-marital births among young working-class women. Abortion patterns, therefore, appear to be the obverse of certain aspects of the non-marital fertility patterns just reviewed and help explain why the incidence of non-marital births declines so much with age and with higher social class.

Religious implications

The changes in demographic behaviour just outlined reflect a weakening of the hold of Catholic belief and practice over social behaviour in Ireland – and indeed for many this may be their most significant feature. Despite the depth of its hold in Ireland, Catholicism proved to be an ineffective bulwark against the liberalising tide of the post-1960s sexual revolution, and the Catholic Church lost many adherents as popular culture shifted in a liberal direction. Certain indicators of Catholic affiliation have shown substantial declines in recent years (weekly church attendance, for example, which in the early 1970s had been practised by more than 90 per cent of Catholics in Ireland, had fallen almost to 80 per cent by the late 1980s and to below 65 per cent by 1995 – Corish 1996). The Catholic Church has also been badly hit by sexual scandals in the 1990s, especially regarding child sexual abuse by clergy.

Yet even with these declines, Ireland can still claim to be one of the most Catholic countries in the western world (weekly church attendance in excess of 60 per cent, for example, is exceptionally high by the standards of other countries) and the Catholic Church is still a potent force in Irish life. In many ways, the sexual revolution has seeped through Irish Catholicism rather than swept it aside. Many new patterns of sexual behaviour have spread quite easily without undermining religious affiliation among Catholics even though they are nominally in conflict with Catholic teaching. The nature and tone of the Catholic approach to questions of family morality has been altered, and traditional Catholic certainties in this area have softened. Data from attitudes surveys show, for example, that disapproval of sex before marriage has collapsed among Irish people, but has done so almost as much among regular church-goers as it has among non-attenders at church (Fahey, forthcoming). For many Irish people, therefore, changes in things such as family and sexual behaviour in recent decades has not meant that they have abandoned Catholicism altogether but rather that they have redefined what it means in their personal lives.

Conclusion

Demographic and social change in Ireland since the 1960s tell a story of a nation breaking away from its past. In the political arena, much of that story has been read as unambiguously positive – it is a past of stagnation and decline, epitomised by the demographic contractions of the 1950s, which is being abandoned and which has been supplanted by vigour and growth in the 1990s. Ireland's population is young and growing, and for the first time since the Famine, it seems possible that all those young people who want to stay in Ireland will have the jobs and earnings prospects to enable them to do so. The major political parties are at one in their welcome for these developments and even in the broad outlines of the strategies needed to promote them further in the future.

But there is a contentious sub-plot to this story. For many, demographic changes show that Ireland is rejecting valuable social traditions, particularly those which underpinned the stable, orderly family life of the past. The growth of such things as unmarried parenthood, marital breakdown and abortion in recent decades are key strands in that side of the story. Divisions over what these trends signify and how public policy should relate to them have played an important role in shaping national politics since the 1970s and have led to a number of highly effective conservative political campaigns on key moral issues. The question of divorce has been settled, for the time being at least, by the referendum of 1995 and the subsequent enactment of divorce legislation. But the abortion issue simmers on, and a pervasive anxiety about declining family stability provides the material for political mobilisation around moral issues which could well be exploited from some quarter in the future.

Chapter 4

Changing values

Niamh Hardiman and Christopher Whelan

Introduction

Studies of value change in Ireland are often framed in terms of a paradigm of modernisation. The central theme of this approach is that economic development entails a variety of changes in patterns of social interaction which weaken the hold of traditional norms and values. The religious world-view typical of traditional societies falls into decline and secularised religious and moral values emerge. This implies the growing autonomy of individuals in developing their own values and norms. Thus economic and technological modernisation is held to give rise to a process of cultural modernisation.

We shall draw upon this basic hypothesis to illuminate some aspects of the Irish experience, while recognising that modernisation theory has shortcomings. For example, it implies a degree of convergence between different societies' experiences which we find implausible – not least because the interactions between countries at different levels of development can cause the late developers, such as Ireland, to take a distinctive course (Bendix 1967). Furthermore, modernisation theory over-simplifies the causal connections between economic and social change. Changes in economic and social structure do not have a single set of consequences for values and norms. 'Modernisation' is not a single category of phenomena, but encompasses a great many facets of social and cultural change, some of which may be adopted without necessarily entailing any of the others. The Irish experience is one of relatively uneven sequencing: modernisation of the society ran well ahead of its industrial development. Under British rule, Ireland acquired a modern state apparatus and a modern financial system. Furthermore, the Catholic Church in the nineteenth century developed as a highly bureaucratic modern organisation and played a critical role in the creation of a modern education system that ensured virtually universal literacy (Fahey 1992).

Some forms of social and political modernisation were well-established, therefore, before significant industrialisation was undertaken. The population pressures resulting from delayed economic modernisation were met, in part, by mass emigration (see Goldthorpe 1992: 417). The Irish experience of emigration, as has widely been recognised, has had pervasive consequences for the shape of the class structure, the nature of family relations, and the formation of national culture and identity (Lee 1989; Mjoset 1992). The significance of emigration provides an example of the importance of the external context as well as internal patterns of development, and further undermines any notion of an inevitable course of development. In attempting to understand the nature and consequences of modernisation in Ireland, 'history must carry at least as great a weight as theory' (Goldthorpe 1992: 414).

A concern with economic and cultural sovereignty ran through Irish politics in the early decades of the independent Irish state. In his famous broadcast for St Patrick's Day in 1943, de Valera, with his emphasis on 'frugal comfort', expressed a yearning for a pre-industrial social harmony. His speech illustrates the strong Catholic suspicion of industrial capitalism and its attendant materialism and consumerism. Lee (1989: 334) has argued that this was a totally unsuitable basis for the construction of national economic policy (see also Girvin 1997). This 'stifling Catholic nationalist orthodoxy' (Kirby 1984: 18) offered little scope for economic dynamism. Paradoxically, after four decades of political independence, Ireland could be characterised as one of the economically peripheral regions of the British Isles (Hechter 1975). The Programme for Economic Expansion, published in 1958, signalled the end of the post-independence search for a national identity and economy rooted in conceptions of traditional Ireland. National economic policy was reoriented towards reaping the benefits of participation in the world economy.

Our previous work (Whelan 1994) showed that the pattern of value change in Ireland has been sufficiently uneven and complex to resist explanation in terms of a unilinear process of modernisation. We must allow for the intentional promotion of change by political means, and for more or less organised resistance to change. We must recognise that Irish society has often responded selectively to new influences, which have in any case been adopted unevenly among different social groups.

Two examples of uneven patterns of change will be explored in this paper. Firstly, we are witnessing a great deal of change in the social significance of religion, specifically Roman Catholicism, in Irish society. Church attendance is in decline, though for mixed reasons. The significance of religious practice itself has changed, with a growing acceptance of the role of individual conscience and a refusal automatically to conform to the dictates of the institutional church. Yet religious values retain a strong hold. Secondly, quite traditional views on the family go together with increasingly progressive views on gender differences and an extremely high rate of lone single parenthood. Issues such as divorce and abortion have revealed deep divisions of opinion. On the one hand, we have witnessed attempts to replace the certainty once provided by social norms by the introduction of, or preservation of, constitutional prohibitions. On the other, we have seen some movement towards more liberal legislation and more flexible responses to individual cases.

These examples illustrate the opportunities as well as the difficulties associated with late and rapid industrialisation, in a society where crucial elements of the social modernisation process had been completed some time earlier.

Data sources

In this paper we draw on two main sources: the *European Values Survey*, which was conducted in 1990 and involved a nationally representative sample of 1,000 respondents; and the *Living in Ireland Survey* which was carried out in 1994 and had a sample size of almost 9,000 respondents, selected by means of the Economic and Social Research Institute's random sampling procedure.

Social structural change

O'Connell (forthcoming) demonstrates that between 1961 and 1991 the overarching trends in the labour market were a contraction in agriculture, expansion of employment in the public sector, a general upgrading of the quality of labour market positions, a substantial increase in the number of women in work, and a marked increase in unemployment. In contrast to the relative stability of the occupational structure from the foundation of the Irish state until the late 1950s, in recent decades Irish society has experienced significant economic transformation. A large shift has occurred away from agricultural employment into manufacturing and services. There has been a steady increase in the level of educational attainment, and a growth in professional and technical occupations. Women's involvement in the workforce has increased. Rapid growth in the 1990s caused the term 'Celtic Tiger' to be coined, evoking comparisons with the newly industrialising Asian countries. A longer-term perspective suggests that a process of social polarisation has been taking place. For those at work, job opportunities, and the rewards associated with them, have been upgraded. Others have found themselves excluded from the labour market because they lack the skills required by the newly created positions (O'Connell, forthcoming; Whelan 1996).

In Table 4.1 we show the distribution of men across the class structure for both 1961 and 1991. In addition to the decline in agriculture, we observe a substantial

Table 4.1 The transformation of the class structure: Percentage distribution of men by class categories in 1961 and 1991

	1961	**1991**
Employers and Self-Employed		
Agriculture	36	16
Non-agricultural	8	13
Employees		
Upper-middle class	8	19
Lower-middle class	16	22
Skilled manual	12	17
Semi-skilled/unskilled manual	21	13
Percentage unemployed	6	16

Source: O'Connell (forthcoming).

Table 4.2 The trend in female labour force participation rates

	1961	1991
All women	29	39
Married women	5	37

Source: O'Connor and Shortall (forthcoming).

increase in the middle class, particularly the upper-middle class, and a significant decline in the non-skilled manual class. Remarkable stability in the class structure for several decades was followed by a period of rapid change over the last 40 years or so. The speed of the change meant that many of the less skilled lost out in the process. By 1991, the unemployment rate for males had risen to 16 per cent, despite the fact that the 1980s had seen the return of large-scale emigration.

At the outset of industrialisation women's labour force participation was well below the European average and the anticipated increase in female participation did not ensue for the first two decades of the process. However, it has been increasing rapidly since the 1980s. The most dramatic change has been in the labour force participation of married women, whose rate of participation, as shown in Table 4.2, rose from 5 per cent in 1961 to over 37 per cent in 1996. The sluggish growth in women's participation prior to the 1980s has been attributed in part to the fact that right through to the 1970s, discriminatory employment policies accorded priority to men as family breadwinners. The increase in the numbers of women at work was facilitated by the explicit abandonment of discriminatory policies, following the removal of the marriage bar in the public service, and the introduction of EU-mandated anti-discrimination and employment equality legislation. Even after the abolition of legal impediments to employment, women's labour-force participation remained low by international standards. This apparent preference for a traditional division of labour within the household certainly owes something to state policies designed to support traditional family structures. The almost complete absence of state support for child care, the lack of tax allowances for child care, and the tax treatment of women, combined to reinforce women's primary responsibility for child care (O'Connor and Shortall, forthcoming; Pyle 1990). Furthermore, O'Connell (forthcoming) notes that a substantial share of the growth in women's employment in recent years has been in part-time employment, with the result that the proportion of women working part-time increased from 11 per cent in 1983 to almost 20 per cent in 1995.

For both men and women, the transformation of the class structure was accompanied by a revolution in educational achievement. From Table 4.3 we can see that, by 1994, while over seven out of 10 of those aged over 65 lacked any educational qualifications, this was true of only just over one in six of those aged 25 to 34. Correspondingly, as one moves from the oldest to the youngest cohort, the percentage having at least a Leaving Certificate rises from less than one in five to over one in two, and the number possessing a third-level qualification rises from 7 to 18 per cent.

Table 4.3 Highest educational qualification by age group

	25–34	35–49	50–64	65+
	%	%	%	%
No qualifications	18	30	48	71
Intermediate certificate or equivalent	30	27	20	12
Leaving certificate	35	28	19	11
Third level	18	16	14	7

Source: *Living in Ireland Survey* (1994).

Changes in the class structure were accompanied by increased urbanisation, with the consequence that almost one-third of the Irish Republic's population now lives in the greater Dublin area. After decades of relative stagnation which gave the country an image of a 'rural conservative and Catholic backwater of post-war Europe' (Breen *et al.* 1990), Ireland experienced an economic transformation of unusual rapidity and intensity. This also meant that a significant part of the labour force found itself at some remove from the new tide of growth. These people lacked the resources to take advantage of emerging educational opportunities and were therefore excluded from access to the higher levels of the new class structure. As a consequence of this uneven development, it is now possible to identify a marginalised working class characterised by long-term unemployment, poverty and fatalism. In short, we have seen the emergence of an increasingly polarised society.

Social change and secularisation

In these circumstances, we might expect to see a decline in attachment to traditional values among both the most and the least advantaged groups. The appeal of traditional values might be expected to decline not only among the economically successful, highly educated and upwardly mobile, but also among those experiencing the sharpest social disadvantages, particularly in the more 'anomic' urban housing developments. However, we would expect to find rather different reasons for a decline in attachment to traditional religious practices among these two groups.

The model of 'secularisation' states that social change weakens the hold of religious values; it may be defined as 'the process by which sectors of society and culture are removed from the dominance of religious institutions and symbols' (Berger 1973: 113). Given the extent of the economic and social transformation it has experienced in the past 40 years, Ireland provides a particularly interesting test case for the thesis that industrialisation weakens religious observance.

The basis for the partnership between church and state in Ireland dates back to the middle of the nineteenth century, when the Church, in close co-operation with Catholic political movements, fought for control over Catholic schools, and developed a substantial role in the provision of hospital facilities. So when the new southern state gained independence, the Catholic Church could build on its base as the 'church of the people', and on the shared experience of the long struggle against a foreign oppressor (Breen *et al.* 1990: 107).

Institutional developments relating to education, healthcare, child services and farm inheritance contributed to the consolidation of the Catholic Church's role in Irish society. The outcome of these processes in Ireland clearly represents a case of what might be termed 'Catholic monopoly'. Inglis, reviewing the situation of the early 1980s, remarks on the scale of the Catholic Church's physical and bureaucratic organisation, and notes that for an estimated Catholic population of 3.7 million (on the whole island of Ireland) there were well over 1,000 parishes, almost 3,000 churches, close to 4,000 primary schools and just less than 1,000 secondary schools. It was the sheer scale of such resources that enabled the Catholic Church to 'control the moral discourse and practice of the Irish people' and maintain a 'moral monopoly' (Inglis 1987: 33). The 1980 *European Values Study* provided what Ryan (1983) described as a general picture of solidarity, with adherence to the faith remaining strong. Ireland remained 'unusual in having a large majority not just of Catholics, but of committed Catholics' (Whyte 1980: 4).

The issue we seek to address is the extent to which such commitment has been sustained in the face of the economic transformation of recent decades, with its attendant occupational shifts, dramatic increases in educational attainment, increasing involvement of women in employment in place of their traditional domestic roles, and the emergence of high levels of unemployment and concentrated pockets of urban deprivation. In this context, secularisation theory would lead one to make a number of specific predictions about differences in religious behaviour and moral values. One might expect that younger age groups which had been exposed more comprehensively to modern 'secular' influences in their formative years would be less completely socialised into church-oriented religion and official standards of personal and social morality. Similarly, one would expect women to be more 'religious' and traditional in their moral values than men, but for these differences to decline as they become more integrated into the labour force. Those with higher levels of education would similarly be expected to diverge more from traditional values and behaviour, because of the rationalising and individualising influences associated with education. Those residing in urban areas would no longer be subject to the reinforcing influences of local community social and religious life, and would correspondingly be expected to be more secularised.

All of these socio-demographic variables serve as proxies for the length and type of exposure to particular kinds of experiences that reinforce or retard the development of meaning systems or 'plausibility structures' for a Christian world-view. Secularisation involves a process of disruption of traditional social structures and the 'taken-for-granted view of the world which they impose as a self-evident truth' (Berger 1973: 55). We would also expect certain kinds of interactions between the socio-demographic variables, which might be expected to reinforce each other, thus strengthening the trend towards secularised values. For example, variables such as age and sex might be expected to have stronger effects in urban than in rural areas.

Table 4.4 Weekly or more frequent church attendance

	Church attendance %	Confidence in the church %
1990	81	72
1994	67	66

Source: *European Values Survey* (1990) and *Living in Ireland Survey* (1994).

Church attendance

Trends in overall levels of church attendance

The 1990 *European Values Survey* found that 81 per cent of respondents attended Church at least weekly, with the corresponding figure for Europe as a whole being three out of ten. The Irish figure represented a position of almost no change when compared with 1981 figures, although there was a significant decline in the percentage attending more often than weekly. The distinctive position of Ireland was far from being explained by the high proportion of Roman Catholics in the population. Despite a radical transformation of the social structure, church attendance was remarkably resilient; a fact which was confirmed by MacGréil's (1991) independent study. Hornsby-Smith and Whelan (1994: 23) concluded that the church attendance figures provided no evidence to support general claims for secularisation, although there were some indications of a cultural shift for those born in recent decades.

By the time the *Living in Ireland Survey* data was collected in 1994, a dramatic change was observed. From Table 4.4 we can see that weekly church attendance fell from 81 to 67 per cent. Furthermore, a detailed comparison of the findings for 1987 and 1994 reveals that this decline occurred rather evenly across sex, age-group and urban-rural location; only among those aged over 65 and located outside the main urban centres was the decline limited to less than 10 percentage points. The extent of the change is dramatic. However, it is not entirely unexpected, since over and above any ongoing process of modernisation, it is necessary to allow for the effect of a series of scandals which rocked the Church in the first half of the 1990s. The Bishop Casey affair became public in 1992, and involved the flight abroad in disgrace of a high-profile and popular senior churchman, following revelations that he had an unacknowledged adolescent son, and amidst allegations of the bishop's misappropriation of church funds to secure the discretion of the boy's mother. This was followed by the 1994 conviction of the priest, Brendan Smyth, for a large number of sexual offences against children; the mid-1990s saw a great many other churchmen brought to trial and convicted for paedophile offences against children in their trust. The Catholic hierarchy struggled to come to terms with their own responsibilities in these cases, and their responses to these problems were

Table 4.5 Weekly or more frequent church attendance in 1994 by sex, age-group and urban–rural location

	Rural %	Urban %	Total %
Sex			
Male	73	46	63
Female	79	60	71
Age Group			
18–34	65	36	53
35–49	78	48	66
50–64	81	67	76
65+	87	82	85
Total	76	53	67

Source: *Living in Ireland Survey* (1994).

subjected to a more public process of questioning by church members and comment from child-care professionals than had previously been customary. Corish (1996: 165) reports figures for 1994 and 1995 which are consistent with the decline in church attendance observed in the *Living in Ireland Survey*, and concludes:

> It seems inevitable and undeniable that these revelations have deeply affected the Catholic community, particularly when the Irish Church has placed so much emphasis on obedience to the Catholic moral code in matters pertaining to sexuality and the family . . . if Catholics could come to terms with accepting that the clergy numbered a small minority of deviants, they found it much more difficult to accept the mishandling of these cases by the hierarchy.

Socio-demographic variation in church attendance

As one might expect from our earlier discussion, the overall church attendance rate conceals some striking socio-economic variation. Table 4.5 shows, as we had anticipated, that sex and age are both related to church attendance but that their impact is significantly greater in urban centres (that is, Dublin, Cork, Galway, Limerick and Waterford). Location is a powerful predictor of church attendance, with barely half the urban respondents attending church weekly or more often, compared to three out of four in rural areas. Within urban centres, men are significantly less likely than women to attend church, the respective figures being 46 and 60 per cent. The variation by age group is even more striking. While over eight out of 10 of respondents aged over 65 in urban centres attend at least weekly, the figure falls steadily to just over one in three of those in the youngest age-group (18–34).

Outside urban centres, the variation is a great deal more modest. The difference by sex is a mere six percentage points, and even among the youngest age group, two-thirds attend at least weekly. Urban-rural differences are thus greatest in the

Table 4.6 Weekly or more frequent church attendance by education, unemployment, poverty and local authority tenure

	%
Education	
No qualifications	73
Secondary	67
Third level	56
Unemployment	
Unemployed	47
Other	70
Poverty	
In poor households	69
Other	55
Housing tenure	
Local authority tenant	49
Other	70

Source: *Living in Ireland Survey* (1994).

youngest age group, with rural respondents being almost twice as likely as their urban counterparts to attend weekly. Very little difference is observed for the oldest group. Taking into account the cumulative influence of these factors, we find that while almost nine out of 10 rural women aged 65 or over attend church at least weekly, this declines to three out of 10 men aged under 35 in urban centres who attend church at least weekly. From Table 4.6 we can also see that, consistent with our expectations, education also has an impact on church-going, with weekly attendance dropping from a high of over seven out of 10 for those without qualifications to little more than one in two for those with third-level qualifications.

Table 4.6 also documents trends which, we would suggest, are not related to the process of secularisation, but which follow from the social polarisation to which we referred earlier. Perhaps the most striking result is the relationship between unemployment and religious participation. Fewer than half of the unemployed attend church weekly, compared to seven out of 10 other respondents. The available evidence shows that unemployed people are substantially more likely to think of themselves as worthless and are less likely to feel that they are playing a useful part in things (Whelan *et al.* 1991). It is therefore hardly surprising that the unemployed are less likely to participate in community rituals such as church attendance. Low levels of religious participation among the unemployed may be understood as an aspect of social exclusion rather than secularisation as conventionally understood.

As Table 4.5 shows, poverty is also a significant predictor of low levels of church-going. Exclusion from ordinary living patterns, customs and activities is a standard way of defining poverty (Townsend 1979). Here we employ a measure of poverty which defines as poor those households which fall below 60 per cent of equivalent average household income and which suffer an enforced absence of at least one rather basic lifestyle item (see Nolan and Whelan 1996). Almost 70 per cent of the non-poor go to church at least weekly, but this falls to 50 per cent of those living in poor households. Finally, members of local-authority households are more likely to be both poor and unemployed and, in addition, are more likely to be located in areas of concentrated deprivation. As expected, we find that fewer than half the members of such households attend church weekly. The cumulative impact of such factors is demonstrated by the fact that only three out of 10 unemployed people living in local authority rented households go to church at least weekly.

Overall, church attendance has shown a marked decline in the 1990s, and this affected almost all socio-demographic groups. However, attendance is sharply differentiated in relation to two sets of factors. The first set of influences is associated with modernisation and includes sex, age, urban-rural location and education. The second set captures socio-economic disadvantage and includes unemployment, poverty and living in public-sector rented housing. Deviation from traditional norms of church attendance is most evident among young urban males, particularly those with third-level education – but it is also evident among the unemployed poor in rented local-authority housing.

What can we infer about changes in value orientations from these findings concerning church attendance? We shall turn now to evidence from the 1990 *European Values Survey* relating to religious, moral and family values. We shall try to explore further the complexities of uneven cultural modernisation, the coexistence of traditional and individualist value orientations, and the effects of social polarisation on value systems.

Religious, moral, and familial values

The 1990 *European Values Study* made it possible to study the relationship between church attendance and religious values. The conclusion which emerged was that failure to attend church did not necessarily involve a rejection of traditional Christian values (Hornsby-Smith and Whelan 1994). More than nine out of 10 people continued to believe in God, although the understanding of the nature of that God was shifting over time from a conception of a personal God to the notion of some sort of spirit or life force. More than nine out of 10 people thought it important to hold a religious service for births, marriage and death, with only modest variation being observed by age group. Eight out of 10 people drew comfort and strength from prayer, and even for those aged under 35, this figure remained close to seven out of 10. Furthermore, Corish (1996: 166) reports that while the sexual scandals of the 1990s damaged the church as an institution, only four per cent of respondents to the survey felt they had a strong impact on their own personal faith.

The complexity and elusiveness of cultural values in Ireland are even more clearly illustrated in connection with issues of marriage, sexuality and the family. On a number of occasions since the early 1980s, such as the abortion referendum of 1983, the divorce referendums of 1986 and 1995, and the further three-part referendum on abortion in 1992, public debate has been convulsed by controversy over the 'politics of the family'. On the surface, the dominant outcome of the conflict has been to provide support for traditional approaches to family matters. The Constitutional referendums in the 1980s installed an anti-abortion clause in the Constitution, and rejected any change to the prohibition of divorce in Irish law, thus placing Ireland in an exceptionally conservative position on these matters in comparison with other European countries. The 1995 constitutional amendment permitting divorce was passed by only the tiniest majority.

However, the surface adherence to tradition belies the shifts that have been occurring in underlying opinion. For example, both before and after the 1986 divorce referendum, opinion polls showed substantial majority support for allowing divorce (Dillon 1993). The defeat of that referendum measure, by a majority of almost two to one, seems rather to have reflected a lack of confidence in the proposed amendment to the laws governing marital breakdown, combined with a profound ambivalence concerning the social consequences of legal change. Somewhat different observations may be made on the subject of abortion, yet here too we see the emergence of deep divisions of opinion in society, as well as considerable ambivalence on the part of many individuals. A strong and apparently unshakeable anti-abortion consensus prevailed throughout the 1980s, yet in 1992 this consensus was thrown into turmoil by the details of the 'X' case which came before the Supreme Court early in that year. The court ruled that a 14-year-old girl who was the victim of an alleged rape had a constitutional right to an abortion on the grounds that her life was threatened by suicidal tendencies arising from her pregnancy. Given the dramatic circumstances of the girl's plight, the court's finding in favour of her right to have an abortion (which she travelled to Britain to obtain) was greeted with public relief and led in turn to a new openness towards the pro-choice point of view in public debate. A three-part referendum was held later in that year to deal with the unsettled constitutional questions concerning abortion arising from the Supreme Court's ruling. In this referendum, the electorate showed a significant shift in a liberal direction. The right to travel abroad to have an abortion, and to disseminate information within Ireland on legal abortion services available abroad, was affirmed, while a proposed new and more restrictive amendment to the 1983 anti-abortion clause in the Constitution was rejected. The effect of this was that the Supreme Court decision permitting abortion in limited circumstances would continue to stand.

However, despite criticism from the senior judiciary, no legislation was enacted to give effect to these constitutional provisions. In late 1997, a highly publicised crisis for a very young girl – aged 13, and pregnant as a result of a rape – exposed the consequences of governments' avoidance of the matter, and further challenged public opinion on the circumstances in which abortion would be considered permissible. The case of the girl, termed 'C', came before the courts because she was in the care of the Eastern Health Board. Despite well-publicised interventions by pro-life activists, the courts gave permission for the Health Board to arrange for her to have an abortion (in England), on similar grounds to those concerning 'X'. Opinion polls after this case showed a two-to-one majority in favour of permitting abortion in circumstances such as these. This result may have been strengthened by an appreciation that legislation was long overdue, and that the option of abortion in Britain was one that many Irish women took each year in any case. However, an openly 'pro-choice' point of view was only tentatively articulated; and a significant minority continued to hold that abortion is never permissible in any circumstances, that the constitution should be amended accordingly, and that the right to travel to obtain an abortion should be curtailed.

There are numerous other instances of complexity and internal contradictions in cultural attitudes towards family matters. In the legal field, strong support in statute and constitutional law for the 'traditional' family has coexisted with decisive moves away from traditional legal concepts in order to accommodate to new patterns of behaviour in family life. The Status of Children Act 1987 abolished the traditional legal disabilities suffered by non-marital children. Similarly, the Judicial Separation and Family Reform Act 1989 introduced what was in effect a liberal no-fault regime regarding separation.

Even from these general indications, therefore, we can see striking change occurring in some areas of family values, but a great deal of uncertainty on many issues. The mixed picture makes it difficult to impose a simple distinction between tradition and modernity as a means of making overall sense of what is happening. Debates about individual issues may take this form in some cases. However, we do not believe it would be accurate to assume any coherent trend away from an integrated, coherent starting point we could term 'traditional', towards an internationally homogeneous end-point of 'modernity'.

It may be more helpful to conceive of societies as organic units, where many customs and values are carried from one generation to the next, and continue to shape developments into the future. The values of the past, its traditions, have an impact in the way change is accepted, rejected or modified. 'Modernisation' is often taken to be in conflict with 'tradition'. But in all but the most exceptional circumstances, the pattern of value adaptation is itself strongly conditioned by past experiences (see Girvin, forthcoming).

It seems more useful to consider, as Dillon (1993) does, that emerging patterns of family values represent a 'pick and mix' approach which blends a variety of traditional and modern value positions. The findings of the *European Values Survey* on issues concerning marriage and the family can offer some insights into these questions. In evaluating the findings, however, we should remind ourselves that people's judgements of what is valuable and acceptable in family matters are far from clear and fixed. Rather, they are fluid, very much influenced by context and thus difficult to identify and pin down in any consistent form. On some issues concerning sexual morality and family values, Irish values are distinctly more conservative than those of the economically more advanced countries – for example on the issue of abortion. The *European Values Survey* data for 1994 show that the only circumstance in which Irish people are willing to approve of abortion is when the mother's health is at risk. Even in this case, only two-thirds approve, compared with nine out of 10 European respondents as a whole. Valid grounds for abortion might include considerations such as not being married, or wishing to avoid having more children. Over one in four respondents in the overall European sample endorsed the former, and one in three the latter, but Irish figures are extremely low for both. While younger respondents are more likely to be tolerant of abortion, only in the case of a danger to the mother's health do we find anything near a majority. Far fewer Irish respondents reject marriage as an outdated institution, and only one in six take the view that individuals should have the chance to enjoy complete sexual freedom compared to one in three in the overall European sample. Furthermore, six out of 10 Irish respondents disapprove of a woman having a child outside a stable relationship with a man, compared to just over one in three among other Europeans.

In contrast, Irish attitudes on sex roles are not significantly more traditional than European views. Almost two-thirds accept that a working mother can establish as warm and secure a relationship with her children as a mother who is not in paid employment, a figure that corresponds exactly to the European average. We find similar results on issues such the relative importance of home-making and employment, the need for women to work in order to be independent, and the need for women to contribute to household income. Similarly, Irish people are just as likely as their European counterparts to stress affection and cultural equality, as opposed to material circumstances, in evaluating the factors contributing to a successful marriage. Irish attitudes in this area continue to reflect traditional values relating to sex differentiation. But the extent of change which has taken place means that they are now in line with broader European patterns.[1]

Kennedy (1989: 1) suggests that many of the behavioural changes in marriage and sexuality have occurred 'notwithstanding the fact that some of them conflict with the professed value system of the majority'. These changes can be summed up by saying that the traditional tight sequencing of marriage, entry into sexual activity, and procreation has been greatly disrupted, if not entirely abandoned. Sex now typically begins before marriage, as increasingly does procreation. One in three first births in 1992 took place outside marriage, although the majority of single mothers apparently marry within a few years of becoming parents. In most cases also, whether inside or outside marriage, sexual activity is not intended to lead to procreation. The annual incidence of Irish abortions had risen to 4,590 by 1994, that is, women having abortions in British clinics who give an Irish address; this figure may understate the true incidence. The standardised way of calculating the abortion rate is to state the number of abortions per 1,000 women aged between 14 and 44. The Irish figures translate into this an abortion rate of 5.8 per cent. This can be contrasted with the British rate of 14.8 in 1994. The known Irish rate, while rising, is still comparatively low. As Fahey notes in Chapter 3 in this volume, the social patterning of abortions appears to be the obverse of that relating to non-marital births. The former are concentrated among single middle-class women in their late twenties or early thirties while the latter are most common among teenage working-class women. The traditional permanence of marriage has also been diluted, with the 1996 figures showing that over five per cent of ever-married people had separated.[2] All of this seems at variance with the professed value system of the majority. Clearly these values have lost the stability and homogeneity of the past – and the will and capacity of an authoritarian church to enforce their observance – and are now in a state of uncertainty and flux.

Confidence in establishment institutions: the role of the Catholic Church

The foregoing discussion demonstrates that there is no straightforward trend encompassing factors such as church attendance and religious, moral, and family values. However, we might expect that trends in church attendance would be linked to confidence in the church. In both the 1990 *European Values Survey* and the 1994 *Living in Ireland Survey*, respondents were asked how confident they were in the Catholic Church, and were offered a range of response categories running from 'a great deal' to 'none at all'. Table 4.4 shows that the trend for confidence in the church has declined in parallel with the trend in church attendance, although the rate of decline is much less sharp, declining from 72 per cent in 1990 to 66 per cent in 1994. By 1994, two-thirds of respondents were attending church at least weekly, and the same number expressed confidence in the church. The overlap, although less than perfect, was substantial. Of those who express confidence in the church, 85 per cent go to church weekly compared to just under 40 per cent who lack such confidence. Correspondingly, almost 80 per cent of those who go to church weekly express confidence in the church, compared to 15 per cent of all others. This size of this association is reflected in the similarity in the variation across age-group, sex and education, in relation to church attendance and confidence in the church.

From Table 4.7 we can see that confidence in the church declines from close to nine out of 10 for those aged 65 or over, to fewer than one in two for those aged under 35. Similarly, among those without qualifications, three out of four fall into the 'confident' category, but this drops to one in two for those with third-level education. For women, the number expressing confidence in the church reaches 67 per cent, but for men it is only 58 per cent. Location also has a strong influence, with seven out of 10 of those outside the main urban centres continuing to express confidence in the church, while for those located in urban centres the figure is close to one in two.

Thus the variables which we suggested would serve as a proxy for exposure to modernisation influences – younger rather than older, more rather than less education, urban rather than rural location – do indeed produce both less frequent church attendance and an erosion of confidence in the church. However, as is apparent from Table 4.7, the socio-economic variables show up a rather different pattern. Unemployment leads to a significant reduction in confidence in the church, with the respective figures for unemployed and others being 48 and 65 per cent. However, among those who are in poverty and those living in the rented public sector, their drop in church attendance, compared with other households, is much greater than their drop in confidence in the church. This is consistent with our earlier discussion of the manner in which deprivation contributes to patterns of social exclusion.

We should not presume that the higher figure found in 1990 reflected an unreserved vote of confidence. In Table 4.8 we report the extent to which, in the 1990 *European Values Survey*, Catholic respondents expressed confidence in the church's ability to give 'adequate answers' to a range of issues. The level of confidence varied from seven out of 10 for 'spiritual matters', to four out of 10 for 'moral problems

Table 4.7 Socio-demographic variation in confidence in the church

	%
Age group	
18–34	49
35–49	56
50–64	68
65+	85
Education	
No qualifications	76
Secondary	57
Third level	50
Sex	
Female	67
Male	58
Location	
Outside urban centre	70
Urban centre	51
Poverty	
Non-poor households	64
Poor households	58
Unemployment	
Unemployed	48
Other	65
Housing tenure	
Local authority tenants	56
Other	64

Source: *Living in Ireland Survey* (1994).

Table 4.8 Percentage of Catholics considering that the church gives adequate answers to problems

	%
Adequate answers to:	
People's spiritual needs	71
Moral problems and needs of the individual	42
Problems of family life	35
Social problems facing the country	34

Source: *European Values Survey* (1990).

and needs of the individual', to one out of three for 'problems of family life' and 'social problems facing the country'. In all areas other than spiritual needs, a significant decline was observed during the 1980s. Levels of confidence in Ireland were no higher than those for Catholics in other European countries. These findings do seem to support the view that there has been a general collapse in the 'moral monopoly' of the church or, at a minimum, a loss of at least some of its moral authority.

However, if the Catholic Church in Ireland is no longer automatically thought to have the right answers, this should not be taken to mean that there is a desire that it should restrict its attention to religious matters. In the *European Values Study*, respondents were also asked their views on the range of issues on which it was appropriate for the Church to 'speak out'. The issues proposed ran from Third World problems, racial discrimination and unemployment, to disarmament and the environment. An additional question referred to 'government policy'. For each of the specific issues, a clear majority considered it proper for the church to speak out. The level of support ranged from over nine out of 10 in the case of Third World problems to six out of 10 in relation to environmental issues. It seems, therefore, to be considered perfectly proper for the Catholic Church in Ireland to express its views on a wide range of issues. However, it appears that Irish Catholics increasingly believe that they may make their own assessments of the adequacy of the response offered by the church. Furthermore, a relatively clear distinction seems to be drawn between the general moral influence that the church can legitimately aspire to have and more specific attempts to influence government policy. Thus, while almost eight out of 10 considered it proper for the church to speak out on unemployment, only about one-third considered it proper in the case of government policy.

The extent to which the evidence we have presented will be taken to support the secularisation thesis is to an important degree dependent on the theoretical perspective that one brings to bear. Even proponents of the thesis do not argue that religion will disappear from the modern world. The contrast they wish to draw is, in significant part, between the public role of religion and privatised belief and practice (Wallis and Bruce 1992: 11). A rather different perspective is provided by those such as Hornsby-Smith (1992: 1) who argue that decline in nominal adherence and social performance of religious rites, and a decline in unnecessary entanglement of religious roles and institutions with secular matters, may leave behind a firmer religiosity in those who continue to practice. As yet, there has been relatively little public discussion of such positive implications for religious practice in a secularising society. In any case, the Catholic Church retains a strong institutional presence in a variety of areas of Irish life, particularly in the education system and in health services. Indeed, there is some evidence that some groups, such as elements of the pro-life movement, would wish to restore the dominance of specifically Catholic teaching in a number of constitutional and legislative provisions. There is much still to be resolved in the relationship between church and social and political life.

An interesting question which arises is whether the recent decline in attachment to and confidence in the Catholic Church in Ireland derives from its own specific difficulties or represents a wider malaise which may be affecting a range of establishment institutions. In Table 4.9 we set out the responses given by people in 1990 and in 1994 when asked to evaluate a number of institutions in terms of the degree of confidence they place in them.

A comparison of Table 4.9 with Table 4.4 shows that, whatever its difficulties, at both points in time the Catholic Church enjoyed a higher level of confidence than the Dáil, the legal system, the civil service and trade unions. The police was the

Table 4.9 Confidence in establishment institutions in 1990 and 1994

	1990 % confident	1994 % confident
The Dáil	50	24
The legal system	47	49
The police	85	78
The civil service	59	55
Trade unions	43	35

Source: *European Values Survey* (1990); *Living in Ireland Survey* (1994).

only institution to enjoy a superior position, and only the legal system maintained its 1990 level. There does indeed seem to be a general malaise in evidence. The most dramatic change clearly relates not to the church but to the Dáil, where the relevant figure declines from one in two to one in four. A relatively small decline in confidence in the church from 72 per cent to 66 per cent can, in this context, be regarded as no mean achievement.

Conclusion

In this chapter, we have profiled some of the complexities of value change in Irish society. We found mixed patterns, where traditional value orientations, largely modelled on conventional Catholic teachings, coexist with more liberal, pluralistic norms. These clusters of values have come into conflict at times since the 1970s over issues of family values and individual sexual morality. Contrasting priorities over sex roles and family structure have been accommodated more easily than conflicts over issues such as divorce and abortion, which convulsed Irish society during the 1980s and 1990s.

Behind these changes we may discern a shift in the role of the Catholic Church in Irish society. The pattern of religious practice and the confidence expressed in the Catholic Church are but a rough guide to shifts in the significance of religious belief to individuals. But they do give some indication of a decline in the Church's traditional centrality in defining the terms of discourse on issues of both public and private morality.

We approached this discussion within the framework of modernisation theory, which posits that economic and industrial change brings about shifts in social and cultural values and practices. We do not argue for any simple unilinear relationship here. We are aware that Ireland experienced extensive institutional and political modernisation long before it encountered the consequences of modern industrial development. Besides, although a late economic moderniser, Ireland was already exposed to an array of social and cultural influences from more economically advanced societies. Nevertheless, it is certainly relevant to note that for several decades after independence, Ireland had a highly religiously homogeneous population, with extraordinarily high levels of religious observance, and that Catholic values and ideals shaped many aspects of political as well as social life.

We have suggested that the rapid changes in the social structure that took place from the 1960s onwards contributed to bringing about far-reaching changes in the value-orientations of Irish people. The consequences are being played out over a long time-scale, with a final shape at which we can as yet only guess. The social-structural changes we have in mind include the rapid transformation of the class structure, offering many more opportunities for the highly skilled, while depriving those with few or no educational qualifications of a meaningful economic role; the greater educational participation of successive cohorts of young people; and, during the 1990s, the retention or return migration of those with higher levels of education and skills who might previously have settled permanently abroad. These trends would be expected to disrupt the transmission of traditional values based on accept-ance of the teaching authority of the Catholic Church, and to facilitate the adoption of value orientations which accord a greater importance to personal choice, indi-vidual conscience, and moral autonomy.

There does indeed seem to be some evidence for a classic pattern of secularisation in Ireland, at least as measured by Church attendance. While formal observance continues to run at quite high levels compared with Catholic populations elsewhere, it declined sharply in the first half of the 1990s, from some two-fifths to about two-thirds. The decline is indeed most marked in the groups predicted by modernisation theory. There may of course be life-cycle effects which are hidden by our data, but we believe that it is safe to say that detachment from Catholic practices is more marked among younger rather than older people, urban rather than rural dwellers, and those with more rather than less education. However, there is another pattern of detachment from participation in church activities which is not due to the effects of modernisation at all, but to the anomic consequences of poverty and social depriva-tion. This is apparent in the low levels of church attendance, and the lower degree of confidence expressed in the Catholic Church, among those who are unemployed or living in poverty, compared with other groups.

Among all groups, the drop in church participation and the drop in confidence in the church happened quite suddenly, and was clearly strongly related to a series of revelations of clerical wrongdoing, particularly those relating to the sexual abuse of children. The unquestioning confidence of many Catholics in the special status of the clergy has certainly been shaken. Once disrupted, the older pattern of strongly formed habits of regular church attendance may not easily be re-established.

We noted that Irish people's attitudes towards family values and the family-based relations between men and women are also changing rapidly, in response to very much the same sets of influences as were apparent when looking at church attend-ance. Irish attitudes towards sex roles in parenting and women's workforce participa-tion are now closer to mainstream European patterns than previously. Irish attitudes tend to be more conservative on the issue of abortion, although public opinion is fluid, and undergoing transition, on this issue. However, it would appear that these value orientations do not result in any single pattern of family life in Ireland. Women having non-marital pregnancies tend to be younger, and working-class;

women travelling to Britain for termination of pregnancies tend to be slightly older, and middle-class. In both cases we see a weakening of the absolute prescriptions and prohibitions of the Catholic Church that once used to prevail in areas of sexual morality and family life.

The institutional hold of the Catholic Church over people's allegiances and values is clearly weakening. However, the difficulties of the Catholic Church itself are not solely responsible. There is a more fundamental shift going on in people's attitudes towards authority, and not only towards religious authority. Almost all major social institutions suffered a drop in confidence levels in recent years. Despite the significant fall from its previous levels, the level of confidence expressed in the Catholic Church is still a good deal higher than the level attained by a number of other social and political institutions. The Catholic Church is no doubt helped in this by its ongoing role in the provision of denominationally based education, which facilitates the socialisation of young people into Catholic values and practices. But there are clearly still considerable numbers of people whose personal religious faith has suffered little or not at all as a consequence of the Church's problems of leadership and example. Quite substantial numbers of Catholics continue to express high levels of confidence in the church's guidance on their spiritual needs.

Nevertheless, evidence of a more private form of religious involvement seems clear. Our surveys show that while most think it quite appropriate for the leaders of the Catholic Church to speak out on issues of principle or on social problems, far fewer want them to comment on specific government policies, and only one-third of Catholics believe that the church is able to give adequate answers either to problems of family life or to social problems facing the country.

We have surveyed significant shifts in patterns of religious participation, in family values, and in attitudes to authority in general. A theme common to all is the decline in the Catholic Church's previous dominance in ensuring observance of traditional religious practices and enforcing traditional morality. But the sources of change are, we believe, more deeply rooted, and may be traced to the social and cultural consequences of economic modernisation. Ireland began this transition fairly recently. Its membership of the European Union has hastened some changes, such as the statutory right to employment equality for men and women, and its exposure to mass communications media has doubtless hastened others.

The result is a mixture of traditional and modern value orientations, sometimes accommodating each other, at other times sharply at odds with each other. It is as yet unclear at what level Catholic Church participation may stabilise. Older, traditional patterns of attachment are in decline. The involvement of socially disadvantaged groups is low. If explored further, this would be seem to form part of a broader disruption of traditional values among the most disadvantaged sectors of Irish society. Where entire communities are subject to the forms of social disorganisation that follow upon economic hardship and social deprivation, many other social problems, such as drug addiction and crime, may flourish. Among poor and unemployed respondents in our surveys, a decline in church attendance is likely to be but one indicator of the hardships experienced by those who have not benefited from industrial modernisation.

Many of the younger, more educated sectors of the population, particularly in urban areas, are likely to move away from religious involvement altogether. Many more of them may well continue to be religiously active, as there is evidence of the enduring importance of spiritual values in the lives of individuals. However, they are likely to be less tolerant of traditional hierarchical authority structures and more committed to the role of individual choice in moral decision-making. The traditional sources of allegiance to the Catholic Church are likely to decline. It remains to be seen what proportion of the younger generations will be retained.

More generally, we would suggest that we are witnessing the rapid development of value pluralism. The liberal emphases on individual moral responsibility, on equality rather than hierarchy, on participation rather than submission to authority, were not much in evidence in traditional forms of Catholicism in Ireland. They are now widely if unevenly shared, with significant consequences for many aspects of social life, including: relations between men and women, both within the family and in the workplace; attitudes to and expectations of marital relationships; patterns of family formation; and overall fertility levels. They do not in any simple sense displace traditional values such as commitment to family life or reservations about recourse to abortion. Instead, we see complex patterns of adjustment going on, and new ways of thinking about fundamental values very much in the process of being worked out.

Endnotes

1 As these results imply, while in relation to a number of these issues we observe variation in relation to variables such as age, sex and education which are consistent with secularisation theory, this is not true for others. For a more detailed discussion of the complexities see Whelan and Fahey (1994).

2 Although as Fahey points out that the available information is far from perfect.

Chapter 5

Religion, ethnic identity and the Protestant minority in the Republic

John Coakley

Introduction

The far-reaching changes that have taken place in Irish society in recent decades have sometimes been so profound that apparently evolutionary transitions have become qualitative shifts. The purpose of this chapter is to examine whether change in the character of the Republic's religious minority might have fallen into this category. For our starting point, we may consider the words of warning published over 50 years ago by the main Protestant religious publishing house, the Association for the Promotion of Christian Knowledge:

> In fifty years Eire may be under a hierarchical autocracy as strict as in ancient Egypt; it may be a completely secularised socialist state; it may be under a military dictatorship; it may be a constituent state in some larger federation; it may be devastated by an intercontinental war; it may be a centre of transatlantic traffic; its population may be doubled or halved; its outlook parochial or œcumenical. None of these can be assumed or ignored when the Church of Ireland looks ahead. In this looking ahead there must be no trimming her sails to suit all winds of politics and economics, but a resolve to meet them with assured inner strength . . . with our roots deep in the soil and history of Ireland we not merely have a hope, but a certainty, of growth and increase if our inner fibre is kept sound. (Stanford 1944: 30–1)

Some components in this forecast may have turned out to be much more true and some much less true than their author could have imagined; this chapter seeks to examine the accuracy of his suggestion that the Protestant community with a sound 'inner fibre' would maintain a strong, independent role in Irish society. This is a particularly interesting question because, at more or less the same time, the same publishing house issued another publication whose conclusions were much more negative. This was a careful study of demographic patterns, which noted that there was a real risk that because of decline in the South, the Church of Ireland would cease to be an all-Irish one, with an all-Irish perspective, with implications for a fundamental change in its character (McDermott and Webb 1945: 22–23). In this chapter, the Protestant minority is seen not merely as a religious denominational one but rather as one with many of the characteristics of an ethnic minority, and it is change in these characteristics that will constitute the primary focus.

Research into ethnic minorities in western Europe has been remarkable for the variety of phenomena that have constituted its subject matter. These have ranged from nationalist movements that enjoy substantial electoral support and the backing of an active military wing, as in the Basque country, to ones whose very existence in the past or present is questionable and whose cultural roots are so slight that any future evolution must be in doubt, as in Cornwall (see, for example, Stephens 1976; Blaschke 1980; Foster 1980; Krejci and Velimsjky 1981). Although the defining characteristic of these movements is linguistic distinctiveness, or at least a minimal consciousness of former linguistic distinctiveness, groups whose identity is now defined in religious denominational terms, such as the Catholics of Northern Ireland, are also frequently included.

The Northern Irish case is, indeed, one of the best-documented of all, the problem typically being interpreted in terms of the failure of the Protestant controllers of the former state of Northern Ireland effectively to assimilate or accommodate a Catholic minority set apart from Protestants by a different sense of ethnic identity.[1] Since the parameters of this problem were laid down by the Government of Ireland Act, 1920, which sought to partition the island along denominational lines but left significant minorities on either side of the boundary, it is surprising that one minority has attracted the attention of scholars and politicians while the other has been virtually ignored.[2]

It is, then, the object of this chapter to examine the position of a forgotten minority: the Protestants left South of the partition line of 1920–21. At the beginning of the century, southern Protestants were only slightly less numerous than northern Catholics (though constituting, of course, a smaller proportion of the total population of the state in which they were to find themselves – one-tenth rather than one-third). While their political values were not necessarily fully shared with northern Protestants, they nevertheless possessed a distinctive British sense of identity that separated them from their Catholic neighbours. Today, signs of this identity are not easy to detect.

In reviewing the changing character of the southern Protestant minority, a comparative examination of its historical evolution is a necessary preliminary step. This is followed by a discussion of the demographic development of this group. The next section examines the declining political profile of the minority. The following section assesses the factors that might have contributed to this diminished role. The last section speculates on the factors that may be associated with a transformation in its identity.

Historical and comparative contexts

As is well known, the depth of the gulf between the two major religious denominations in Ireland had its origins in the events of the sixteenth and seventeenth centuries. The definitive conquest of Ireland under the Tudors, epitomised by the defeat of the major Gaelic chieftains in the wars of 1594–1603, was followed by a policy of settling English-speaking Protestants from Britain over much of the country with a view to copper-fastening English rule, especially in the more Gaelic parts of the North in the early seventeenth century (other settlements had taken place in East Ulster and, on a less ambitious basis, in the South in the sixteenth century). By the beginning of the eighteenth century most of the land of Ireland was in the hands of the new settlers or of the growing group of native landowners who became Protestant to avoid losing their estates under the terms of 'anti-Popery' laws.

The new Protestant landed class inevitably came quickly to acquire not merely monopoly of control over the economy but also domination over the social, cultural, religious and political life of the country. Their church was the state church, and Catholics were permitted neither to vote nor to become members of parliament. In the three southern provinces, however, the great bulk of the population remained Catholic; it was only in the most northerly province, Ulster, that Protestants constituted a majority of the population, since the seventeenth century 'plantations' had included substantial settlements of all classes. Unlike their Anglican counterparts in the South, most Ulster Protestants were not members of the state church; Presbyterians accounted for the greatest number.

The southern Irish Protestant minority closely resembled certain privileged linguistic minorities elsewhere in Europe with whom it also shared a common political fate (Coakley 1980). The Swedish-speaking minority in Finland and German-speaking minorities in Estonia, Latvia and Czechoslovakia, for instance, had traditionally occupied a position of economic, cultural and political dominance as complete as that of the Protestant ascendancy in Ireland. In the late nineteenth and early twentieth centuries, this dominance was steadily undermined. The landed power-base of the minority collapsed as estates were broken up among peasant proprietors; its dominance in the towns and in the secondary sector of the economy disappeared under pressure from a new, expanding middle class drawn from the majority; its cultural superiority was threatened by the linguistic development and official recognition of the majority language (or, in Ireland, erosion of the privileges of the minority religious group); and its control of government (especially at local level) collapsed as the franchise was extended and political institutions were democratised. Like most of the other minorities, Irish Protestants did not share the nationalist views of the majority and remained hostile to the new state; but, unlike the others, including the much smaller Baltic German communities, Irish Protestants did not organise politically after independence, nor were their voices heard during the wave of ethnic protest in the late 1960s, when even minuscule minorities elsewhere raised their heads.

In accounting for this change, one of the most obvious factors with which to begin is the actual size of the minority. The extent of the hegemony that it established at the end of the seventeenth century disguised its numerical weakness. But the political mobilisation of Catholics, manifested in violent rebellion in certain counties in 1798 and in electoral revolution from the late 1820s onwards, drew attention to the relatively small number of Protestants, especially in the southern part of the country. By the middle of the nineteenth century, it was clear that

Protestants constituted only a quarter of the population of the island of Ireland, and just a tenth of the population of the present territory of the Republic. The political settlement of 1921–22 was a double blow to southern Protestants: in addition to losing the security provided by membership in an explicitly Protestant state under the Act of Union with Great Britain, they were deprived of the strength of numbers that their northern co-religionists would have supplied had the island not been partitioned. It is appropriate now to examine the demographic character of the southern Protestant minority.

The changing profile of the Protestant minority, 1861–1991

Since a question on religious affiliation was first asked in the Irish census in 1861, the number of Protestants has declined in absolute terms over each intercensal period until the most recent one. This may be seen from Table 5.1, where, for the earlier years, the entire non-Roman Catholic population is taken as constituting an approximate equivalent to the Protestant population.[3] It will be seen that as the number of Catholics has also fallen over each intercensal period until recently,

Table 5.1 Protestants as proportion of the total population, present territory of Republic of Ireland, 1861–1991

Year	Population	No information on religion	All Protestants[1]		Church of Ireland[2]	
			number	per cent	number	per cent
1861	4,402,514	–	468,939	10.7	372,723	8.5
1871	4,053,187	–	436,531	10.8	338,719	8.4
1881	3,870,020	–	404,688	10.5	317,576	8.2
1891	3,468,694	–	369,691	10.7	286,804	8.3
1901	3,221,823	–	343,552	10.7	264,264	8.2
1911	3,139,688	–	327,179	10.4	249,535	7.9
1926	2,971,992	–	220,723	7.4	164,215	5.5
1936	2,968,420	–	194,500	6.6	145,030	4.9
1946	2,955,107	–	169,074	5.7	124,829	4.2
1961	2,818,341	5,625	144,868	5.2	104,016	3.7
1971	2,978,248	46,648	125,685	4.3	97,739	3.3
1981	3,443,405	71,983	126,156	3.7	95,339	2.8
1991	3,525,719	99,704	111,699	3.2	89,187	2.5

Notes:
1 Total non-Roman Catholic population excluding those refusing to state their religion, those claiming no religion and adherents of non-Christian faiths, where these are identifiable. In 1991, the figure for 'no information' includes those listing their religion as 'Christian'.
2 For 1991, the Church of Ireland figure includes those describing themselves as 'Protestants'.
Source: Calculated from *Census of Ireland* for the dates in question.

Protestants did not necessarily decline as a proportion of the total population. In fact, from 1861 to 1911, they constituted a relatively stable percentage of the population, hovering about the 10 per cent level. The traumatic 1911–26 period, however, saw this community reduced by a third, and since then the inexorable decline has continued to the point where Protestants now account for approximately two-fifths of their number in 1911.

Decline on this scale of a formerly privileged minority is not without parallel in Europe, particularly in the instances mentioned already. Between 1880 and 1970 the Swedish-speaking population of Finland dropped from 14.3 per cent to 6.6 per cent; between 1881 and 1934 the German-speaking population of Estonia fell from 5.1 per cent to 1.5 per cent; and between 1881 and 1935 the German-speaking population in Latvia dropped from 8.4 per cent to 3.2 per cent (Coakley 1980: 221). In these cases, three reasons have been put forward to explain the change: a relatively low rate of natural increase, assimilation to the majority group, especially through mixed marriages, and a relatively high emigration rate (Allardt and Starck 1981; von Rauch 1974: 166). To what extent have these factors been of significance in Ireland?

The first factor clearly has been of some importance: one study has shown that between 1946 and 1961 Protestants experienced a natural decrease in population; deaths exceeded births (Walsh 1970). An analysis of the rate of natural increase of the largest Protestant group, the Church of Ireland, over a 45-year period revealed a consistent pattern of natural decrease, the excess of deaths over births running from 4.4 per thousand (1926–36) to 5.5 (1936–46), 3.3 (1946–61) and 3.8 (1961–71) (Bowen 1983: 29). It seems clear, though, that a rapid drop in the Catholic fertility rate beginning in the 1970s will have the effect of greatly reducing the fertility differential between Catholics and Protestants (Ó Grada and Walsh 1995: 263–4).

Assimilation to the majority group has also clearly depressed the proportion of Protestants in the population. In principle, such assimilation can take two forms, personal and generational. The former tends to be more characteristic of linguistic minorities, language shift frequently being associated with entry to a linguistically alien labour market. Pressure in the direction of religious conformity is obviously much less; conversion to Roman Catholicism has been infrequent and has certainly not matched the frequency of conversions from Roman Catholicism to Protestantism in earlier periods. The importance of assimilation across generations, especially through mixed marriages, has, however, been more pronounced. Although the rate of mixed marriages was negligible in 1946 (when fewer than 2 per cent of Protestants who married took Catholic spouses), by 1961 this figure had increased to 16 per cent and by 1971–73 to an estimated 34 per cent (Bowen 1983: 41). Because of the tendency for the children of such marriages to be brought up as Catholics, this factor contributed significantly to an erosion in the minority's position. More recently, however, as the Catholic Church relaxed its long-standing insistence on observation of the provisions of the papal decree *Ne temere* (which dated from 1908, and required the non-Roman Catholic spouse in mixed marriages to agree to bring the children of the marriage up as Catholics), the freedom of parents to decide

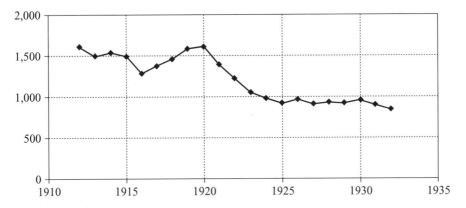

Figure 5.1 Population decline: number of Protestant marriages per annum, 1912–32
Source: Calculated from Registrar General 1922–35.

on the religion in which their children would be brought up has increased significantly and the outcome has become more unpredictable. This position was further reinforced by the growing secularism of Irish society, a development that was particularly obvious in the case of the Catholic community.

In terms of migration patterns, the Protestant population appears to have gone through three phases in the twentieth century. It is clear that during the 1911–26 period the rate of Protestant decline was well above the national average, and during the two intercensal periods 1926–36 and 1936–46 it continued to be significantly higher than the average. From 1946 to 1971, however, the estimated Protestant emigration rate has been lower than the Catholic one (Bowen 1983: 29). This relationship appears to have been reversed once more after 1961, with Protestants slightly more likely to emigrate than Catholics (Ó Gráda and Walsh 1995: 264). The first phase is of particular interest. While withdrawal of the military and of their dependants accounts for part of the sharp drop in the Protestant population in this period, it by no means explains it; indeed, it has been estimated that the departure of the security forces accounted for only one-quarter of the total decline during this period. Examination of local church records in Cork suggests that, after a small rise immediately after the end of World War I, there was a very sharp drop in the years 1921–23 (Hart 1996: 83). This is confirmed by an examination of Protestant marriage rates over this period, as may be seen in Figure 5.1. While there are obvious drawbacks to the use of marriage data as an indicator of population size, the sharp decline in the early 1920s offers plausible confirmation that a general population decline took place at this time.

Two main sources of pressure on the Protestant community in this period may be distinguished. The first is the deep ideological and cultural gulf between the political elite of the new state and the old elite, with the result that, over and above withdrawal of the army and disbandment of the Royal Irish Constabulary (RIC), a large number of civil servants, other administrators and members of the landed

Table 5.2 Protestant male occupied population by occupational group, Southern Ireland, 1911 and 1926

	1911			1926			Change 1911–26	
	no.	% of all	% of Prots.	no.	% of all	% of Prots.	no.	%
Security forces	20,698	59.9	20.1	1,239	5.6	1.7	−19,459	−94.0
Banking and insurance	1,674	45.4	1.6	1,928	30.8	2.7	254	15.2
Professions	4,959	27.3	4.8	3,322	18.7	4.6	−1,637	−33.0
Public administration	3,263	20.7	3.2	1,373	12.5	1.9	−1,890	−57.9
Farmers	26,065	6.6	25.3	27,075	6.6	37.3	1,010	3.9
Farm labourers etc	6,382	2.5	6.2	3,549	2.8	4.9	−2,833	−44.4
Other	39,927	14.0	38.8	34,102	9.2	47.0	−5,825	−14.6
Total	102,968	10.2	100.0	72,588	7.2	100.0	−30,380	−29.5

Note: For 1911 and 1926, the first set of percentages refers to Protestants in a particular occupational group as a proportion of all employed in that group; the second set refers to Protestants in a particular occupational group as a proportion of all Protestants. The occupational categories in 1911 and 1926 do not always correspond exactly to each other.
Sources: Calculated from *Census of Ireland*, 1911, and *Census of Ireland*, 1926.

gentry left the state out of a sense of alienation from the new regime. Second, the revival of agrarian unrest during the Truce and Civil War periods (1921–23), most visibly manifested in a wave of mansion-burning, had a sectarian as well as an economic and a political dimension; there were reports of attacks on Protestant homes in towns and in the countryside. Protestant farmers, landowners, merchants and others, no longer confident of the protection of a sympathetic government, left in considerable numbers.[4]

An effort is made in Table 5.2 to assess the effects of the political changes of this period on the structure of the occupied population. This embarks on the hazardous attempt to compare the cross-tabulation of religion and occupation in the 1911 census with that in 1926. Recalculating the 1911 data so that they cover only the 26 counties is relatively straightforward; ensuring that the occupational categories correspond is much more demanding, so the table must be read with some caution. Certain patterns nevertheless emerge clearly. The impact of the withdrawal of the security forces (caused by the departure of the army and the disbandment of the police force) is obvious, as is the sharp shift in the composition of the public administration sector. While the Protestant component may have declined in other areas, there continued to be areas, such as banking and insurance and the professions, where the minority continued to be over-represented.

Of course, the figures presented in Table 5.2 disguise certain qualitative shifts. The Protestant farming sector actually increased in absolute terms during this period. Two aspects of this sector merit further comment. On the one hand, Protestants continued to be overrepresented in the upper echelons of this sector. The 1926 census showed that of farmers with holdings below 30 acres, only 4 per cent were Protestants, but this proportion climbed to 8 per cent for holdings of 30–50 acres, 10 per cent for 50–100 acres, 16 per cent for 100–200 acres and 28 per cent for holdings with over 200 acres. On the other hand, however, the landed gentry, core of the so-called Anglo-Irish community, had suffered a grievous blow. Its economic base had already been undermined before 1922, but the loss of its political connection in 1922 was a contributory factor in its further marginalisation. To the extent that the Anglo-Irish gentry had provided the political leadership of the Protestant community, this was a heavy blow. It is appropriate now to turn to the political role of this community.[5]

The decline of Protestant political power

The disappearance of the hegemonic control exercised over all aspects of political life by Protestants was, in fact, a phenomenon of the pre- rather than the post-independence period. Between 1840 and 1898 Protestant control of local government was swept away. Catholic Emancipation and franchise extension contributed to a gradual contraction of Protestant parliamentary power outside Ulster, a process that was completed by the 1884 Reform Act. The role of the minority will now be looked at in a number of areas: at local government level and at parliamentary level up to 1922, in the transitional period while the new state was being created, and subsequently in the Dáil and in the Senate.

Local government

It was in the urban local government structure that the Protestant Ascendancy was first challenged. The Catholic Relief Act of 1793 had allowed Catholics to become members of corporations, but the closed nature of these bodies rendered this reform ineffective. Forty years later, only four of the country's 60 corporations had any Catholic members, and in one only (Tuam) did Catholics constitute a majority. This situation was brought to an end in 1840, when the Municipal Corporations Act abolished all existing corporations and re-established the 10 largest towns as municipal boroughs with elective councils; although the franchise was restricted, this facilitated a decisive shift away from Protestant control.[6] In the countryside, county government was controlled by the Grand Juries, selected from among the leading property owners in each county and *ipso facto* predominantly Protestant. This powerful political group continued to have a significant judicial and policing role even after the abolition of its functions in local government in 1898, and its Protestant character carried over into the twentieth century.[7]

Throughout the second half of the nineteenth century, many of the local administrative functions of the embryonic welfare state were handed over not to the Grand Juries but to the Boards of Guardians of Poor Law Unions, established under the 1838 Poor Relief Act. Each of the country's 160-odd unions was administered by a board consisting partly of large ratepayers (normally Protestant landowners) who were guardians *ex officio*, and partly of guardians elected on a weighted ratepayers' franchise. Initially securely controlled by Protestant and conservative interests, the boards increasingly came under electoral assault in the late 1870s, in particular from the Land League and the Irish National League. Between 1879 and 1886, popular control of most boards was achieved; one study has shown that, by 1886, only 43 per cent of the key offices (chairman, vice-chairman and deputy vice-chairman of the board) remained in landlord hands in the 26 counties, though in the six counties the corresponding figure was 82 per cent (calculated from Feingold 1975).

It was, however, the Local Government Act of 1898 that dealt the death blow to Protestant influence in local government. This act transferred the administrative functions of the still-Protestant county Grand Juries to elected county councils, established a tier of district councils below county level, and democratised the franchise for all local authority elections. The consequences of the act were revolutionary: in the first elections of 1899, Nationalists or Nationalist sympathisers won complete control of practically all authorities in the 26 counties. Aside from rare or even accidental victories in the countryside, it was only in the towns that Unionists were able to win a handful of seats after this date.

Parliamentary politics to 1922

The year 1885 represented a turning-point in the involvement of Protestants in parliamentary electoral contests. It would not be too gross an exaggeration to suggest that before that date they enjoyed a modest degree of electoral success with minimal organisation; after 1885 their electoral successes were negligible despite the existence of a well-organised party machine. Catholics had been allowed to vote in 1793, and to sit in parliament in 1829. As early as the 1820s an association between the Protestant interest and the Tory party had clearly emerged in Ireland, Catholics tending to favour the Whigs and later the Liberals. It is not surprising that, in view of the regional dimension to the religious cleavage, party support in Ireland gradually became spatially polarised, a process that got underway even before the 1832 Reform Act.

As the nineteenth century progressed, the relationship between party support and religious affiliation became clearer; indeed, in the 1832–80 period, the Tory party was able to win an average of only 15 per cent of the southern Irish seats that had a Catholic electoral majority.[8] The Reform Act of 1884 completed the process of the destruction of Protestant parliamentary power in the 26 counties: by introducing in effect householder suffrage, it shifted the ratio of Catholic to Protestant voters decisively in favour of the former. The 1885 election was the last at which Tories/ Unionists contested a majority of seats in the 26 counties, and their electoral setback then was devastating. It became clear that there were only three constituencies where they had a realistic chance of winning a seat, and that Catholic–Protestant political polarisation was almost complete.[9] While there continued to be some

Catholics (especially members of the landed gentry and persons in public service) who supported the union and a handful of Protestants who were nationalist, we should not be blinded to the fact that by the 1880s prominent nationalist Protestants were unrepresentative of the community from which they were drawn.[10]

If the 1884 Reform Act spelled the virtual end of Unionist parliamentary representation in the 26 counties, it also, paradoxically, gave birth to organised Unionism in the South. While Tory or Conservative electoral organisations had existed since the 1830s, when the Irish Protestant Conservative Society (1831), modelled on O'Connell's associations, sought to give cohesion to electoral planning, they tended to be ephemeral bodies whose main object was to maximise support in a specific election. The establishment in 1853 of the Central Conservative Society of Ireland was an important stage in the further evolution of electoral organisation (Hoppen 1984: 278–332). Finally, in the 1880s, coinciding with the Reform Act, Unionists, in common with supporters of other parties, developed a systematic organisation. This took shape as the Irish Loyal Patriotic Union (1885), which was re-organised in 1891 as the Irish Unionist Alliance (IUA).

In structure, the IUA resembled an orthodox modern political party. It consisted on paper of individual members, district branches (whose areas corresponded to polling districts), branches (corresponding to the areas of parliamentary constituencies), a General Council (comprising representatives of members, branches, affiliated constituency organisations, other affiliated loyalist organisations such as the Orange Order, and the multi-member presidency and vice-presidency of the party, which consisted mainly of titled landed gentry), and an Executive Committee selected by the General Council.

In practice, this blueprint had to be altered to take account of the dispersed nature of the loyalist community, and the electoral consequences of this demographic factor caused the IUA to come increasingly to resemble a British-oriented pressure group rather than Irish political party. It sponsored teams of speakers who travelled through Britain warning of the dangers of Home Rule, especially in marginal constituencies at election time, and it published a huge volume of pamphlets and broadsheets exposing alleged Nationalist incompetence, sectarianism and disloyalty. The title of the Alliance's journal sums up this negative aspect of its activity. Unlike the journal of a more normal political party, its focus was not on the activities of the party itself, but instead on those of its opponents. Its full title was *Notes from Ireland: A Record of the Sayings and Doings of the Parnellite Party in Furtherance of their Separatist Policy for Ireland; and of Facts Connected with the Country. For the Information of the Imperial Parliament, the Press and the Public Generally.*

The electoral collapse of Southern Unionism after 1885 was compensated for in large measure by the close connection between the IUA and the British (and especially Conservative) governing elite, which ensured that its viewpoint would certainly be heard and would probably be of some weight. Down to 1914, this viewpoint was uncompromisingly Unionist, but the perceived possibility that Home Rule would be implemented, together with shared experiences during the war, encouraged a more flexible attitude towards Nationalists. Despite a temporary reaction after the 1916 rising, the IUA under the leadership of the Earl of Midleton was able to play a constructive role in the Irish Convention (1917–18), a last attempt by the British government to bring the competing groups in Ireland together with a view to agreeing on a constitutional compromise. Such a realistic role, however, inevitably compromised the unionism of the leading actors, and tensions within the IUA led to the withdrawal of Midleton and supporters of his moderate policy in 1919. These secessionists established their own Unionist Anti-Partition League and subsequently played a major role in arranging the negotiations that led to the Anglo-Irish Treaty of 1921 and in representing southern Unionist interests to the draftsmen of the Free State Constitution.

Political change and minority organisation

The absence of an external guarantor of the minority's position after 1922 threw that community onto its own resources, and appeared to make necessary the re-assertion of a Protestant political role. Under the terms of an agreement between the Unionist leadership and the new government of the Irish Free State, the minority's position was to be safeguarded by two devices: the introduction of proportional representation for Dáil elections, and provision for substantial minority representation in a powerful Senate. We examine these two areas below. There were also other areas of political life where the issue of Protestant political representation was an issue.

At the level of local government, the introduction of proportional representation in 1920 raised the prospect of the return of a Unionist voice on local councils. While this voice was heard, however, the language had changed: the demise of Unionism as a defensible ideology was followed by the splintering of political Protestantism. Protestants could exercise some influence by standing as candidates for existing political parties (such as Ratepayers' or Business groups) or as inde-pendents, but only in a few areas – mainly in the border counties – did political organisations survive. The most notable such group has been the Donegal Progress-ive Party, which represents Protestant interests in the East of Donegal.

Another area is the presidency of the state, an office created in 1937. Of eight incumbents of the office of president since the post was first filled in 1938, two have been Protestants. It must, however, be noted that neither was elected as a Protestant as such. The first, Douglas Hyde (1938–45), had been prominently in-volved in the cultural nationalist movement as founder and president of the Gaelic League. The second, Erskine Childers (1973–74), was best known as a leading member of Fianna Fáil.

Dáil politics since 1922

If the electoral system of the new state were fully proportional, an organised party drawing on Protestant support might have expected to win 16 Dáil seats on the basis of the 1911 census figures or 11 on the basis of the 1926 data. Yet no such party appeared, even though there existed two Unionist political bodies, one of them with a nationwide organisation. The more realistic Unionist Anti-Partition League was also the more elitist of the two: supported by the wealthier elements in the Unionist community, by aristocrats and big businessmen, its members tended to adopt a condescending attitude to the state-building efforts of the new rulers of the 26 counties. In 1921 the League had declined to combine with a group of dissident Nationalists in forming a new centre party, and in 1922 the organisation dissolved itself following internal dissension. The attitude of many formerly powerful ex-Unionists has been summarised as follows:

> Anglo-Ireland pointed out with a sneer that the new Ministers, if they had been to any University (and most of them were exceedingly well-educated), had attended the National University, not Trinity College; it pointed out that they spoke with a brogue and not in the refined cadences of Rathgar or Aylesbury Road; it wondered whether they understood the ordinary decencies of polite society, did they know how to tackle an oyster, was it true that they eat peas with a knife? Even when Anglo-Ireland grudgingly admitted ability in the Ministers it sneered at their wives, at their clothes and at their manners. (Robinson 1931: 147–8)

The IUA remained uncompromising to the last, and found itself unable to adapt to political life in the new state. As late as 1921 it had refused to consider transforming itself into a conservative party to contest seats in a Home Rule parliament, believing that 'if, as is extremely probable, Southern Ireland refuses to work the Act, the restoration of the Legislative Union can only be a matter of time'. Its misreading of the political barometer left the IUA impotent in 1922; in the general election of that year its most positive contribution was a call on loyalists to abstain. It abandoned politics in 1922 and became simply a British-oriented pressure group for loyalist interests.

That the main Unionist electoral organisation should survive a 37-year period of almost entire exclusion from Parliament and break up precisely when reform of the electoral system guaranteed it a number of parliamentary seats is ironic. The gap thus created was not bridged; ex-Unionist electoral organisation remained fragmented, and was based on two important surviving segments in the Protestant community, the farmers and urban business interests. These found political expression through small class-based parties. The Farmers' Party (1922–32), child of the Irish Farmers' Union, represented the interests of larger commercial farmers of the South and East and, its opponents alleged, had been colonised by ex-Unionists and ex-Nationalists. While the Farmers' Party undoubtedly enjoyed substantial Protestant farming support, there were more obviously Protestant-oriented groups. In 1922 a Business and Professional Group had two of its five candidates in Dublin and Cork elected; in 1923 the Dublin Chamber of Commerce created a Business Men's Party, two of whose five candidates were elected, while in Cork a Cork Progressive Party sought to represent business interests and had one of its two candidates elected. The personnel involved in these initiatives makes clear their largely ex-Unionist character, but their policies related mainly to economic matters (the Business Men's Party, however, was opposed to the Government's compulsory Irish policy). No such group contested any election after 1923, business parties' support presumably being absorbed by the government party, Cumann na nGaedheal.

The most visible representatives of the ex-Unionists in the Dáil after 1922 were a group of independent deputies. Dublin University returned three (normally Protestant) independents until it was disenfranchised in 1936. Elsewhere, on the assumption of Catholic and Protestant turnout rates proportional to their distribution among the population in 1926, Protestants could expect to gain four-fifths of an electoral quota, and thus have a realistic chance of winning a seat, in six constituencies under the 1923 Electoral Act: County Dublin (1.90 Protestant quotas), Donegal (1.63), Dublin City South (0.90), Monaghan (0.86), Dublin City North (0.81) and Cavan (0.80). County Dublin was able to return two ex-Unionists until 1927 and one subsequently, while the three border counties returned one each. The number of Protestant independents peaked at nine in 1927 but, though sharing distinctive opinions on many matters (such as church-state relations, legislation in the areas of divorce and censorship and policy on the Irish language), this group never behaved as a political party in the Dáil.

Apart from the declining numbers of potential Protestant supporters, two of the constituencies, Counties Dublin and Donegal, suffered from the effects of the Electoral Act of 1935, which bisected each county, thus raising the electoral quota. No Protestant independent was elected subsequently in Dublin. In Donegal the independent Protestant candidate had slowly built up his support base, and the lower threshold of representation allowed him to be elected more easily. After the 1935 division of the county, Protestants were concentrated in the four-seat constituency of East Donegal. This continued to return an independent Protestant deputy until 1943, when the Protestant vote was seriously divided. The sitting independent Protestant lost his seat to another Protestant who stood for a small agrarian party, Clann na Talmhan, and this contest was replicated at the next election with the same result. By 1948 the new agrarian Protestant had broken with his party and inherited the Protestant independent seat, which he held down to 1961. Believing that a further re-districting in that year would make his election impossible, he retired from the Dáil (Sacks 1976: 65), bringing to an end the phenomenon of independent Protestant representation. The position in Cavan and Monaghan was more straightforward. In the early years, Protestants were able to secure the return of a representative of their own community even though their share of the population implied that they would not have a full electoral quota. As the Protestant population continued to drop as a proportion of the total population, however, it became increasingly difficult for independent Protestants to secure election, and after a succession of failures, independent Protestants ceased to attempt the impossible.

Senate politics since 1922

Ex-Unionists played a much more active role in the second chamber than in the first. The senate of the Free State was to consist of 60 members elected for a 12-year term, one-quarter retiring every three years. Candidates were either to be former senators or were to be nominated by the Oireachtas (parliament) 'on the grounds that they have done honour to the Nation by reason of useful public service or that, because of special qualifications or attainments, they represent important aspects of the Nation's life', but the election was to involve all persons aged 30 or more, the territory of the Free State comprising a huge, multi-member electoral area. The description of the criteria for the nomination of candidates was intended to indicate the need for representation of a particularly 'important aspect of the Nation's life', the Protestant minority; but since the ultimate choice would be the people's, the most the Oireachtas could do to secure the return of ex-Unionists would be to weight the ballot-paper in their favour. In a proportional representation election fought along denominational lines, Protestants could expect to win one or possibly two seats at the triennial elections, making a probable total group of between four and eight Protestants in the Senate – hardly a formidable number.

The first Senate could not be formed by this means. Half of its members were nominated by the President of the Executive Council and the remainder were elected by the Dáil. While several prominent Unionist peers declined to serve, WT Cosgrave's 30 nominees included no fewer than 16 ex-Unionists; in all, non-Roman Catholics accounted for 24 of the 60 new senators. The prominent role this group would play was symbolised in the election of ex-Unionist Lord Glenavy as the Senate's first chairman (the first vice-chairman being a Quaker, Senator Douglas).

Clearly-defined party groups emerged in the Senate only after 1928, but even before that time there was an 'Independent Group' consisting mainly of ex-Unionists and under the chairmanship of (ex-IUA) Senator Jameson. The power of this group was damaged in successive elections – it dropped to 12 members in 1928, 10 in 1931 and 7 in 1934. Several Protestants and ex-Unionists remained as independents (i.e. outside the Independent Group), but they, too, were casualties of the electoral process and heightening party polarisation. The total number of Independents in the Senate dropped to 15 (1928), 9 (1931) and 4 (1934) (O'Sullivan 1940: 447).

The combination of ex-Unionists with others in forming a general pro-Treaty Senate majority was a factor in provoking the abolition of the house itself in 1936, following a number of clashes with the Dáil. The new Senate established under the Constitution of 1937 was a much less satisfactory body from an ex-Unionist perspective; though again consisting of 60 members, 43 of these were to be indirectly elected to represent five vocational panels (but in practice they have always reflected the party political divisions of the country), six were to be directly elected by graduates of the two universities and 11 were to be nominated by the Taoiseach. The Taoiseach's nominees tend to include one or two Protestants, and to these in the past could be added three Dublin University representatives; but no Protestant or ex-Unionist bloc emerged at any time in the new Senate.

Impediments to Protestant political mobilisation

As a small minority, southern Irish Protestants might have been expected to suffer from certain of the disadvantages of political minorities in general. Demographic decline is not, however, a sufficient explanation of their political passivity. While this lessened the electoral prospects of any party based mainly on the Protestant minority, it does not explain why Irish Protestants failed where the relatively weaker Baltic Germans succeeded. Three types of circumstance appear to have inhibited Protestant political organisation after 1922: institutional, cultural and contextual factors.

The principal *institutional* factor has been the electoral system. While the introduction of proportional representation lowered the threshold of representation by an enormous extent, the type adopted in Ireland contrasted in two important respects with the normal continental European list systems. In the first place, the single transferable vote form, with its demanding condition that candidates be ranked and its complex counting procedures, imposes a practical limit on constituency size. The practice in Ireland has been to keep constituencies small and thus to keep the electoral quota relatively high (in a three-member constituency a party needs at least 25 per cent of the votes to be sure of a seat, in a four-member constituency 20 per cent, and so on). This factor clearly erected a barrier in the way of Protestant representation, as the example of the division of County Dublin in 1935 has shown. Second, until 1963, voting in Ireland was, in theory, for candidates rather than for parties; in continental Europe, by contrast, the exigencies of the list system force electoral alliances and institutionalise political parties. It was not, in other words, necessary for Protestants to form a party in order to secure Dáil representation.

Second, there was also an important *political cultural* difference between Ireland and the East European cases where there were minorities comparable to the Irish Protestants. The long British two-party tradition of government – opposition alternation made this model seem natural in Ireland; in the other cases, either a non-party or a multi-party tradition was the norm. When Irish Unionists were no longer part of one of the major British parties, it could be argued, it seemed more appropriate to seek out allies among the major Irish parties than to attempt to secure sectional representation.

Third, the *political context* within which the Irish minority operated contrasted with that characteristic of similar minorities in central or eastern Europe. The most important consideration was that the economic position of the Protestant minority was not under threat. Like the other minorities, its power had traditionally been based on control of the land. In Ireland, however, its grip over the primary sector of the economy had been eroded before independence, and the 1923 Land Act completed a process that was only being initiated in 1919 and 1920 in Estonia and Latvia, a process that urgently demanded the existence of strong Baltic German parties. In addition, several other cases had their 'Ulsters' – the Åland Islands in Finland and the Sudetenland in Czechoslovakia being the most obvious examples. In such regions, the 'minority' was, in fact, a majority, and the population was disposed to be more assertive than in regions where it was swamped by the rest of the population. In Ireland, however, the minority problem had been 'solved' by the exclusion of Northern Ireland, which had the effect of serving as an alternative focus of Protestant loyalty, siphoning off the most vigorous opponents of Home Rule, and removing from the jurisdiction of the government in Dublin the main territories that were cohesively Protestant.

Furthermore, the ideology in particular of the German minorities was not redundant after independence. Pan-Germanism was not merely a starry ideal; it could be seen, as events showed, as a realistic goal. In Ireland, by contrast, Unionism was acknowledged to be irrelevant after 1922 not only because of the finality of the break with Britain but also because, as dismayed and betrayed Irish Protestants saw it, the Union had been dissolved by the British themselves. Finally, there was not, in the East European cases, any continuing threat to the state of a type that the minority found both objectionable and immediate, and of such a nature as to call for the sinking of differences between minority and majority. The defeat of the Red forces in Finland, Estonia and Latvia in 1918–19 appeared to be decisive. In Ireland, however, the Free State appeared to be under serious attack from the outset and, objectionable though Protestants found the Treaty, it was infinitely more satisfactory than the Republic; a closing of ranks with the defenders of the Treaty seemed, consequently, to be appropriate.

The identity of southern Protestants: from ethnic minority to religious minority?

The weak political articulation of southern Irish Protestants after 1922 and the changed character of their self-expression contrasts so sharply with their vocal and self-confident performance before that date that the question arises as to whether this might not constitute a rare example of the successful assimilation of an ethnic minority. To defend the view that such a process of assimilation has indeed occurred requires us to establish at least two points: that southern Protestants *were* an ethnic minority in the past, and that they *are not* today. We present some impressionistic and other evidence in the following paragraphs in support of these points. This is followed by a discussion of certain other objectively traceable changes that we might expect to lead, inevitably, precisely to such assimilation. These changes constitute elements of a causal explanation of this transformation, but they also provide support for the view that assimilation is likely to have taken place even if direct evidence for this is lacking.

Of the strength and direction of southern Protestants' political views in the later nineteenth century, there can be little doubt. Near-unanimous opposition to any measure of devolved government for Ireland is an example. This had been made clear by Protestant reaction to the second Home Rule Bill, which was passed by the House of Commons but blocked by the House of Lords in 1893. Apart from vigorous opposition from Ulster, the entire Irish Protestant establishment seemed opposed to the measure. The local authorities of almost every southern county (still controlled, in general, by Protestants) passed resolutions of protest, and 'immense demonstrations' against Home Rule in Dublin, Cork and Limerick were reported by the main unionist political organisation.[11] Further denunciations were forthcoming from the predominantly Protestant educational, medical and commercial establishments: from the Senate of Dublin University, the fellows of the Royal College of Surgeons and of the Royal College of Physicians, the Council of Dublin Chamber of Commerce and the Dublin Stock Exchange. The Church of Ireland, whose name implied a particularly close connection with the country, made known its determined opposition at a General Synod convened for the purpose and at special meetings of all but 39 of the country's 1,229 select vestries (parish councils); and virtually all adult Quakers signed a petition against Home Rule. To underline the point, the Irish Unionist Alliance (which in 1897 was to claim 270 branches and 40,000 members outside Ulster) collected 127,000 signatures for an anti-Home Rule petition in the provinces of Leinster, Munster and Connacht alone.[12]

That the configuration of Protestant attitudes extended well beyond a distinctively Unionist response to a particular political issue is not in doubt. The myths and symbols that were shared by this community set it apart from the nationalist majority. Its national anthem, in an emotional as well as a formal sense, was 'God save the King!'; its flag was the Union Jack; and the version of history to which it was attached was distinctly 'British'. This is clear from autobiographical and other writings of the period, as well as from the kind of debates that took place within the educational sector over precisely these issues.

The 1920s and 1930s appears to have been a period of sharp transition for the minority. Protestants found themselves in a new state whose ethos they regarded as objectionable. Adjustment was probably easier for urban Protestants involved in extensive commercial relations with their Catholic neighbours than for the remnants of the landed gentry, or, if it was not easier, it was certainly more necessary. Literary evidence from the period suggests that Protestants came to a reluctant accommodation with the new regime, even if it was one from which they remained emotionally detached (see Brown 1981: 107–37). This aloofness, accompanied in Protestant enclaves in such areas as Malahide by attachment to values of 'Englishness', survived at least into the 1940s and 1950s (Inglis 1962; Viney 1966).

By the 1990s, evidence of a separate Protestant ethnic identity in the Republic of Ireland is difficult to find. There is no organised political articulation of the values traditionally associated with the minority. External expressions of traditional loyalism are almost never to be seen in public, though they may exist in milder forms in private. While survey evidence on the subject is limited, it is not incompatible with the view that southern Protestants identify themselves unambiguously as 'Irish' and that they now tend to be more or less indistinguishable from Catholics in their political priorities (though they may follow a slightly different pattern of party preference). There are, of course, exceptions, and these are most likely to be encountered in the border counties. In part because of proximity to Northern Ireland but also because of the existence of Protestant communities there that are demographically more powerful, expressions of separate cultural identity (such as the existence of Orange Lodges and pronounced patterns of voting for Protestant candidates) are commonly to be found in these counties. Whether such patterns of identity will survive through the next century remains to be seen; but the long-term trend seems to be one of steady assimilation.

There are strong reasons for expecting precisely this kind of change. Survival of minority ethnic identity depends in large measure on the maintenance of separate social institutions capable of sustaining this identity. It is precisely the survival of such institutions among Finland's small Swedish-speaking minority that has been credited with a central role in the maintenance of that group's separate identity (Sundberg 1985: 173). Many of these institutions have long disappeared among southern Irish Protestants: for example, political organisations (except in isolated areas) in the 1920s, and the Orange Order more gradually, though less completely. Protestant clubs, social organisations and sporting bodies gradually opened up their membership to Catholics, and began to change fundamentally in character from the 1950s onwards, to the point where their identity has been transformed. The once-flourishing Protestant press has virtually disappeared, as its original readership has been replaced by a predominantly Catholic one – the provincial papers decades ago, the *Irish Times* in the 1960s. Even the Protestant school system, at all levels from the primary school to Trinity College, has been a victim of the growing secularism of the Catholic community: children of Catholic parents increasingly attend these institutions and steadily contribute to a significant change in their culture. Not even the Protestant churches (as places of worship) themselves are the staunch bulwarks that they once were against Catholicism; many are attended regularly by worshippers of Catholic background.

Much of the difficulty that the Protestant community has encountered in maintaining a separate identity arises from the fact that religion constitutes a less secure barrier than language against penetration from the dominant culture. Religion has been of dual significance in Irish politics. First, it has set apart people whose perceptions of the appropriate role of the state were in conflict. As 'Rome Rule', Home Rule signified to Protestants an unacceptable type of state intervention in the areas of education, medicine and family law. The terms of the Treaty and of the Constitution of 1922 gave some guarantees in this respect, but the passage of time afforded many examples of strong influence of specifically Roman Catholic theology on legislation and on the administration of the state. As we have seen, though, these were not taken so seriously by Protestants as to justify the formation of a distinct party or defence organisation. In recent years, the need for such defence has greatly diminished: as religious belief and practice have declined, the character of Catholicism has changed, with a pronounced growth in the secularisation of Irish social life and the 'Protestanisation' of Catholic belief and practice (by which is meant a growing tendency to reject the authority of the church and to devise one's own path to spirituality and morality (Inglis 1988: 203–42)).

The second significance of religion was to set apart two ethnic groups, though not with the same degree of clarity as was the case with language in central and eastern Europe. Both Unionists and Nationalists rejected religion as an ethnic label, but there was no set of terms with which to replace it (a linguistic deficiency whose success in impeding the development of 'Protestant' self-consciousness should not be under-estimated). The literary and autobiographical output of Irish Protestant authors seems to provide evidence of a slow evolution of Protestant self-consciousness. Up to the late nineteenth century, when their dominance was unquestioned, Protestants appear not to have been concerned by questions of national identity. The revolution in Catholic consciousness that coincided with Catholic social and political mobilisation in the 1880s forced Protestants to reconsider their status; there was a tendency for the two communities to see themselves as part of separate heritages, to adhere to incompatible myths of history and to hold conflicting cultural and political aspirations. Yet, southern Protestants did not opt unambiguously for one of these alternatives, and this unwillingness to see themselves as a distinct national group from Catholics has, no doubt, added to Protestant reluctance to play an autonomous political role in the public life of the 26 counties after 1922.

This ambiguous attitude towards the wider community within which they are located also appears to be confirmed by current sociological research into the group identity of the Protestant minority in the Republic. Preliminary results based on analysis of structured group meetings of Protestants using a combination of sociological and psychoanalytical techniques have pointed to a certain ambivalence: on the one hand, consciousness of a separate identity from Catholics, but, on the other, an anxiety to be accepted as part of the wider community.[13] Furthermore, the view that the boundary between southern Protestants and southern Catholics cannot now be described as an *ethnic* one is not incompatible with the view that significant *ethnographic* differences between the two communities remain. There is evidence of such surviving differences, often subtly expressed, in a range of domains, including speech patterns, eating habits, attitudes towards waste, interest in genealogy, attitudes towards alcohol and death rituals, not to mention differences rooted in two very different religious belief systems.[14]

Conclusion

The remarks above on the changing character of the southern Protestant minority are based in large measure on impressionistic evidence. This minority, it has been suggested, has undergone a fundamental change in its ethnic orientation; life in independent Ireland has resulted in a steady shift from British to Irish ethnic allegiance. This change, though, has taken place in a wider context of value and attitudinal change. It is not only southern Protestants whose values have shifted; many of the changes within this community must be seen in the context of changes within the majority community.

In assessing change within the Catholic community, we encounter some of the same difficulties as in the case of the Protestants. For the contemporary period, survey evidence is available in abundance, but this extends backwards in time in years rather than in decades. It is clear that 75 years of partition have taken their toll: Catholics north and south may have constituted a single community in the early years of this century, but it would be difficult to find contemporary evidence to suggest that this pattern has continued. On the contrary, survey data from 1988–89 show that southern Catholics appear to feel that they have much in common with southern Protestants, and the social psychological distance that separates them from northern Catholics is, strangely, greater than that which separates them from the English (Mac Gréil 1996). Quite apart from intergroup attitudes, though, it is clear that the character of southern Catholicism has changed profoundly. Not only is a majority of the population prepared to distinguish more clearly than in the past between appropriate jurisdictions for the church and the state, as referendum results and public opinion polls show; even the quality of religious life has changed, with a decline in church attendance and an enormous drop in clerical recruitment.

In fact, much of the change in the identity of southern Protestants may well be a response to change in the Catholic community. As Catholics become more secular in orientation, they are in the process of acquiring values that were once largely a monopoly of Protestants. But as ecumenism develops and the social significance of religion declines, the barriers that helped to sustain the culture of a separate Protestant community have been undermined. The ultimate irony is that a community whose abiding fear 100 years ago was the spectre of 'Rome Rule' may itself have fallen victim not to this ogre, but rather to the fact that, in the long term, the menace of monolithic Catholicism turned out to be an unthreatening variant of Christian or post-Christian belief.

Endnotes

1 There is no need to review the vast literature on Northern Ireland; for overviews see, for instance, Whyte 1991 and O'Leary and McGarry 1996.

2 See Jackson and McHardy 1984. The literature on the political role of the southern minority is well developed for the period up to 1922 (see, for example, Akenson 1991; Buckland 1972; McDowell 1997), and is reinforced by publications that deal more specifically with religious issues, or with the history of the main Protestant church (for example, Bowen 1995; Ford, McGuire and Milne 1995; Hurley 1970; McDowell 1973; Milne 1966). Literature whose primary focus is on the post-1922 period includes a short historical review (Lyons 1967), a sociological overview (Bowen 1983) and a number of overviews directed at a more general readership (for example, Viney 1966; White 1975).

3 In 1991, for instance, the six most important Protestant denominations accounted for 98.8 per cent of those belonging to religions other than Roman Catholicism, made up as follows: Church of Ireland (including 'Protestants'), 79.8 per cent; Presbyterians, 11.8 per cent; Methodists, 4.5 per cent; Baptists 1.0 per cent; Lutherans, 0.9 per cent; and Society of Friends, 0.7 per cent. See Census of Population of Ireland, 1991.

4 See Hart (1996) for an examination of the impact of the events of this period on Protestant communities in Cork, and Dooley (1990) for the position in the very different context of the border county of Monaghan.

5 On the Anglo-Irish tradition, see especially Beckett (1976). For a vivid schematic overview of the differences between this community and Catholic society, see McConville (1986: 247–54).

6 For local studies of the effects of the act see Daly (1984: 203–21) for Dublin and d'Alton (1978), and d'Alton (1980) for Cork.

7 This group was drawn from the same class as the justices of the peace, who had an important judicial and policing function. In 1884, 73 per cent of justices of the peace in southern Ireland were Protestant; notwithstanding the subsequent appointment of large numbers of Catholics, by 1910 the proportion of Protestants had dropped only to 60 per cent (calculated from House of Commons (1884) and House of Commons (1910: 28)).

8 Calculated from Smith (1973) and Walker (1978).

9 The three constituencies were Dublin University, South County Dublin and the St. Stephen's Green division of Dublin City. The significance of religious

affiliation in determining electoral preferences is confirmed by an analysis of the statistical relationship between the percentage of Protestants in 1891 and the percentage of voters in each of the 51 contested constituencies in 1885 in the 26 counties supporting Conservative candidates: the correlation coefficient (Pearson's) between the two is 0.95. For a local study of the relationship between religion and political mobilisation in this period see d'Alton (1973).

10 On the phenomenon of Catholic unionism, see Biggs-Davison and Chowdharay-Best (1984). Protestant nationalists have been more extensively studied; see, for instance, Ó Broin (1985).

11 *Annual report of the Irish Unionist Alliance*, 1893, pp. 6–14, 42.

12 *Annual report of the Irish Unionist Alliance*, 1897, p. 11.

13 See Mennell (1997), which reports on some preliminary findings of the research team examining the topic 'Threatened bonds: a study in the sociology of emotions and the dynamics of group identities'. I am grateful to the research team for making these preliminary findings available.

14 I am indebted for this insight to Deirdre Nuttall, graduate student, Department of Irish Folklore, University College Dublin.

Chapter 6

The changing role of women

Yvonne Galligan

Introduction

Ireland's image as a 'rural conservative and Catholic backwater of post-war Europe'
(Breen *et al.* 1990: 1) was shattered in 1990 with the election of feminist and liberal reformer, Mary Robinson, to the office of President of the Republic of Ireland.
The image of a modern, self-assured country with a role in international politics
was cultivated by Robinson for the duration of her seven-year term. In November
1997, many traditionalists expected that with the election of Northern nationalist,
Mary McAleese, as successor to Robinson, conservative Catholicism was ready
to reassert itself once more. This was not to be. Shortly after taking office, McAleese
reaffirmed the independence of thought and action which had characterised the
presidency of her predecessor. She challenged the doctrine of the institution with
which she had been closely identified during her presidential candidacy, the Roman
Catholic Church. It was clear that by 1997 the old certainties of Irish political and
social life were open to scrutiny. It is no accident that two female presidents have
done much to redefine and empower the Republic's most conservative political institution. In acknowledging the positive, creative achievements of communities on the
island of Ireland, Robinson and McAleese were laying the ghosts of an Ireland of
the past, facilitating the emergence of a modern, diverse society and renewing links
between Northern Ireland and the Republic.

That this should come from two women is not surprising, given the development
of women's consciousness regarding their status in society over the last two decades. There is little doubt that the role of women in Ireland today is very different
to the social role and function assigned to their mothers, even if attitudes towards
that new role remain staunchly traditional. Women's aspirations in the 1990s are
not confined to home and family. Increasingly, Article 41 of the Constitution,
which defines women's citizenship in orthodox patriarchal terms, is seen as an
irrelevant portrayal of the reality of Irish women's experiences. Nevertheless, the
gains in women's rights and the revaluation of women's role and status in society
did not come easily to a people steeped in the twin conservatisms of nationalism
and Roman Catholicism. Progress in this area was slow, with modest advances

being made within an incremental framework of policy making. That such was the case is not surprising, and even today, the fashioning of women's civic and social roles takes place in the context of complex views on gender equality. A similar pattern of conservative hegemony is evident in Northern Ireland, where McWilliams (1993: 79) observes that 'church and state have combined together at various times to ensure that the prime role for women was as home-makers and mothers'.

The subject of this chapter is the extent to which conservative, traditional and religious attitudes influencing the role and status of women in society hold sway at the close of the millennium. The tensions between slowly changing attitudes towards traditional gender roles and the visible progress on women's political representation and rights is explored. While the focus of the chapter is primarily on the Republic of Ireland, comparisons are drawn between the situation of women in the Republic and Northern Ireland. The first part of the chapter provides a picture of women's participation in the economy and politics and considers the response of parties and the modification of political institutions to women's demand for political participation. The second section of the chapter explores the attitudinal context underlying the efforts of women to secure a rightful share of the civic space. The study concludes by suggesting that women's participation in civic society on the island is set to continue to grow into the new millennium, that political institutional and policy responses will also evolve in the direction of ensuring gender equality, but that developments in egalitarian attitudes within society will emerge more slowly, indicating that for the foreseeable future at any rate, the tension between women's changing role and social expectations will continue.

From parlour to parliament

In 1973, in a study of Irish political and social culture, Schmitt characterised Irish society as being male dominated, where 'within the home the major decisions are traditionally made by the male head-of-family, whose word – especially in economic matters – is absolute' (1973: 46). Although Schmitt observed some lessening of male autocracy in urban areas, a strong tradition of female deference to family males was clearly the order of the day, with women and girls accorded 'a secondary and less favoured position within the Irish family' (46). This set of attitudes towards gender relations within the family translated into an unambiguously gendered social and economic division of labour, where 'the mature adult woman has a specific place in the community and she knows it and keeps it. That is, briefly, at home looking after her husband, house and family' (46). Schmitt was not alone in this assessment of gender relations in Irish society at a time when Europe was still 'swinging' to the sixties and 'flower power', peace movements and protest politics were gripping the United States of America. The Commission on the Status of Women (1972: 12) identified a 'cultural mould' which encouraged the view 'that there are definite and separate roles for the sexes and that a woman's life pattern will be predominantly home-centred while the man's life pattern will be predominantly centred on employment'. The Commission went on to argue that underlying this view was the 'broader question of traditional male attitudes to women's role in society and male reluctance to accept women as an equal partner on either a social or domestic level' (13).

Since then, dramatic changes have come about in women's position in society, particularly in terms of women's participation in the workforce (CSO 1997). In 1971, just over a quarter of a million women aged 15 or over were at work in the Republic, accounting for just over one-quarter (26 per cent) of the total workforce. By 1996, this figure had increased by 170 per cent, representing almost four in ten (38 per cent) of those at work. This was equivalent to the rate of women's economic activity in Northern Ireland in 1971 (EOCNI 1993). When compared with male employment patterns in this time interval, the increase in women's labour force participation is even more striking. In 1971, men in employment outnumbered women by almost three to one. In 1996, the number of men in the workforce had hardly changed from 1971, registering an increase of less than one per cent. In contrast to the pattern of women's economic activity in the Republic, women in Northern Ireland have a higher level of workforce participation, with almost half (47.7 per cent) of working-age women in employment (EOCNI 1993). It is evident, then, that while there have been significant increases in women's overall participation in the labour force in the Republic, it is still significantly lower than in the North, suggesting that there may be stronger social constraints operating to inhibit women's economic participation in the Republic than in the North. This view is borne out in a closer examination of the pattern of women's employment in both jurisdictions.

The increase in women's participation in the workforce in the Republic over a 25-year period can be almost wholly accounted for by the entry of married women into employment. In 1971, married women made up 14 per cent of the female workforce, a figure kept low by the existence of an extensive public sector ban on the employment of married women. Following the lifting of the 'marriage bar' in 1973, the number of married women at work grew substantially, and by 1996 accounted for just half of the female workforce (CSO 1997). This illustrates a convergence with the employment pattern for married women in Northern Ireland. In 1971, 29 per cent of married women were working in the North, four times as many as in the South (McWilliams 1993: 86). By 1993, over one half (55.3 per cent) of married women were employed outside the home (EOCNI 1996: 9).

Marriage was not the only significant feature of women's employment profile in the 1990s. Motherhood was also a growing characteristic. Evidence of a growing participation of mothers in the labour force emerged during the 1990s in the Republic, accounting for well over one-third (36.6 per cent) of the female workforce in 1996, compared with just over one quarter (25.7 per cent) in 1991. However, the Republic has some way to go to match maternal employement levels in Northern Ireland, where mothers comprised just over one half (51.2 per cent) of the female workforce (EOCNI 1996: 11). In the Republic, mothers of one or two children are more likely to be in paid employment than mothers of three or more children. In Northern Ireland, a noticeable fall-off in labour force participation rates for mothers occurs when there are five or more children in a family. Thus, mothers in Northern

Ireland are more integrated into the workforce than mothers in the Republic, suggesting an underlying difference in social attitudes towards working mothers in both parts of the island.

In considering these figures, however, we need to be aware that these official statistics mask women's complex employment patterns. As Smyth points out:

> measures of the numbers of women in employment and unemployment cannot be regarded as unproblematic, however. It has been argued that official statistics present labour market participation in 'male' terms (ie, as a permanent, full-time relationship), thus leading to a distorted or inadequate coverage of the female labour force. In particular, using figures based on women's 'usual employment situation' underestimates less regular forms of employment, such as seasonal or casual work, some types of part-time work, as well as unpaid labour carried out in the home, farm or business. (1997: 65)

On closer examination, we find that, in 1993, while four-fifths (81.5 per cent) of women in regular employment in the Republic had a full-time job, more than nine out of ten men (96.1 per cent) held regular full-time positions. The remaining one-fifth of employed women (18.5 per cent) worked part-time, significantly more than the 4 per cent of men in this category. In the case of women working in regular part-time employment, almost three quarters (71 per cent) were married, while married women constituted two in five (44 per cent) women holding full-time regular positions (EEA 1995: 4). In 1993, almost twice as many women in Northern Ireland worked part-time (37.3 per cent) as compared with the South, reflecting the higher participation of mothers in the workforce in the region (EOCNI 1996: 15, 16, 18). In sum, then, the marital status of women is a factor in determining the nature of female employment patterns, with part-time regular work being dominated by married women and full-time regular positions filled by a majority of non-married women in both parts of the island. These patterns clearly show the effects of family responsibilities and the absence of organised child-care and family-care facilities on women's employment opportunities.

In the political arena too, women have made measurable, if modest, strides since the 1970s. In 1969, there were three (2.1 per cent) women TDs (parliamentarians) in Dáil Éireann (lower house of parliament) and five (8.3 per cent) women senators. In 1997, 20 (12 per cent) women were elected to the Dáil, there were eleven (18.3 per cent) women senators, three (20 per cent) women held government ministries and two (11.7 per cent) held junior ministries. These advances are in marked contrast to the situation for women in political life in Northern Ireland, where only three women have been elected to parliament from the region since 1945 and none were successful in the 1997 United Kingdom general election (Galligan and Wilford 1998a).

In 1967, women's representation in local government in the Republic, at 3.3 per cent, mirrored that in the Dáil. Although this had increased to just under 15 per cent in 1997, the hoped-for breakthrough following the Robinson presidential success in 1990 did not materialise. These figures are similar to the representation of women in local government in Northern Ireland, where in 1997, women's membership of local councils stood at 14.1 per cent (Galligan and Wilford 1998a, Heenan and Gray 1998).

State boards are an important area of public authority on both parts of the island. In the Republic, such boards comprised 27 per cent women, with 35 per cent of the government nominees being women (*Irish Times* 15 October 1997). In Northern Ireland, state boards are particularly significant sites of public decision-making, with responsibility for the delivery of major services such as education and social services. Despite women's poor electoral record in the province, they were represented in greater numbers on nominated boards (31.1 per cent in 1997) than in the Republic. Referring to the opportunities for women's political participation in Northern Ireland, Heenan and Gray (1998: forthcoming) remark that:

> it is rather paradoxical that while there is justifiable concern about the under-representation of women on public bodies, women have achieved considerably greater representation *via* the system of appointed public bodies than through electoral politics.

Explanations for the modesty of women's participatory record in public life in Ireland are rooted in social and cultural attitudes towards women's role in society which will be discussed later in this chapter. However, the presence (or absence) of women from sites of economic and political decision making is not the only measure of women's political and civic engagement. While representational matters are important in that they give a quantifiable picture of women's participation in clearly defined political and economic sites, women's activity has taken other, equally significant, forms as well.

From kitchen table to negotiating table

The growing modernisation of Irish society throughout the 1960s created a space for the emergence of new political discourses, in particular, discourses based around new social movements. Ireland was not immune from the civil liberties and feminist protests elsewhere in the world. The civil rights movement in Northern Ireland and the revival of nationalist politics in the province in the late 1960s encouraged the development of an emerging critique of women's rights on the island. In the Republic, action campaigns which focused on the grim social and housing conditions in Dublin's inner city acted as a further catalyst for feminist politicisation and mobilisation. A significant network of traditional women's groups also existed, some organised on a national basis and others with connections to a world-wide network of established women's groups. Leaders of these groups, some with a history dating back to the turn of the century and with experience in the feminist campaigns of the early years of the state, were open to advancing the cause of women in a more overt manner than previously. Although there were inevitable tensions between the older, more institutionalised feminists and their radical sisters, Connolly notes that there was little difference in their political agenda:

> The primary difference between the two derived from preferrd strategy – persistently lobbying the state for moderate, gradual legislative change on the one hand, and engaging in controversial, direct action tactics (pickets, protests, expressive action) on the other. However, even though these methods were more concentrated in each sector,

each drew on the same repertoire of tactics (and symbols, ideologies and resources) in a strategic fashion when the need arose. For example the fight for change through the courts was utilised both by mainstream and autonomous feminists, as were petitioning, mass meetings and demonstrations. (1996: 55)

Irish feminists, old and new, placed the issue of women's rights on the political agenda of the Republic – the former through lobbying for the first Commission on the Status of Women and participating in its deliberations (Fitzsimons 1991), the latter through direct action campaigns for contraception and equal pay (Galligan 1998; Smyth 1993: 252–3). Although the feminist movement had largely evolved into single-issue pressure groups by the mid-1970s, these groups quickly became adept at advocating legislative changes on women's status in public and political fora (Galligan 1998). In Northern Ireland, the development of feminism was more circumscribed due to the dominance of politicised religious and nationalist ideologies, resulting in a cultural context described as 'armed patriarchy' (Harkin, cited in McWilliams 1995: 15).

Central to the strategic success of women's groups in influencing public policy in the Republic was a willingness to work within existing political structures while maintaining a strong feminist identity. One of the most significant organisations in that respect is the National Women's Council of Ireland (NWCI), formed in 1973 (as the Council for the Status of Women) shortly after the fragmentation of the women's movement by a feminist coalition which had the aim of improving the status of women in Ireland. Since its inception, the NWCI has campaigned at national level for women's equality. It has sought to develop a consensus among its members (which comprised over 135 women's organisations in 1997 representing an estimated 300,000 women) on women's issues. This consensus has been reached with difficulty on some occasions, particularly on abortion, where there was a clear split between affiliated groups holding an anti-abortion stance and others with strong pro-choice views. It is a mark of the resilience of the organisation that it has succeeded in surmounting internal tensions and in expanding its membership base among women's groups (Fitzsimons 1991).

Perhaps the most significant success of the NWCI is the role it has played in bringing about the establishment of two government commissions on the status of women, one in 1970, the second in 1990. The report of each commission has been hailed in its time as a blueprint for women's rights in Ireland. Today, renamed the National Women's Council of Ireland (NWCI), the organisation is recognised by government as the official representative of women's interests and is consulted on a diverse range of policy issues with a potential impact on women (Galligan 1998). The expansion of corporatist-style bargaining structures on pay and socio-economic issues during the 1990s brought the NWCI into an arena from which it had been previously excluded (see Chapter 7), thus reinforcing the position of the organisation as a significant player in national economic- and social-policy making.

Other feminist organisations have made their mark on specific policy areas. Among them, AIM (Action, Information, Motivation), a direct offshoot of the women's liberation movement, highlighted the gross inequalities in rights between women and men in family law and exerted a critical influence on policy reforms in this area. Cherish, a support group for unmarried mothers established at a time when having a child out of wedlock attracted social stigma, has had a direct influence on the development of social policy on children and lone parents. The Rape Crisis Centre groups have made a significant contribution to reforms in the law on sexual violence while Women's Aid has played a similar role in raising public and political awareness of domestic violence and in bringing about substantial policy change (Galligan 1998).

Elite feminist groups with a national profile and a focus on government lobbying often obtain media attention at the expense of smaller, more localised and less high-profile women's organisations. Although there is little research on the extent, nature and form of women's sub-national agencies, there is evidence that, since the 1970s, Irish women have become involved in local political action, often with the needs of their children as catalysts for political engagement. Women have also assessed their own needs and have developed a range of support groups and services at local level, assisted in the 1990s by funding from the state and state agencies. The mushrooming of adult education activities and community writing workshops, along with extensive participation in the EU-sponsored New Opportunities for Women (NOW) programme for women wishing to return to employment attest to this desire for self-improvement.

Whether these groups can be seen as part of the women's movement is a difficult question, for, as recent research by O'Donovan and Ward (1998) shows, not all women's groups are comfortable with being identified as feminist or with an overtly political agenda. The pattern of women's activity at local level is defined in very specific terms, is issue driven and avoids confronting the major social and political questions of the day in the interests of group unity. Group activities are seen as ends in themselves, not necessarily the beginning of a broader level of political involvement, as the dearth of women in local politics attests.

The growth of feminism and women's representative associations in Northern Ireland has been much more restricted than in the Republic due to a combination of political and historical circumstances shaped, as has already been noted, by the dominance of a conservative consensus within state and religious institutions. McWilliams summarised the obstacles facing women in the North who sought to carve out a feminist space in the following terms:

> When traditional religious attitudes were combined with the absence of a liberal
> democracy, and where the political parties on both sides of the sectarian divide formed
> a united opposition to the above legislation, then it is not difficult to appreciate why the
> question of women's rights came far down on the political agenda. At the same time,
> the high degree of social deprivation in Northern Ireland meant that there was a very
> strong community development movement but one in which any connnection with
> feminism was strenuously resisted. (1995: 18–19)

Yet the fragmentation of feminism (stemming from the unresolved question of competing nationalisms) from the mid-1970s to the mid-1980s was gradually replaced by a growing network of community-based women's centres, committees and single-issue organisations that stressed the commonality of women's situation rather than the political differences that divided women. This way of working across the sectarian divide has found its most forceful political expression in the Women's Coalition, formed in 1996 to give women a voice in the peace process (Hinds 1998, Wilford and Galligan 1998). Coalition candidates contested the 1997 General Election on the basis that women could make a difference to the political context of the North. Although unsuccessful in obtaining a seat in parliament, the Women's Coalition is represented in peace-talk negotiations within the Forum talks, where it continually challenges the anti-woman bias in the attitudes of other political party members towards its presence.

Institutional responses

From the establishment of the first Commission on the Status of Women in 1970 in the Republic of Ireland to the publication in 1997 of the deliberations of a government task force on violence against women, the political and party systems have provided a muted response to the continuous pressure from women seeking a representational voice in decision-making. The demand-response process, while clearly visible, was not solely the business of two groups, state and women, but involved a much more complex interaction of national, international and European forces for change. In the 1970s, pressure from feminists in Ireland through the NWCI, along with recommendations from the United Nations, led to the establishment of the first Commission on the Status of Women. In 1977, the representations of feminists, many of whom were based in trade-union politics, combined with a requirement to fulfil European Union directives on equality in employment led to the establishment of the Employment Equality Agency (EEA) on a statutory basis (Galligan 1998).

In the 1980s, institutional responses took the form of the establishment of the junior ministry for women's affairs (an office held by a former active feminist) and the creation of the parliamentary committee on women's rights in 1982 and 1983, respectively (Mahon and Morgan 1998). In the 1990s, the development of women's policy machinery within government structures was considerably advanced with the creation of a full ministry for equality and law reform which pursued a proactive agenda on women's rights. Other initiatives included a second Commission on the status of women; increased state funding to established groups providing a service for women, such as the Rape Crisis Centres and Women's Aid; funding support for women's community initiatives; the introduction of a 40 per cent gender quota on state boards; and the development of the NOW programme and attention to women's needs in the development of a national health policy. The foregoing is not a complete list of woman-specific initiatives introduced by govenments in the 1990s, but it is clear that the advancement of women's concerns went further than the development of women's policy machinery and included a woman-related perspective in the policy concerns of a range of government ministries.

Political initiatives taken in 1997 subsequent to the installation of a Fianna Fáil-Progressive Democrat government point to some dilution of institutional commitment to women's agencies. The ministry for women's affairs and family law reform was demoted to a junior portfolio and placed within the remit of the Department of Justice, Equality and Law Reform. The long-standing parliamentary committee on women's rights was incorporated within a restructured committee on Justice, Equality and Law Reform. However, the government did reaffirm the commitment of its predecessor to implementing the 40 per cent gender quota target on state boards. By 1997, then, government, parliamentary and party structures had changed to accommodate the representation of women and women's concerns. Within the formal institutional structure, women's presence at the negotiating table is a tenuous one, open to being advanced or impeded by the extent of government commitment to women's affairs.

Parties too, could ignore women no longer after the 'discovery' of the 'women's vote' in 1977. Although some were more reluctant than others to incorporate women into senior party decision-making sites, by the late 1990s all parties in the Republic had made some provision for women's representation within internal party structures (Galligan and Wilford 1998a). If the level of women's representation on a party's national executive is taken as a measure of the integration of women into party decision making, Fianna Fáil, with 17.9 per cent women among the party elite in 1997, emerged as the least open to including women at the top. The two other long-established parties, Fine Gael and Labour, had, respectively, 23.5 per cent and 26 per cent women among national executive members. The more recently formed parties, the Progressive Democrats (PD), Democratic Left (DL) and the Green Party, indicated a more positive attitude to the incorporation of women in leadership roles. All were close to, or exceeded, significant minority levels, with 38.8 per cent of the membership of the PD national executive being women, 41.6 per cent in the case of the Green Party and 42.3 per cent women at the top in DL.

However, these stark figures mask a more complex process at work within each party, suggesting that the old party–new party divide presented by the figures for women's participation at élite level is not the only factor determining women's presence or absence among party leaderships. Levels of women's representation in the upper echelons of party organisations were also determined by party attitudes towards women's political advancement. In the application of this perspective, a bi-polar alignment again emerges, based on party ideology and cutting across the old party–new party model. This time, a clear distinction can be made between the facilitatory policies of the Green Party and the social-democratic parties, Labour and DL, and the diverse range of policies held by the centre-right parties, Fianna Fáil, Fine Gael and the Progressive Democrats (Galligan 1998). The former group of parties have adopted gender quota strategies varying from 25 per cent to 40 per cent as a mechanism for boosting women's representation in their decisison-making ranks and in electoral politics. The latter group indicates a preference for a variety of non-quota strategies. For the PD party, merit is the key factor in deciding participation at elite level and the party adopts a neutral position on the issue of gender. Fianna Fáil, long accustomed to making rhetorical exhortations to women to come forward for party and political office, have begun to shift ground towards a more interventionist policy in recognition of the need for a more structured approach to facilitate women's presence among party elites. Within Fine Gael, the embrace of a positive-action programme aimed at increasing women's participation within party decision-making sites, and the adoption in 1997 of an affirmative action strategy to secure that objective, point to party recognition of the structural obstacles to women's paths to power.

Women's representation in parties in Northern Ireland reveals a similar dynamic to that operating in the South, despite a significantly different political context and party system. Wilford and Galligan noted that:

> those parties that occupy space towards the 'right' of the ideological continuum tend towards the old certainties . . . they favour the reinforcement of orthodox gender relations . . . By comparison, those on the nominal 'left' . . . have tended to gravitate towards the facilitation of women both 'in-house' and in terms of public policy . . . Those parties that claim to occupy a more 'centrist' ideological position, or at least a more liberal one, are more likely to endorse gender recognition as their perspective. (1998: forthcoming)

Yet, parties in Northern Ireland, unlike their counterparts in the Republic, do not attract the confidence of women when it comes to representing women's interests. Admittedly, their record in this area is something less than inspiring. However, the parties are victims of their own environment as the zero-sum nature of politics in the region 'frustrates the active and local pursuit of equal opportunity policies' and perpetuates the political impasse (Wilford and Galligan 1998). Hinds (1998), however, viewed women's experience of political exclusion in a positive light:

> The long painful experience of exclusion and marginalisation suffered by women [in Northern Ireland] makes them ideal champions for new structures, relationships and arrangements which can accommodate people's multi-faceted identities composed of gender, class, culture, race, religion, age, sexual preference; reflect different life experiences, allegiances and analyses; and give voice to different aspirations and expectations. The energy, experience and commitment exhibited by women will not be contained solely within traditional structures. Women have played and continue to play their part in the transformation of Northern Ireland and expect to reach beyond the traditional towards something more innovative and forward looking. (1998: forthcoming)

At the close of the twentieth century, women in Northern Ireland remain marginal to grand-scale politics. Ironically, it is on the foundations of their years of cross-community co-operation that a peace process with real stability has the most chance of success.

A woman's place? Attitudes towards the role and status of women

In the Republic, surveys measuring changes in men's and women's attitudes towards gender roles pinpoint the existence of two contradictory sets of cultural values which, as Whelan and Fahey (1994: 48–50) suggest, are best illustrated in the interplay of women's family and economic roles. The view that women should be accorded equal status with men in society co-exists with the expectation that women will also carry the major responsibility for family affairs. That this should be the case comes as no surprise, given the context of Irish society. The historical influence of a hierarchical and authoritarian culture, in which women's place was defined by the Catholic Church, reinforced by the constitutional framework and circumscribed by conservative attitudes towards women's civic role, led to women's political interest and engagement being among the lowest in the EU during the 1980s.

This disempowerment of Irish women as citizens is clearly seen in studies which measure the popular sense of political competence. Gardiner (1993: 62–3), for instance, highlighted the fact that Irish women felt much less competent than their menfolk in their ability to change or influence an unjust local law. This subjective incompetence in the civic arena is a reflection of findings by Wilcox (1991: 131) and Hardiman and Whelan (1994: 108–11), pointing to attitudes in Ireland towards women's participation in public life being less egalitarian than those in other EU countries. This general observation is modified, however, by indications of strong support among Irish women for female participation in parliament, an egalitarian-ism matched only by women from Denmark (Wilcox 1991: 131). Yet, of the eight EU countries, Irish women were the least supportive of women in non-traditional roles and rivalled German women in the holding of traditional attitudes towards family roles. When compared with attitudes among Irish men, the Wilcox survey indicated that Irish men had even more difficulty than Irish women in expressing confidence in women performing non-traditional roles, while both genders shared common conservative views on family roles.

A series of EU surveys on popular attitudes conducted during the 1970s and 1980s yielded findings on situational constraints which reflected the observations of Wilcox. The results consistently showed the dominance of the traditional model of women in the home in Ireland, where a majority of married men preferred their wives not to work in paid employment (Commission of the European Communities 1987). Paradoxically, surveys also charted increasingly favourable attitudes towards women and men having equal status in society. This trend appeared to be driven by Irish women, particularly those engaged in work outside the home, be they married or unmarried. On the whole, men (with the exception of married men with working spouses) stated a preference for a traditional role for women, indicating an emerging gender gap in popular attitudes.

This view is given some qualification by more recent studies. One of the most significant contributions in this area is the European values systems study, which allows for cross-national comparisons in attitudes among respondents in all EU countries towards a wide array of issues. This research is analysed for the Republic of Ireland by Whelan and others (1994), measuring Irish attitudes towards aspects of religious, economic, political and social life in Ireland and placing them in a comparative context with the EU average response on each dimension. A particular value of this study is the extensive gender breakdown in the analysis of responses. Adherence to traditional religious values was found to be strong on both parts of the island and significantly higher than in other European countries (Hornsby-Smith and Whelan 1994: 42–4). In interpreting sex-role attitudes in Ireland, Whelan and Fahey concluded that:

while Irish attitudes [on sex roles] are not significantly more traditional than European views, the pattern of results does point to the continuing influence of values that underpin sex-role differentiation. Thus while attitudes to women's employment are generally positive, substantial proportions of the adult population consider that there are negative effects for children. Furthermore, significant majorities consider that women can be fulfilled in the role of housewife and indeed that this, rather than jobs outside the home, is what they really want. (1994: 51–2)

Whelan and Fahey (1994: 52–9) also pointed to variations within this overall finding which could be accounted for by the variables of gender, employment status, education and age. They found only modest differences between men and women on attitudes towards women at home and in employment. These differences were more pronounced when analysed by age and education, with younger age groups and groups with third-level education indicating more egalitarian views on women's role. Women, however, were clearly divided in their pro-home, anti-employment views. Women engaged in home duties indicated a consistently traditional attitude towards women's place in society, seeing women's work within the home preferable to a role which involved paid employment. In addition, women in the home emerge as having more conservative attitudes towards working mothers than do their working sisters, while husbands' attitudes towards gender roles reflect a greater level of traditionalism than those held by their wives (Whelan 1994: 97–8). Gardiner encapsulates the complexity of this mix succinctly in the observation that 'Irish women are becoming more liberal minded on a range of issues, moving ahead of Irish men, many of whom still cling to traditional attitudes. There is evidence, however, that traditional attitudes still prevail among many women, highlighting a generation as well as a gender gap' (1993: 73).

The persistence of a strong degree of traditionalism underlying an apparent liberalisation of views on social and sex role matters carried through to other areas of civic life. The Irish position on divorce and abortion, for instance, became more tolerant over time, but overall support for a liberal position on these issues was significantly less than in other European states. Indeed, as O'Donoghue and Devine (1998) show, women on both parts of the island were more likely to adopt a less liberal stance than men on both issues.

In terms of political culture, Hardiman and Whelan (1994: 106–9) confirmed a long-standing observation that women in the Republic were found to be less interested in politics than men. They also observed that gender difference in political participation could be accounted for by the lower level of women's participation in the labour force (1994: 115), suggesting that work is a significant site of politicisation. Overall, though, gender and political participation is given scant treatment in the European values study. To gain a deeper understanding of the dynamics of women's involvement in public arenas, it is necessary to assess the findings of a separate body of literature.

The factors operating to inhibit women from holding public office are a reflection of the larger forces which place obstacles in the way of women's equal participation in civic society as a whole. The constraints on women's political engagement have been extensively studied in recent years and this research provides a picture from which general observations on women's role in Irish society, North and South, can be made. In the Republic, Randall and Smyth observed that 'Irish women have until the very recent past been subject to a particularly intense, if complex, process of socialisation, through the agency of family, school and Church, into an acceptance of an extremely traditional division of labour between the sexes and its implications for women's political role' (1987: 200). They highlight the practical restraints on women's political participation imposed by their family commitments, absence of educational or occupational criteria and lack of personal finance as contributing to the dearth of women seeking political careers (1987: 200–1). Research on attitudes towards women's political participation among women party activists by Brown and Galligan (1998) also confirmed a consensus on the importance of women's traditional family role and pointed to the financial dependency that attends it, presenting women interested in a political career with an additional obstacle to be overcome. In addition, this study observed that the cultural ethos of party politics, which presumes a supportive background network, flexibility of time, late hours and a tolerance of a 'pub' setting, are often incompatible with women's lives, reflecting the situational constraints on women's political activity highlighted by a study on women's underrepresentation in Northern Ireland (Miller, Wilford and Donoghue 1996).

Evidence from Northern Ireland suggests that personal factors, such as lack of experience or confidence, were not relevant in considering reasons for women's absence from political life in the region. However, as in the South, women were less likely to present themselves for selection as party candidates. Parties were perceived as discriminating against women in their selection processes and in their wider organisational cultures. The time-consuming and unsocial hours of a political career were also seen as disadvantaging women, reflecting a constraint on women's political participation identified in many other countries (Galligan and Wilford 1998a).

Attention has also focused in the South on the parties and on their 'gatekeeping' practices which have institutionalised a bias against the selection of women as candidates and the promotion of women within party structures (Randall and Smyth 1987; Galligan 1993; Brown and Galligan 1998; Fawcett 1992). One general finding is the significance of local politics as a stepping-stone to the national arena. Indeed, for women, it has replaced the political family and the 'widow's seat' as the key route of entry to the Dáil. Related to this observation is the finding that Fianna Fáil and Fine Gael are extremely resistant to selecting women as candidates in significant numbers. Furthermore, the two major parties have, in the past, been reluctant to change party institutional rules to advantage women, although Fine Gael has a record of being more open to promoting women within party ranks. There is evidence to show that one of the main conditions for the successful promotion and selection of women is through party elite support. In Fianna Fáil, this seldom extends beyond an occasionally voiced rhetorical commitment, a reflection of general societal attitudes towards women's role. In Northern Ireland, there is a general move among the parties towards an awareness of the structural and situational constraints operating to exclude women from the public realm. Within this overall framework, there is considerable variation. The two main unionist parties, the Ulster Unionist Party (UUP) and

Democratic Unionist Party (DUP) tended to reinforce conventional gender roles. At the other side of the ideological spectrum, the Social Democratic and Labour Party (SDLP) and Sinn Féin were more positive in support of positive action for women within their ranks (Wilford and Galligan 1998a).

Conclusion

We find, then, that in the Republic of Ireland and in Northern Ireland a series of constraints operating to reinforce women's under-representation in political life and in civic participation. Personal factors are a significant initial barrier in determining women's political ambitions in the Republic. Situational factors, related to views on women's social roles, can be seen as impeding women's political opportunities in both jurisdictions on the island, while the structural obstacle of party selectoral preferences serves as an additional barrier to women's political participation. Yet, increasingly, Irish women, North and South, are challenging traditional social, political and economic norms. What is also clear is that political parties on the island act as 'gatekeepers' to the political institutions. In most cases, they are only slowly incorporating an egalitarian approach into their organisational cultures.

In 1973, Schmitt characterised Irish society, in gender terms, as being dominated by the twin pillars of hierarchy and patriarchy. Two decades and more later, a study of Irish society shows the persistence of patriarchy and a weakening of social and religious hierarchy. Political and economic hierarchies have proven more resistant to change in both parts of the island and for different reasons. In the Republic, the overall persistence of conservative attitudes towards the role and status of women have led to women finding themselves in a double bind. It has been found that the level of women's participation in the public sphere (most often represented as political life, though not exclusively so) was related to their participation in the workforce. Traditional attitudes towards women working outside the home, particularly in the case of married women, still persist and are quite strong. Thus, cultural constraints operate to reinforce the tendency for women to focus on home life rather than on public life; political parties reflect this bias in their organisational cultures. As a result, there are few women in politics and public life in Ireland. Many women prefer to direct their energies towards single-issue groups, community organisations and local activity – sites of civic participation which can be more readily reconciled with home and family obligations than can national political and economic leadership. In Northern Ireland, the persistence of traditional attitudes towards women's role and the dominance of the debate on nationalism in political life has excluded women from politics in spite of a high level of workforce participation among women in the region.

In recent decades, women's role in society has changed, largely through the efforts of women in becoming involved in economic, social and political activities. They have not found assistance in this endeavour from cultural attitudes towards women's role. If anything, views supporting a traditional gendered division of labour have persisted and are finding new forms of political expression. In this context, it is not surprising that the political response to women's changing role has been a muted one for the most part. While a range of institutional initiatives have been developed within the state system and a considerable amount of women's-rights legislation has been placed on the statute books, these responses cannot be seen as mould-breaking and role-challenging ventures. Tensions remain between women's expectations of partaking in full citizenship, cultural values which seek to inhibit that role, and institutional and policy responses which offer a modest and piecemeal response to the place women are claiming in civic society.

Chapter 7

Inequality and the representation of interests

Niamh Hardiman

Introduction[1]

For some time now, there has been a common commitment among the major political parties in Ireland to accord priority to tackling a range of social inequalities. From the mid- to late-1980s, the channels through which issues of inequality may been raised within the policy-making process have been widened. During the 1990s, Ireland experienced high and sustained growth, to the extent that comparison with the high-growth 'tiger economies' of Southeast Asia did not seem far-fetched. While it might have been argued that resources to tackle inequalities were constrained during the 1980s, these limits no longer existed by the second half of the 1990s. This was a time of unprecedented national prosperity. It would appear that conditions were uniquely favourable for making significant progress on a range of social problems.

Growth brought improvement on some measures, particularly in the expansion of employment opportunities and reduction of the numbers unemployed or emigrating. Governments introduced a range of policies designed to tackle social inequalities. However, the effects of these policies were insufficient to make a significant impact. The hardships of fiscal adjustments in the 1980s had been far from equally shared; it would appear that the benefits of growth in the 1990s were also far from equally shared. A large and indeed growing section of the population was left behind in relative terms.

This chapter explores some of the reasons for the persistence of serious social inequalities in Irish society. The first section outlines some of the reasons why we might have expected inequalities to be tackled and redressed effectively. The second surveys some of the dimensions of social inequality which have remained very much in evidence. The final section argues that we may find at least part of the explanation for the relative lack of progress in redressing these inequalities may be found in a closer analysis of the patterns of interest representation, in the form of both party politics and interest group activity.

The commitment to tackling inequalities

A commitment to dealing with social inequalities is a continuing theme in Irish political life. The terms on which parties compete for votes would suggest that parties have little to gain electorally from policies that are perceived as socially divisive, and more to gain from seeking to integrate diverse sections of the electorate in their own support base. What parties themselves say about these matters in their election manifestoes supports this view. The evolution of the centralised pay agreements since 1987, and the greater involvement of less advantaged groups in policy processes, also points towards a strengthening of the mechanisms through which issues of social inequalities can be raised and addressed.

Party politics

The main political parties in Ireland all profess to be committed to a concern for the least advantaged in society.[2] This is due, at least in part, to the absence of a clear left-right divide between the largest political parties, Fianna Fáil and Fine Gael, and to the weakness of social class as a predictor of support for parties. Fianna Fáil draws on a cross-class support base; this is also true of Fine Gael, though to a lesser degree. The small parties have a more conventional profile – on the left, the Labour Party and Democratic Left, on the right, the Progressive Democrats – though these can only hope to govern in coalition with one or other of the larger parties. Alternative governments thus need the support of a broad social coalition. This could well be expected to make them averse to implementing potentially divisive policies.

It did not always prove possible to avoid hard choices. During the 1980s, governments imposed spending cuts in response to fiscal difficulties, and lost electoral support as a consequence. However, governments explicitly rejected the Thatcherite policies adopted by Conservative administrations in Britain during the 1980s. Shifts in electoral support for one party or another therefore tended to be volatile and not to settle into clear new patterns (Marsh and Sinnott 1990: 127; Sinnott 1995: 155, 166).

A consensus emerged during the 1990s that unemployment and poverty constitute fundamental problems in Irish society, and that they need effective government intervention. For example, the Fianna Fáil–Labour *Programme for a Partnership Government 1993–97* identified its priorities in terms of the need to 'develop a strong sense of partnership . . . in the economy, society, community', 'put the country back to work', and 'create greater equality . . . and the elimination as far as possible of social disadvantage and poverty'. The policy agreement negotiated by the 'Rainbow Coalition' of Fine Gael, Labour and Democratic Left, *A Government of Renewal* (December 1994), was even more emphatic on the subject of social inequalities. It stated that 'continued commitment to the employment needs of all our people – especially the long-term unemployed – is a clear priority if we are to successfully address the causes of poverty and marginalisation in our society'.

It said that 'prudent economic management alone will never reach into those communities and families who have suffered from disadvantage or have been bypassed by growth', and promised 'full support . . . for economic and social partnership at all levels of Irish economic and social life'. A National Anti-Poverty Strategy, launched by the Fine Gael–Labour–Democratic Left coalition government in May 1997[3], announced that it was to be a government priority to halve the number of 'consistently poor', halve the proportion of unemployed and long-term unemployed, and end early school leaving within 10 years.

Public opinion

There is some evidence that egalitarian values are a feature of Irish political culture, and that there would be broad support for greater government commitment to the welfare of the least well-off in Irish society. In a major study of Irish political and social attitudes, conducted in the late 1980s, MacGréil found 'overwhelming support' for the view that 'the Government should see to it that differences between higher and lower incomes are greatly reduced'. He found an 'overwhelming rejection' of the statement that 'the poor person is responsible for his/her state of poverty'. This, he claims, 'is encouraging for those who would like to see more active support of a more radical approach, i.e. the location and removal of the causes which are outside the victims in the inequitable distribution of wealth, jobs and facilities, and the removal of such causes' (MacGréil 1996: 360–1).

The broadening of social partnership

A key feature of the management of the Irish economy since 1987 has been the negotiation of a series of centralised pay agreements (Chapter 2). These agreements also played a part in bringing issues of social inequalities into the political process, and in facilitating the direct representation of disadvantaged groups in the negotiating process.

The role of the consultative body, the National Economic and Social Council (NESC), proved to be vital in setting the context for the agreements. It provided the forum within which the main social partners (unions, employers, farmers) came to a shared understanding of each other's expectations and to a shared analysis of the functioning of the economy. NESC's reports provided the background documentation which informed the negotiations. These documents also stressed the importance of tackling issues of social inequality effectively (cf. NESC 1986, 1990, 1993, 1996).

Each agreement broadened the scope of the negotiations. The first in the series was the 1987 'Programme for National Recovery', born of economic crisis; that pay agreement was mainly intended to secure macroeconomic stability. The second, the 'Programme for Economic and Social Progress' (PESP), included a commitment to a wider range of social policy issues, including 'a substantial increase in employment;

a major assault on long-term unemployment' (par. 6). Employment and unemployment assumed greater prominence in the following agreement, the 'Programme for Competitiveness and Work' (February 1994). This stated in its opening paragraph that 'The key challenge in this Programme is to increase the number of people at work within our economy and to reduce the level of unemployment'. It also contained a range of policy commitments in the area of Social Equity (Section VI).

By the mid-1990s, the pay agreements had become linked to the ongoing process of policy analysis at NESC, on the one hand, and to the range of policies developed within the civil service, on the other. At this point, the fact that they were exclusively negotiated by the traditional social partners began to come into question. Submissions on each agreement had been received from many groups outside the conventional social partnership. These now acquired a more coherent voice and a more formal input to negotiations over pay and diverse social-policy issues.

One development in this direction was the formation of the National Economic and Social Forum (NESF), arising from a manifesto commitment in the Fianna Fáil–Labour *Programme for a Partnership Government 1993–1997*, whose brief was 'to develop economic and social policy initiatives, particularly initiatives to combat unemployment, and to contribute to the formation of a national consensus on social and economic matters'. The NESF comprised representatives not only of government and the 'social partners' (unions, employer and business interests, and agricultural and farming organisations), but also a 'third strand', consisting of representatives of women's organisations, unemployed, disadvantaged, youth, the elderly, people with a disability, environmental interests, and academics.

In the next three-year agreement, 'Partnership 2000 for Inclusion, Employment and Competitiveness' (December 1996), this 'third strand' was included in the negotiations for the first time, rather than making their submissions through government as previously (Partnership 2000, pars 3, 4). The 'community platform' and other representatives of groups outside the usual network of influence thus acquired formal recognition as participants in shaping the overall agreements. Partnership 2000 also contained commitments to a variety of policies intended to tackle social inequalities, including the National Anti-Poverty Strategy (pars 4.7–4.14).

The growth of participatory initiatives

The inclusion of a more diverse range of interests in the national-level talks leading to Partnership 2000 mirrored other developments that had been taking place at local or community level. A number of initiatives tended to converge on issues of local community development, and the promotion of social and economic development from the 'bottom-up'. Some arose from European Commission policies on poverty and unemployment. The terms of the debate in Ireland were coloured by this EU concern with 'social exclusion' conceived not only as income deprivation but also as exclusion from networks of participation and influence over decisions affecting one's own life and the life of the community.

One strand of these initiatives was formed by what were known as Area-Based Partnerships. Twelve were originally established under the PESP in 1991; some 26 others were subsequently established, jointly sponsored by government and by EU Structural Funds. Their composition varied, but typically involved representatives of a variety of local community interests, local representatives of the national employer and union organisations, representatives of the state organisations responsible for such functions as training and industrial development; and representatives of local government. All these groups were committed to involving local communities in identifying their own priorities to overcome disadvantage, especially endemic high unemployment. Some partnerships focused on methods of improving the provision of social services and welfare resources; others became involved in starting up experimental productive enterprises (see, for example, ADM 1997; Sabel 1996).

This complex institutional web was able to develop in large part because local government structures were relatively weak in European terms (Coyle 1996). There was scope for institutional innovation, emphasising 'local networking among statutory, community and voluntary interests, together with dialogue between the local and national levels' (Harvey 1994: xiii). Sabel (1996: 17) terms this 'democratic experimentalism'. He argues that organisational flexibility of this sort is the hallmark of successful innovation in manufacturing, and suggests that it provides a good model for a much wider range of economic, social and administrative functions. The variety of projects initiated since the late 1980s therefore brought a broader range of community groups, voluntary organisations and local branches of national organisations into the political process in initiatives that were funded and sponsored by a combination of national and EU schemes.

The priorities of deprived areas and disadvantaged groups were also given political expression through the growing involvement of some Catholic Church agencies in advocacy on their behalf. Many community development projects and many voluntary sector activities based in deprived areas were backed by Catholic religious social activists. In addition, the Justice Commission of the Conference of Religious in Ireland (CORI, previously the Conference of Major Religious Superiors), which is the co-ordinating body of religious orders, contributed their critique of priorities in economic and social policy in a series of position papers, pre-Budget submissions, and radical policy proposals on topics such as Basic Income (Clarke and Healy 1997).

Summary

In summary, we have seen that several developments in Irish politics since the mid-1980s have tended to work together to bring issues of social inequality into sharper focus. Party competition appeared to favour policies that had a broad appeal. Parties of the left were involved in government between 1992 and 1997. Social partnership processes broadened out to cover social policy issues. Many deprived groups acquired official representation at the policy-shaping talks. Policy initiatives, both domestic and European-led, aimed to tackle 'social exclusion' in its many guises;

in particular, they supported 'bottom-up' economic and social development in order to improve the opportunities available to people in deprived areas or neighbourhoods. In the context of strong economic growth, it would appear that conditions favoured progress in redressing a range of social inequalities as never before.

Persistent inequalities

However, many social inequalities remained stubbornly in evidence. Three such issues can be identified which were much debated in the public domain. These are a continuing problem of high unemployment and especially long-term unemployment; the extent of poverty in the overall context of income growth; and finally, the profile of tax revenues and the particularly heavy tax burden placed on low-paid employees.

Unemployment

Even prior to the unemployment crises of the 1970s and 1980s, Irish unemployment was several points higher than in other European countries. But the situation worsened dramatically during the 1980s: unemployment rose from 10 per cent in 1981 to over 17 per cent in 1985. It dipped slightly in the early 1990s, but rose steadily again to 16 per cent in 1994 (Sexton and O'Connell 1996: 20). Thereafter, rapid economic growth contributed to improving the situation both relatively and absolutely. There was a big increase in numbers in work – from 1.1m. in 1992 to 1.3m. in 1997, according to the Labour Force Surveys. Unemployment fell to just over 13 per cent in 1995, and by the end of 1997, the Live Register showed unemployment dipping below 10 per cent for the first time in 20 years, which was also below the EU average.

From the mid-1980s onwards, however, long-term unemployment (lasting for more than one year) emerged as a serious and persistent problem, and on a much larger scale than in most other developed countries. About one-third of the unemployed were long-term unemployed in 1983, but this proportion rose to 62 per cent in 1985 and 65 per cent in 1989 (Sexton *et al.* 1996: 48). It dropped slightly over the next five years. Economic buoyancy gave many of the unemployed new opportunities. The introduction of job subsidy and work allowance schemes helped the integration of the long-term unemployed into the labour market.

However, in 1996, the long-term unemployed in Ireland still accounted for some 60 per cent of the total (compared with 48 per cent in Germany, 40 per cent in Britain and France, and 9.5 per cent in the USA: *cf.* OECD *Employment Outlook*, July 1997: 180). A sizeable group remained who, for whatever reasons, were unable to take advantage of the newly available opportunities. At the end of 1997, the Irish Live Register figures showed that some two-fifths of the registered long-term unemployed had been unemployed for more than three years. Most had low levels of educational attainment and, at a time when skills command a premium (Barrett *et al.* 1997), few marketable skills either (*Report of the Task Force on Long-Term Unemployment* 1995; NESF 1997). Breen and Whelan, in their study of poverty and deprivation, identified a hard-core group of those who had become 'marginalised' from the labour force by having had a long spell of unemployment and an intermittent work history. About 12 per cent of non-farm households fell into this category (Breen and Whelan 1996: 162–4) – a significant section of the population.

Economic growth alone will do little or nothing to improve the labour-market situation, and consequently the social situation, of those suffering the most pronounced labour-market disadvantages. Contrary to the liberal optimism once again in evidence in the 1990s, the 'rising tide' would not 'lift all boats'. Those left behind were likely to be regarded by employers as among the least desirable employees. The bridges that had been built between welfare dependency and work often did not reach these people. A number of studies have concluded that specially designed programmes would be required. These would include systematic reform of the taxes levied on low levels of pay, and a review of the cash and non-cash benefits available on a means-tested basis, because the interaction between taxes and benefits, and the withdrawal of income support or medical benefits beyond certain income thresholds, can cause disincentives for people to make the transition from welfare to work (*Report of the Expert Commission on Integrating Tax and Social Welfare* 1996). They would also include extensive investment in education, both to prevent early leaving in future and to provide second-chance opportunities for those with few skills; closely targeted training programmes; and a big increase in social employment schemes for those otherwise unable to find work (Breen and Whelan 1996; *Report of the Task Force on Long-Term Unemployment* 1995). A highly targeted set of reforms along these lines would require considerable co-ordination of policies across government departments. It would also be expensive.

Income distribution and poverty

Most Irish people would probably hold that Ireland does not experience extremes of wealth and poverty, and that income inequalities are less marked in Ireland than in other countries. However, the data series compiled by the Economic and Social Research Institute (most recently in 1994) suggests that this is not so, and that Ireland has quite severe problems of poverty.

The numbers identified as 'poor' will vary depending on the measure used. However, recent studies have revealed that the numbers experiencing poverty did not fall between the 1980s and the 1990s. On the contrary – they either remained static or rose.

Despite the difficulties in making cross-national comparisons, it would appear that in the mid-1980s, Ireland had a larger problem of poverty than any other EC country except Greece and Portugal. Some 23 per cent of persons had incomes below half national average equivalent income, compared with fewer than 10 per cent in Belgium, The Netherlands, and Germany, and 12 per cent in Britain, and 17.5 per cent in France (Nolan and Callan 1994: 39). Over the following 10 years or so, the proportion of people in poverty rose sharply in Britain (up to approximately Irish levels), and was not reversed; increases in poverty levels in other European countries in the late 1980s showed some reversal in the 1990s (Atkinson 1997: 18–20). But by 1994, the numbers of people experiencing poverty in Ireland had not fallen, remaining at about 22 or 23 per cent (Callan *et al.* 1996: 73). In real-income terms, the situation of the least well-off improved.[4] Fewer people fell very deeply below the lowest income threshold, so the severity of poverty was somewhat alleviated for those on the lowest incomes. But overall, real incomes had grown between 1987 and 1994, while the living standards of those with below-average incomes had not kept pace. A bigger and growing number of people had been 'left behind' in relative terms.

It is hardly surprising, in view of the trends in unemployment outlined in the previous section, that the composition of those experiencing poverty changed over time. In the 1970s, the single largest category of people at risk of poverty had been the elderly. By the time the Economic and Social Research Institute (ESRI) undertook its surveys of poverty and income distribution in 1987 and 1994, poverty was far more likely to be associated with unemployment and labour market situation than with old age. Unemployment rose from about 6 per cent of the labour force in 1973 to 18 per cent in 1987 to some 16 per cent in 1994. The risk of poverty for the unemployed had not changed, but the large rise in the numbers unemployed exposed far more people to that risk. Others at risk of poverty, besides the unemployed, included lone parents, those in home duties, and households headed by people otherwise not in the labour force, such as the ill or disabled. Households with children were now much more exposed to income poverty, and low-income households tended to have more children (Callan *et al.* 1996: 78–9, 84–6; Breen and Whelan 1996: 53–5). In fact, the problem of child poverty had increased significantly. In 1973, approximately one in six children lived in households below the poverty line (50 per cent of average incomes). In 1987, the figure was one in four, and by 1994 it had reached almost 30 per cent (Callan *et al.* 1996: 92).[5]

Low income is not the only indicator of poverty. Social security policies are geared towards maintaining incomes, but we can get a better idea of the extent of real difficulties being experienced by households by taking account of the extent of basic lifestyle deprivation as well. In 1987, approximately one in seven households experienced income poverty and severe lifestyle deprivation, and this figure had not changed by 1994 (Callan and Nolan 1996: 116). Of these, 36 per cent were unemployed and almost 30 per cent were 'in home duties' (119).

The risk of poverty therefore varies strongly with employment status, and especially with unemployment: 'The poverty risk rises strongly as one goes down the class hierarchy . . . Poverty is increasingly associated with long-term labour market difficulties, which in turn are disproportionately borne by households in particular social classes and from a similar class background' (Breen and Whelan 1996: 150). There is a long-term and persistent problem of poverty which is mainly caused by unemployment.

At the other end of the income scale, relatively small numbers enjoyed quite considerable incomes. On the basis of cross-national data gathered in 1987, Ireland ranked with Britain and the USA in having the most unequal distribution of primary income, and inequality in the distribution of per capita income was matched only by Switzerland and the USA (Atkinson *et al.* 1996: 89–92). Since then, Ireland has experienced rapid growth in national wealth. But the growth in average per capita GDP clearly outstripped the progress made in reducing inequalities and in distributing the fruits of that growth more equitably.

Taxation and equity

The incidence of income taxation, and especially the burden placed on those with low and middle incomes, was the focus of ongoing concern from the 1970s onwards. Indeed, in 1979 and 1980, mass protests were organised on the streets of Dublin and other urban centres, focusing on the disproportionate reliance on income tax, the level and incidence of income tax, and the narrowness of the income tax base.

Between 1970 and 1980, taxation revenue from personal income jumped from about 18 per cent of the total to just under one-third, most of it from employees. A prominent analyst of the tax system commented that 'an unsustainable trend in Irish taxation was the increasing number of taxpayers liable to tax rates that were above the standard rate. By 1983, over 40 per cent of Irish taxpayers were faced with marginal rates of 45 per cent or higher, whereas before 1975 less than 5 per cent of Irish taxpayers paid tax at above the standard rate' (O'Toole 1993). A further burden on those on relatively modest incomes was the fact that employees' social insurance contributions have a cut-off ceiling, which makes it regressive in its impact. Despite the tax protests, the situation actually worsened for employees during the years of fiscal difficulties in the 1980s. By 1987–88, the peak year in terms of the employee tax burden, the average tax rates on all income bands had grown significantly. For someone on average industrial earnings, the average tax rate had gone up from 27 per cent to 35 per cent since 1980. For someone earning half of average industrial earnings, the average tax rate had grown from 14 per cent to 22 per cent, proportionately a bigger increase (Ruane and O'Toole 1997: 11).

The narrowness of the tax base was a particular matter of concern. The erosion of the employee tax base by tax expenditures and tax allowances chiefly benefiting higher income earners was brought into question (O'Toole 1993). The self-employed and farmers were perceived to enjoy preferential tax treatment, resulting in substantial evasion and under-payment of taxes by these groups.

During the 1980s and into the 1990s, widespread agreement developed that the profile of the tax system was both unfair and inefficient. The narrow allowances and high marginal rates faced by those making the transition from welfare to low-paid employment resulted in unemployment traps, whereby a person taking paid work would take home less money than by remaining unemployed. They created poverty traps where a very high marginal rate of tax might apply as income levels went over certain thresholds which, combined with the withdrawal of welfare benefits, could result in the individual being worse off though nominally earning more. These features of the tax and benefits systems operated as a deterrent to taking paid work. Numerous reports advocated reform of the income tax system – especially as it applies to those on the lowest incomes (Commission on Taxation 1982; Sandford 1993; O'Toole 1993; *Report of the Expert Commission on Integrating Tax and Social Welfare* 1996).

During the 1980s, there was a marked lack of political will to tackle reform of the tax system, despite its increasingly evident shortcomings. Indeed, government leaned all the more heavily on employee income to raise extra revenues in the face of large deficits and a mounting public debt. By the late 1980s, though, all political parties had committed themselves to tax reform, including those measures that would be of greatest benefit to those on lower incomes, such as increasing allowances and broadening tax bands. This is evident in Fine Gael policy from its 1987 election manifesto onwards, where it stated that real tax reform must 'enhance the incentive to work', reduce the initial rate of tax, and raise the level at which the higher rate applies. Fianna Fáil, in its 1989 manifesto, referred to the need to 'reduce rates and broaden bands'. Fianna Fáil, in government with the Progressive Democrats, committed itself to 'a programme of pro-jobs tax reform' (*Review of Programme for Government 1989–93*, 1991). In government with Labour, it stressed the plan to 'continue the process of tax reform: remove the low-paid, especially families, out of the tax net' (*Programme for a Partnership Government 1993–97*). The 'Rainbow Coalition' of Fine Gael, Labour and Democratic Left committed itself in December 1994 to 'targeting lower-paid workers . . . taking them out of the tax net . . . reform PRSI . . . widen the standard rate band . . . increase personal allowances by significantly more than inflation' (*A Government of Renewal*).

Average tax rates did indeed come down for all employees from 1987–88 onwards. However, the evidence shows that the tax reforms of the late 1980s and 1990s benefited those on higher incomes more than those on low or medium incomes. Furthermore, by the mid-1990s, tax rates still exceeded those which had been in effect in the early 1980s, which had themselves been the occasion of worker protests. 'Many taxpayers appear to be facing a higher, rather than a lower, average tax rate' than they did in 1980 (Ruane and O'Toole 1997: Table 5.3). The exceptions were the very highest income-earners: those on five times average industrial earnings were the only ones paying lower average tax rates in 1994–95 than in 1980–81.

Yet it would appear that relatively few of the highest earners paid anything like their full tax liability, given the opportunities available (both legal and illegal) to shelter their income. Tax compliance was a persistent problem, despite administrative reforms from the late 1980s on. A 'tax amnesty' was introduced in 1988 as part of these administrative reforms, whereby previously undeclared income could be brought into the tax net without risk of prosecution for past evasion. A second tax amnesty was introduced in 1993. Both brought in unexpectedly large sums. But they weakened the authority of the revenue system because confidentiality was guaranteed to those who availed of them, and because they generated the expectation, particularly in the case of the second one, that further amnesties would follow. The Revenue Commissioners acknowledged that they were unable to trace considerable amounts of outstanding tax (*Report of the Comptroller and Auditor General 1997*). Public Tribunals such as the Beef Tribunal and the Dunnes Payments to Politicians Tribunal almost incidentally revealed widespread and serious tax evasion by businesses, by wealthy individuals holding offshore bank accounts, and by individuals active in political life. These revelations strengthened the view of many critics that the tax system contained many inequities, both in its structure and in its implementation.

Income tax reforms were undertaken, but they fell far short of targeting those on low and middle incomes, despite the recommendations of many policy experts. There are two reasons for the regressive impact of the income tax reforms. First, allowances and bands were not indexed and were eroded by inflation. While producing buoyant revenues through 'fiscal drag', the effect was particularly hard on lower earners. Secondly, tax reform during the 1990s paid more attention to reducing rates than to widening bands and increasing allowances. The number of rates was reduced and simplified, and the rates themselves were brought down. But the net effect was to give more benefits, both absolutely and in relative terms, to those on average and above-average incomes, than to those on lower incomes (O'Toole 1997). Meanwhile, the tax collection system applied to the highest income earners continued to be very porous.

Summary

Successive governments made claims about the priority they would accord to addressing social problems such as unemployment, poverty, and the taxation of those on low incomes. But despite some policy measures, each of these problems continued to be a major feature of Irish society.

Social inequalities and conflicts of interest

We might consider a number of possible reasons for the apparent inability or unwillingness of governments to make a more significant impact on social inequalities. The argument advanced in this section is that the impact of organised interests on political decision-making has a major bearing on political outcomes. Those who are most organised are best placed to ensure that their interests are adequately protected and that policies they oppose do not make much progress on the political agenda.

The role of organised interests in the policy process

Policy priorities in democracies are shaped to an important degree by the demands and pressures emanating from the electorate, whether through party politics, through the activities of organised pressure groups, or through the more diffuse means of public opinion and public debate about current issues. This is not to say that all interests are equally capable of getting organised, still less that all interests have equal access to the decision-making process. Far from it: some interests are organised into politics, while others are organised out. Also, systematic bias in the system of representation may favour the preferences of groups that are already advantaged, whether in terms of command over resources, or direct access to the arenas of agenda-setting and decision-making.

This paper does not claim that policy decisions and outcomes are wholly explained with reference to which social groups or which organised interests exercise most influence in the decision-making process. A comprehensive model of the decision-making process must allow for the strategic calculations of those in positions of political leadership where responsibility for decision-making ultimately lies. Policy decisions entail choices between competing options, and the political leadership has latitude and discretion in deciding upon outcomes. In addition, the institutional framework within which policy is made and implemented may shape future decisions in important ways, by making some courses of action seem more practicable, while others are seen to entail unacceptably high costs in administrative adaptation. As March and Olsen have argued (1984: 739): 'The bureaucratic agency, the legislative committee, and the appellate court are arenas for contending social forces, but they are also standard operating procedures and structures that define and defend interests'. This can result in a 'path-dependent' development of policy in particular areas, where new developments build upon older ones and alternative possibilities are not seriously considered.

Some authors have suggested that we should view government policies as expressions of the interests of the state itself (for example, Skocpol 1985). This approach would tend to minimise the role of organised interests in influencing the decision-making process, and to stress the possibility that the state may possess interests and projects of its own (for example, O'Connell and Rottman 1992). I wish to argue here that it is inappropriate to attribute autonomous interests to the state as such. Firstly, the state is in any case composed of a diversity of administrative divisions and agencies which may well have conflicting priorities among themselves. Secondly, actual policy decisions become the responsibility of ministers and thus of government, and are subject to the electoral calculations referred to above. We must take seriously the difference that organised interests may make to shaping the policy priorities of government.

There are two channels through which social conflicts may work their way through to influence policy-making. One is through influencing the terms of electoral competition and the priorities of political parties; the other is through interest-group activity.

The priorities adopted by political parties are largely shaped by parties' own calculations of their electoral best interests. Parties seek to build up a basis of support through the policies they make their own. In the Irish case, I have suggested that parties themselves describe their objectives in terms of social inclusiveness. In the section which follows, I shall suggest that the pressures on parties in fact make it more likely that they will cater to social interests in a far more selective manner. In the process, the interests of the least advantaged in society are over-looked, or are sacrificed to those of middle and upper tiers. Evidence of a politics of social inclusiveness among Irish parties is no guarantee of a strong commitment to the politics of redistribution.

Turning to the role of organised interests, we can see that there are many reasons here, too, why the least advantaged may not be able to influence decision-making effectively. It is difficult for people in disadvantaged situations to become organised: their circumstances make it hard to build up networks of involvement. There are many aspects of social disadvantage, making it difficult to establish common concerns between organisations. These organisations may themselves face challenges as to how representative they really are. The trade union movement may champion some issues on behalf of the disadvantaged. But it also has obligations to its own membership which may at certain points limit how vigorously it can press issues pertaining to social disadvantage.

Even where the disadvantaged acquire a voice with which to lobby government, they do not necessarily gain influence, at least not when their objectives are held to conflict with those of business. The Irish economy is small and very open, and is particularly dependent on retaining and expanding investment in the multinational sector. Business interests do not necessarily oppose government initiatives to reduce social inequalities. But they can bring a powerful influence to bear on the priority which governments accord to redistributive issues, both through direct lobbying, and through what we might think of as the particular structural advantage they enjoy in the Irish economy. The possibility also exists that business interests may influence government priorities indirectly, through the financial donations they make to political parties.

Finally, the prevailing style of setting priorities and deciding upon the distribution of resources within the Irish political system tends to favour those best able to promote their group's interests and claims. Within the established way of doing things, radical policy innovations are not so much resisted as never seriously contemplated.

Electoral considerations: parties and the politics of the median voter

Governments have proven reluctant to commit the volume of resources needed to alleviate social disadvantage and inequalities. The principal explanation must be because they fear that this will not be to their electoral advantage. This is at odds with the hypothesis raised at the outset of this paper that the relative weakness of class patterning of party support in Ireland, and the growth of electoral volatility, would make parties more and not less inclined to embrace policies of social inclusiveness. This may well be so at the level of rhetoric. But it proves not to be so in hard decisions about 'getting and spending'.

One factor must be that poor and disadvantaged voters are not very 'visible' electorally. The political values of unemployed people are more left-wing than those of the electorate in general, and more so too than those of employed people with comparative class and educational backgrounds. They are considerably less likely to support Fianna Fáil or Fine Gael and more likely to support the left-wing parties (Hardiman and Whelan 1994: 179–81). However, they are also more likely to be non-voters. Sinnott and Whelan (1992) found strong correlations at the aggregate level between low electoral participation and social deprivation in the Dublin area, and they argue that the association is real, despite the limitations inherent in ecological data. Using individual-level data, Marsh (1991) shows that long-term non-voters are far more likely to be socially disadvantaged and to lack knowledge of and interest in political institutions than regular voters and 'accidental', short-term non-voters. Even where geographically concentrated in localities with high concentrations of welfare recipients, unemployment and local authority tenants, their lower tendency to participate electorally dilutes their presence on a constituency-wide basis. There have been initiatives by community activists to increase electoral turnout. For example, the Vincentian Partnership for Justice organised a pilot programme in five deprived areas in Dublin which it describes as 'very positive and hopeful'; it ran workshops to encourage people to become better informed about local issues and local political candidates, and to work out where they stood on issues and candidates. Nevertheless, as journalist and broadcaster Olivia O'Leary commented while launching the project, 'politicians simply don't bother to canvass some areas because of their low turnout' (*Irish Times*, 11 April 1997).

Swing voters – those who do exercise their vote and who are likely to change allegiance between one election and the next – occupy far more of politicians' and party activists' attention. These voters are more likely to be urban, middle-class, and articulate about their interests and preferences (Marsh and Sinnott 1992). The social services and social transfers that are needed to alleviate social inequalities, and which require extra public spending, are likely to affect these voters as taxpayers, but to bring them no benefit as recipients. Ireland's social security system tends to segment people's interests: most of the programmes on which the disadvantaged rely heavily (especially the long-term unemployment benefits, disability benefits, and non-contributory old age pensions) are likely to be drawn on relatively little by the great majority of employees and self-employed. While ESRI researchers found that 28 per cent of people had experienced unemployment at some point in their careers, a much smaller group with over five years of unemployment had experienced almost half of all the years of unemployment (Nolan *et al.* 1994: xi).

For similar reasons, other income transfers were at risk of being squeezed – for example, support for state non-contributory pensions and widows' allowances, which rose during the 1980s, but fell back somewhat in the 1990s. The budgetary commitments required to make real progress in tackling the underlying causes of poverty were, it seemed, even less likely to be forthcoming. The NESF, in its evaluation of the National Anti-Poverty Strategy, commended the overall objectives, but concluded pessimistically that 'it seems that additional budgetary resources will not be made available for the NAPS' (1996a: 3.5).

Korpi and Palme (1997) suggest that the electoral calculations made by political parties are not exclusive to Ireland. They argue that there is a generally observed 'trade-off between the degree of low-income targeting and the size of the redistributive budget, so that the greater the degree of low-income targeting, the smaller the budget tends to be'. Hence the enduring fears among governments that they will face electoral backlash for increasing the number and size of targeted provisions, however socially desirable they may otherwise seem to be as methods of reducing social inequalities.

Parties tend to concentrate their election campaigning on middle- and upper-income earners. This was particularly apparent in the terms in which the election campaign of 1997 was conducted by all parties. Taxation was one of the most prominent issues in debates between the parties: the concerns of the relatively advantaged were very much to the fore. Another example is the case of education policy, where inequalities in participation and opportunity are well documented (Lynch and Drudy 1993; Clancy 1996; NESF 1997). The Labour Minister for Education between 1992 and 1997 committed extra resources to primary schools in deprived areas, and initiated a pre-school early-learning programme, as the best place to begin to break the cycle of educational under-achievement.[6] However, there appears to be a limit to the extent to which governments are prepared to concentrate resources on the most needy in this way. The bulk of that Minister's additional spending on educational provision went on the abolition of university fees (albeit accompanied by the abolition of tax-sheltering educational covenants). There were good reasons to believe that this was not in fact the most egalitarian way to improve access to third-level education, and that extra targeted spending, for example on increasing maintenance allowances, and raising the threshold for grants, would have been more beneficial to lower-income families. However, 'free third-level education' is a simpler concept, with resonances of the more clearly egalitar-ian second-level scheme of the 1960s. And most relevantly for present purposes, it benefited many families in the mainly middle-class constituencies in which Labour had reaped large electoral gains in 1992. Although the election of 1997 revealed that the initiative did not consolidate that electoral support, it is not unreasonable to suppose that the calculation of electoral advantage played some part in the decision to commit education spending in this way.

Representing the unorganised

Activists on behalf of the least advantaged became more organised during the 1990s, and they acquired formal representation in the talks leading to the Partner-ship 2000 agreement in 1997. However, the capacity of these groups to press for greatly increased resources and a more fully developed political programme to address issues of poverty remained very limited.

Organisations claiming to speak for disadvantaged groups such as the unem-ployed, or the poor or the disabled do not have the same claim to representativeness as the functional organisations of unions, employers or farmers. The Irish National Organisation of the Unemployed (INOU) does not 'represent' the unemployed in the same way that the Irish Congress of Trade Unions (ICTU) and its constituent unions 'represent' trade union members. They have a more unstable and inchoate constituency, there are no formal criteria for determining their representativeness, and they have little claim to authority over their support-base. Even though these organisations had a voice within the policy process, through NESF and the 'community platform', they had nothing to 'trade' in negotiations. As Aneurin Bevan wrote in *In Place of Fear* (1952), 'silent pain evokes no response'; only the ability to exercise some power forces decision-makers to make significant concessions. The organisations who would represent the most deprived can exercise very little direct pressure, and they lack organisational structures that command attention as 'legitimate' representatives.

We would expect spontaneous community self-organisation among deprived groups and in deprived areas to be quite rare, since social networks typically do not flourish where people are under severe financial and personal stresses of these sorts. An exception, therefore, is the network of anti-drug activists in a number of deprived areas of Dublin. However, these groups tended to mobilise around highly specific local issues, and to engage in discussions with the local authority and the police about these and closely related issues only. In general, their concerns were not widened to include other issues, nor did they seek more mainstream political influence.

The bishops of the Catholic Church, and more organised pressure groups backed by the Church, such as the CORI Justice Commission, found themselves in the same position: they had no exclusive access to government on matters of social policy as once they might have had. Others who claimed to speak on behalf of the deprived included social workers, community development activists and anti-poverty campaigners. They would hope to exercise moral influence, but little else.

There was also a limit to the representational effectiveness of the local partnership initiatives. Local initiatives were likely to suffer from a 'democratic deficit' within their own communities (CORI 1997: 64), since the basis on which they claimed to represent community interests was opaque. Groups that were already organised, such as the local branches of union and employer or business groups, often played a prominent role. Sabel (1985) praised the institutional innovations embodied in these partnerships, but he too recognised that they could also expose conflicting interests within communities, particularly as they lack any clear relationship to the mechanisms of democratic accountability, whether national or local. Many locally based anti-poverty or development initiatives could be seen as prepolitical; the issues arising within the project may not even reach the stage of being articulated through to national political debate. It would appear therefore that both the direct and the indirect representatives of deprived groups carried little political influence.

In any case, however valuable they may be as a means of channelling community energies into improving the quality of life in a locality, area-based initiatives are likely to be of limited value as a means of making a serious impact on poverty and unemployment. Poverty is not confined to the main urban centres (Breen and Whelan 1996: 164–8). Unemployment is a 'spatially pervasive' phenomenon, not geographically concentrated in socially isolated pockets. Only a minority of poor people, or unemployed people, live in such 'black spots'.

Many area-based anti-poverty initiatives are based in disadvantaged urban communities. There are certainly serious concentrations of poverty, unemployment and social deprivation in inner-city flats complexes and in large housing developments in the outer suburbs of the main cities. Other social problems may flourish in these localities, such as drug addiction and involvement in criminal behaviour. However, community-based projects can have only a limited impact on alleviating poverty, and, realistically, very little impact on unemployment. The problems faced by people in areas of concentrated social deprivation are not ones they can realistically resolve through their own efforts. As Breen and Whelan firmly conclude, 'structural factors producing poverty have to be tackled primarily at national and EU level' (1996: 212).

The trade union movement and the politics of redistribution

Within the context of the social partnership agreements, the trade union movement took part in promoting the interests of the least advantaged. Most commentators would agree that the centralised agreements in the 1990s held wage drift in check, and prevented further wage dispersion at a time when this would have been expected, even if they did not reverse the widened dispersions of the early 1980s (Sheehan 1996; Sexton and O'Connell 1996). Most also agree that this contributed to the strong growth in jobs of the mid-1990s, although many other factors, of course, also affect employment levels (O'Donnell and O'Reardon 1996).

However, the interests of trade union members and those of the least advantaged – who were often outside the labour force altogether – were not always easy to reconcile. The trade union leadership experiences pressure from its own membership to deliver increases in real disposable incomes. Increased expenditure on welfare payments or on social services is not necessarily experienced as an improvement in personal living standards.[7] Modest tax reforms targeted at low and middle incomes, resulting in increased take-home pay, have formed part of the pay agreements. But the unions' budgetary influence on these matters wanes for the duration of each agreement.

Within organised labour itself, conflicts of interest over how resources are to be shared were also apparent, particularly with regard to employees in the public as against the private sector. Increases in public-sector pay and pensions mean that extra taxation must be levied from the private sector. Additional spending on public sector pay means that tax reductions must be foregone, or social spending deferred.

Public-sector employees were a powerful influence within the trade union movement during the 1990s. Approximately half the country's trade union members were public sector employees (Roche 1997). More than 70 unions were affiliated to ICTU; about half of these had a membership confined wholly or mainly to the public sector. But public-sector employees were also organised by other unions which were not primarily public-sector unions. It was estimated that only about 15 unions had no public-sector members (Cox and Hughes 1989). The leadership of the trade union movement comes under pressure to accommodate these divergent interests; it cannot or will not try to impose a normative view of the relationship between public and private-sector pay increases.

The negotiating structures in the public service enabled various groups to pursue parallel pay claims outside the terms of the pay agreements, through comparability or other 'special' claims. Public-service increases outpaced those in the private sector between 1987 and 1993. To some extent this is attributable to changes in the occupational structure of the civil service, with an increase in the number of higher-level grades, and sometimes large increases in their remuneration. But this would not explain all the divergence. Sexton and O'Connell (1997: 63) concluded that 'the size of the difference suggests a genuine divergence which cannot be attributed to differences in coverage or changing occupational structures'.

In summary, the trade union movement is not a single, unified actor with a single set of objectives; various interests contend for dominance. The leadership seeks to promote issues of social justice, but it must also respond to pressures from its own members to ensure real pay increases. Trade union members were also far from being a homogeneous group. Skilled workers experienced minimal pay drift during much of the 1990s, despite strong profitability in many private-sector firms. Public-sector employees carried considerable weight within the trade union movement, and were able to press for improvements in real income. This has implications for tax policy, for employment levels in the public service, and for social spending on facilities other than pay and pensions. The trade union leadership finds it difficult to take a stance on these issues on equity grounds. It cannot be as powerful an advocate on behalf of the least advantaged as some of its leaders might wish.

Politics and business interests

Looking at the various aspects of inequalities outlined above, we could argue that business interests seem to receive especially beneficial treatment from government in a number of respects. In particular, the tax regime to which personal wealth and corporation tax are subject constrained government's scope for serious tax reform.

There are some who would argue, within a marxist framework, that producer interests necessarily enjoy special advantages because of their centrality to economic success, and perhaps because of the 'structural dependence' of the state, both in terms of electoral advantage and in terms of revenue flow, on the continuous growth of the economy (for example, Offe and Ronge 1982). This may be true in general, but it gives us no guidance as to the particular policies that are essential to provide business with a satisfactory context in which to operate. Generous welfare-state provision has not proved to be a deterrent to economic success in many countries (Block 1990; Atkinson and Mogensen 1993; Korpi 1996). The notion that business performs most successfully in something approximating to free-market conditions, in which welfare provisions are minimal, proves illusory (Kenworthy 1996; Soskice 1990). There is no single set of conditions that is optimal for business performance, but rather a range of variation within which business interests can prosper.

The development strategy adopted by successive Irish governments since the late 1950s, which is premised upon attracting mobile international capital investment, accords business interests many privileges in the shape of industrial grants and tax incentives (Jacobsen 1994; O'Hearn 1989). Overall, this strategy has not been seriously questioned, given its successes in attracting inward investment and boosting job creation in manufacturing and services. Corporate tax revenues were very buoyant during the 1990s.

What followed, however, was a tendency – especially on the part of the Progressive Democrats and Fianna Fáil – to accord greater priority to business than to redistributive priorities, even during the high-growth phase of the mid- to late 1990s. All governments expect to be lobbied by organised interests. It may also be that business interests enjoy an additional advantage because of the prior commitment of all governments to ensuring the continued success of Ireland's industrial development strategy.

What is much less obvious is the extent of influence over government decisions obtained through donations to political parties. Two public Tribunals in the 1990s provided evidence of the very close mutually beneficial relationships between some business interests and some politicians. This evidence raises the possibility that an unknown degree of political influence may have been obtained through business donations to political parties.

Legislation requiring disclosure of political donations, whether to individuals or to parties, and mandating state financial support for parties, was under consideration for several years during the 1990s, though its passage was delayed partly because of concerns that sections of it might be unconstitutional. The outstanding difficulties appeared to have been resolved with the Electoral Act 1997. A number of commentators concluded that enactment of this legislation was long overdue. As long as political parties relied so heavily on corporate donations for their funding, they pointed out, there would always be some suggestion of direct business influence being improperly brought to bear, resulting in a systematic bias in political decisions, and worse, the possibility of political corruption distorting the substance of policy making.

Setting policy priorities

In attempting to explain why policies to alleviate inequalities may not in fact be implemented, or why those policies that are introduced may fail to make much impression on the problem, it is perhaps relevant to consider the ways in which decisions about the allocation of resources are taken in general. Two observations may be made here. Firstly, policy-making in Ireland tends to be driven by the struggles between interests for their share of available resources, and governments tend to respond most actively to the most audible or most prominent of those interests. Secondly, the public bureaucracy in Ireland is generalist rather than 'technocratic' in character. Policy-making tends to be made in response to events. This can result in a certain lack of coherence in the overall strategic approach to particular problems.

The implication of the first of these observations is that despite the 'proliferation of organisations desiring to participate in the policy process' (O'Halpin 1993: 201), groups representing the disadvantaged have not been among the most successful in gaining access and influence.

Irish policy-making, like that in Britain, tends to be departmentally based. Ministers themselves tend to become drawn into promoting the concerns of those interests with which they deal most frequently. Departmental policy-making means that many aspects of resource allocation are likely to be decided through 'policy communities' (Marsh and Rhodes 1992), that is, where contacts are close and regular between a specified set of interests and government, and where the style of policy-making is consultative. The interests involved in consultations are there as of right. Like the 'functional' economic interests in social partnership negotiations, they enjoy legitimacy because they cannot be excluded. Their co-operation is likely to be essential to ensuring the implementation of the policy, because they are involved in that implementation themselves. Policy-making in the area of education, for example, tends to take this form. In the Irish case, it might involve church interests, local authorities, and more recently, parents' representatives, in consultations with the Minister and officials from the Department of Education. Another example might be the special role accorded to medical professionals in making and implementing health policy (Eckstein 1960; Lehmbruch 1984). The influence of these groups is likely to be considerable, but limited to the policy domain to which their participation is related.

In contrast, the input of organisations representing the most disadvantaged is likely to be treated as a 'residual category', confined to securing whatever is left over after the established interests have had their say. For example, the Community Platform, which represented the 'third strand' of interests in the talks leading to Partnership 2000, pointed out that they had a consultative role, had some degree of participation, but did not have full negotiating status. They explicitly stated that they wished to secure the sort of role now accorded to farming interests within the social partnership process – not involved in shaping the package of pay and tax, but intimately involved in setting the overall priorities. The Community Platform held that several 'limiting parameters' kept them away from where they believed the real decisions were being taken. They complained that there was a 'segregation of core policy areas between the different "Rooms" in the negotiations'. Tax and pay were negotiated first, with issues of social inclusion and equity being given residual status, instead of being discussed jointly with the others. The macro-economic framework to the negotiations had already been established by the main social partners through NESC. This resulted, they believed, in an unspecific and aspirational commitment to social inclusion issues, compared with quite specific commitments on the management of public finances, and on the pay and tax package. The scope for major spending commitments on issues of poverty or unemployment was therefore already circumscribed before the Platform had a chance to make its input (Community Platform 1997: 12–15).

However, even where there is a willingness to devise new measures to deal with aspects of social disadvantage, policy-making in Ireland tends to be rather ad hoc in character and all too often lacks coherence. There were numerous initiatives on issues of unemployment, poverty and social deprivation during the 1980s and 1990s. A variety of programmes were developed to retrain unemployed people, to reintegrate the unemployed, especially long-term unemployed, into the workforce, and to top up family income to encourage labour-force participation. But there were many schemes of this sort – over 30 in 1997 (OECD 1997: 77) – and they were were not always either well-designed or well coordinated with each other. The ESRI labour market analysts concluded, in relation to schemes designed to help the long-term unemployed, that 'the entire range of publicly sponsored measures directed at the long-term unemployed lacks coherence (especially from the administrative point of view) and is not sufficiently focused on the most disadvantaged' (O'Connell and Sexton 1996: xxvii). It appears that policy-makers only take a radical and thorough-going approach to solving problems at moments of great crisis, or in the wake of a great shock to the established way of doing things.

Conclusion: inequality and conflicting interests

This paper has argued that although Ireland experienced a period of unprecedented prosperity during the 1990s, and despite the consensus that social inequalities must be addressed, no political response on anything like the scale required proved to be forthcoming.

Representatives of the most disadvantaged were able to exercise a growing consultative 'voice' within the decision-making system, through mechanisms such as NESF and the Community Platform in the Partnership 2000 negotiations. But this form of representation proved not to be enough to change policy priorities.

Decision-making within governments is primarily responsive to the most organised voices in society, and to the interests with the most effective negotiating sanctions. Whether we look at the electoral representation of interests, or at the way other organised interests get involved in conflicts over the distribution of resources, we see that the interests of the most disadvantaged are treated as residual concerns, not as core issues.

There is evidence of a widespread concern in Irish society at the scale of social inequalities, and a growing awareness of the ways in which poverty, unemployment, and poor educational attainment may combine to create severe social deprivation. To deal effectively with these issues would require radical changes to 'normal' policy priorities, beginning with targeted tax reforms, and would undoubtedly require considerable increases in targeted spending. Our analysis has outlined some of the reasons why, despite widespread agreement on the importance of these issues, very little progress was made in tackling them systematically. The fruits of growth were shared very unevenly, and Ireland continues to be a society riven by serious social inequalities.

Endnotes

1 Thanks to Bill Cox, Eithne Fitzgerald, Francis O'Toole, Pat Sykes, and Chris Whelan, for their various helpful comments on an earlier draft of this paper.

2 The exception is the Progressive Democratic Party, which accords priority to pro-business fiscal and administrative reforms. It has been credited with giving impetus to tax reform policy (Sandford 1993: 192). But it is very small, and even when in coalition government with Fianna Fáil (1989–92, and from 1997 to the time of writing), its influence over other issues is limited.

3 Commitment to this strategy followed from the government's participation in the United Nations Summit on Social Development in Copenhagen in 1995. Governments were asked to tackle poverty with reference to measurable targets and specific time-scales.

4 This was mainly because the long-term unemployment benefits had been increased – though still not to the real levels recommended by the Commission on Social Welfare in 1986.

5 This situation may have been improved in the mid-1990s by the increases in Child Benefit introduced by the 'Rainbow Coalition' government – although the rate at which it was paid still fell short of comparable payments in most other European countries.

6 A programme called 'Breaking the Cycle' directed extra spending towards primary schools designated as disadvantaged; 'Early Start' was directed at pre-school children in areas of social disadvantage.

7 As a former senior union leader commented: 'If there are 16 per cent unemployed, there are still 84 per cent at work, and they want their pay increase' (Hardiman 1988: ch. 5).

Chapter 8

Patriots and republicans:
an Irish evolution

Tom Garvin

Introduction

Ireland in 1957 was a quiet place, both North and South. The revolution of 1913–23 had burned out, leaving behind it a quiet, if often sullen, acquiescence in the partition settlement that had emerged between 1920 and 1925. De Valera, the iconic hero of the 1916 rising and leader of Fianna Fáil, the natural governing party of the Republic, became Taoiseach (prime minister) for the sixth and last time in that year. His cabinet consisted substantially of the same group of old comrades who had sided with him in the split of 1922 and who had been in his first cabinet in 1932. De Valera, the firebrand radical of the twenties, had become the grey-haired leader of a nationalist and republican gerontocracy by 1957. And old hatreds derived from the bitter little civil war of 1922–23 still dominated much political debate a generation later.

Politics and culture intersected in peculiar ways in this small, peripheral, ingrown and post-revolutionary polity. Fianna Fáil, in particular, presented itself as a party which was the true and loyal heir of the separatist and heroic tradition of 1916. It also represented itself as being the true defender of the Catholic faith of the ordinary people of Ireland. This combination of fundamentalist Catholicism and purist all-Ireland 'republicanism' formed a 'blended ideology', to use the term of Robert Dahl.

A national Catholic tradition of cultural defence was ensconced in power in both the state and the Catholic Church to which the state was so closely allied. This tradition defended itself by using the leaders of both church and state against both internal and external perceived enemies.[1] Religious traditionalism, a small-town and rural nationalism and a political and cultural isolationism attempted to preserve itself against its perceived enemies of liberalism, cosmopolitanism and non-Catholic, commonly British, freethinking. Battles were won or lost in the democratic arena, but the process was one of a continuous politics of cultural defence which certainly dated back to the late nineteenth century. In many ways, that battle is still being waged in the late 1990s, although the defenders have suffered very substantial, perhaps decisive, defeats.

This chapter outlines the process by which a popular nationalist alliance between fundamentalist Catholicism and 'republicanism' gradually crumbled. It is suggested that it has been replaced by a general Irish patriotism which does not need to attach itself to religious or tribal identity. Unfortunately, this new secular identity is one that is little understood in Northern Ireland or among some Irish-Americans. Indeed, it is little understood in parts of the Republic itself, or if it is understood, is disliked and feared.

The process is not one that is peculiar to Ireland, although it has taken a particularly well-articulated form there. In the United States, for example, movements of cultural defence have reacted to social change much as they have in Ireland over the last hundred years. The populism of William Jennings Bryan in many ways was echoed by the nationalist republican alliance of Faith and Fatherland offered the Irish people by de Valera between 1922 and 1959. Again, Prohibition between 1920 and 1933 in the United States was to a considerable extent a nativist reaction to the growth of great cities and of non-Protestant and somehow 'un-American' ethnic communities with social values derived from recent European experience (Lipset and Raab 1971: 78–80 and passim). The difference was that Ireland was, as a nation, reacting to social change being transmitted to her in apparently almost irresistible form from Great Britain and, to a lesser extent, America and mainland Europe.

Ireland has seen a succession of waves of reaction to secularism and other by-products of modernisation and economic development in the last hundred years; the continuity between the travails of the period since 1957 and the politics of the previous two generations is quite striking. Fundamentalist Catholicism interacted with separatist nationalism ('republicanism') to produce a series of moralistic political movements often of impressive organisational effectiveness, intellectual forcefulness and political sophistication.

Priests and patriots

The ideology as originally formulated in post-Famine Victorian Ireland portrayed the country as being a Catholic nation, symbolised as a green island washed by the pure waters of Ocean, innocent, virginal and, as yet, unpolluted by the modern and secular world of the Enlightenment. It further postulated that Ireland would not remain long in this pristine condition unless Catholic patriots defended it. Other versions – secular, socialist, liberal and individualist – of Irish separatist nationalism existed, but all were to lose out after 1922 to the essentially religious version proposed by Catholic ideologues. Erhardt Rumpf summarised de Valera's version of this Victorian ideal as represented by the policies put forward by the Fianna Fáil during its rise to power in the late 1920s.

> The [Fianna Fáil] programme was well calculated to appeal to the smaller Irish farmers: a frugal, Gaelic Ireland, as little despoiled as possible by the forces of civilisation, especially English civilisation; a state in which there would be no rich and no poor, but rather a countryside scattered with small farmers and small industries. (Rumpf *et al.* 1977: 103)

Such a 'Jeffersonian' programme, he might have added, tied in well with the ambitions for the Catholic Irish harboured by the Catholic Church. Ireland was seen by the church as her beachhead in the English-speaking world, as a source of young men and women who would be, collectively, the vehicle for the conversion of England and America and the British Empire to the true version of Christianity. Even demographically, Ireland was bent to Catholic purposes by the social engineering of the Victorian Irish Catholic Church. The proportions of males and females in religious orders in Ireland were, by 1900, the highest in the West, and possibly the highest in the world. For a variety of reasons, many of them related to the Great Famine of the 1840s, the religious life was of great attraction to many young people. Ireland was a highly religious country, and also a *popularly* religious country. The main menaces to this happy condition were the outside world and any tendency toward dynamic internal economic development uncontrollable by ecclesiastical authorities.

Cultural defence and the fear of the modern

From the 1880s to the 1960s, nationalist and nativist themes were used to erect ideological and organisational defences against the cultural and political assaults seen to be emanating from the Anglo-Saxon world and elsewhere. Sometimes these influences were seen as being mainly literary and cultural; sometimes as being carried by secret societies and political movements such as Freemasonry, Communism or liberalism; sometimes they were seen as internally generated by local sceptics, anti-clericals or extreme radicals.

In particular, the fear of secular individualism, seen as threatening Irish communal values, was often associated with a fear of the modern and an imperfectly camouflaged hatred of Protestant culture. To be fair, this hatred was returned with interest by the more anti-Catholic Irish and English power-holders and voters. Catholic anti-secularism dates from the French Revolution and became clearly visible in the form of a series of *Kulturkaempfe* over clerical control of education in the period 1832–50. These conflicts resulted in the churches in Ireland acquiring control over primary and secondary education. A further struggle over third-level education resulted in the delaying of the concession of university education to any considerable number of Catholics until the early twentieth century. A sixty-year long bishop-led boycott of Protestant and secular third-level institutions was partially lifted only in 1908. In that year the nominally secular National University of Ireland was founded, which provided third-level instruction of a type acceptable to the Catholic Church. Protestant and other secular third-level education remained generally under ban.

This extraordinary assault on higher education by the priests had incalculable but huge effects on the mentality and capabilities of lay Catholic political leadership in the first half of the twentieth century. Among these effects was the intellectual subordination of many lay leaders to ecclesiastical direction, combined with a general deference toward Catholic social and cultural ideas.

The ideology of cultural defence, combined with an intense nationalism of the Faith-and-Fatherland type, was disseminated with great enthusiasm by the priests, brothers and nuns who dominated the education of the bulk of the population. The ideology was accepted to varying extents by the young men and women who were to become the elites of independent Ireland. Through the Christian Brothers and primary-school teachers it also became the ruling ideology of a large part of the general population. It is scarcely an exaggeration to claim that the achievement of independence in 1922 meant, almost incidentally, the triumph of the Catholic lay and clerical forces which adhered to this blended ideology of Catholicism, cultural defence and Gaelic revivalism. The ideology, now with the state behind it, pitted the stereotypic puritan, clean-living and heroic Irish nationalist against both the equally stereotyped effete and corrupt aristocratic world of the British and Anglo-Irish establishments and the vulgar, drunken and anglicised Irish of the big towns (Garvin 1987: 56–7).

C. S. Andrews has given us a vivid picture of his own group of young, mainly pro-de Valera, republican activists in the 1920s, products of the Christian Brothers' schools, the Gaelic League and its programme of cultural and moral rearmament, Sinn Féin (the national liberation front of 1919–22) and, of course, the armed struggle of 1916–23:

> We were a doubly bonded group. We had been close to one another from early boyhood. We were dyed-in-the-wool Republicans. We held strongly to the social ethos of Republicanism in that, with one exception, we were puritanical in outlook and behaviour. We didn't drink. We respected women and, except for the amorous Earle, knew nothing about them. We disapproved of any kind of ostentation. We disapproved of the wearing of formal clothes – tuxedos, evening or morning dress and above all silk hats. We disapproved of horse racing and everything and everyone associated with it. We disapproved of any form of gambling. We disapproved of golf and tennis and the plus-fours and white flannels that went with them. We disapproved of anyone who took an interest in food. We ate our meals in the same spirit of detachment with which we washed and shaved each day. Eating was accepted as an inescapable part of the act of living but served no other purpose. We disapproved of elaborate wedding ceremonies requiring bouquets and buttonholes, red carpets and train bearers. We disapproved of women 'making up' or wearing jewellery. (Andrews 1982: 29)

Impelled by attitudes such as these, an extraordinary apparatus of legal and extra-legal cultural censorship was set up after independence. This regime was to last until the 1960s. The censorship of books was particularly draconian and became, even during the period, internationally notorious. In May 1954, the list of books whose sale was illegal in the Republic of Ireland included books by: the British Government (*Report* of the Royal Commission on Population), James Branch Cabell, Truman Capote, Joyce Cary, the Church of England (*Threshold of Marriage*), Simone de Beauvoir, John Dos Passos, Theodore Dreiser, William Faulkner, F. Scott Fitzgerald, C. S. Forester, Anatole France, Sigmund Freud, Oliver St John Gogarty, Henry Green, Graham Greene, Ernest Hemingway, Aldous Huxley, James Joyce, Arthur Koestler, W. Somerset Maugham, Bryan Merriman (*Cuirt an Mhean-Oichdhe* in English translation from the Gaelic by Frank O'Connor; it was legal in Gaelic), Kate O'Brien, Sean O'Casey, George Orwell (*Nineteen Eighty-Four*), J. D. Salinger, George Bernard Shaw, John Steinbeck, H. G. Wells and Herman Wouk (*The Caine Mutiny*). Film was subjected to a similar censorship (Blanshard 1954: 89–121).

At an informal, extra-legal level, the discouragement or suppression of 'foreign ideas' was carried to further, sometimes grotesque, extremes. The Catholic Church and its allies denounced and intimidated individuals who stepped out of line and expressed ideas or behaved in ways disliked by the establishment. Education for most was controlled directly or indirectly by ecclesiastical agencies or their allies. A static and unchanging mainly rural economy underpinned a democracy and public policy which attempted to prevent cultural change. In reality, the post-revolutionary alliance between priests and patriots was behaving rather like a collective King Canute.

The thaw

Sometime in the period between 1945 and 1960 something snapped. This was a period of economic stagnation relative to the newly booming postwar economies of Britain and mainland Europe. The old men were still in power, and increasingly came to be seen as having outlived their time. The social forces that were eventually to liquidate most of the extraordinary system of social control that had been built up since Victorian times were complex. Many commentators have pointed to increased education of lay people, to increased prosperity and therefore increased mental independence, to media blanketing from Britain and elsewhere, as well as to the events within the Catholic Church commonly termed 'Vatican II', which undermined fundamentalism and antimodernism inside international Catholicism.

There was, however, a deeper reason for the disintegration. A mutual disaffection was growing between the two sides of the nationalist establishment: priests and patriots ceased to see eye to eye. The alliance of separatist nationalism and fundamentalist Catholicism which dominated the state during the first generation after independence began to show signs of decay. Essentially, the nationalist and developmentalist component of the alliance came increasingly into open conflict with the puritan, culturally defensive and quietist component. By the late 1950s, they were in open opposition. The patriots had come to the conclusion that protectionism would have to be abandoned in favour of multinational capital, and education for pious citizenship would have to take second place to education for economic growth.

The nationalists wanted to create a strong, modern nation with industries, cities, a growing population and 'a place among the nations of the earth', as the old slogan had put it. Spreading what little wealth was available around equally in a stagnant rural and small-town protected local economy was not going to work any more. Furthermore, ideas were needed badly in an atmosphere of intellectual bankruptcy; baiting the intellectuals and the unorthodox did not impress the newly educated young on whom the younger nationalist leaders in Fine Gael and Fianna Fáil increasingly had to count. Puritans wished to preserve and reproduce a certain social type – pious, familial, loyal to the native acres, culturally ingrown and obedient to clerical authority in matters moral and intellectual. By the fifties, this latter project could be, and increasingly was, accused of being a threat to the nationalist one, and was increasingly seen as such even by some younger priests.

A certain undercurrent of doubt about the socio-cultural policies espoused by the clerical and lay puritans had always existed in the nationalist tradition, going back particularly to founding father Arthur Griffith's doubts about the rural arcadias beloved by so many of his political allies in the early Sinn Féin. His paper, *United Irishman*, complained as early as 1903:

> This cocky disparagement of the work of modern thinkers is characteristic of the shoddy side of the Irish revival. According to this gospel we are to keep our eyes fixed on the Middle Ages – and then wonder we are decaying . . . The world outside has been thinking and growing, Ireland preserves her picturesque ignorance – which her smart young men, who know better themselves, tell her is more sacred than the wisdom of an infidel world – and Ireland emigrates. We require the breath of free thought in Ireland. (*United Irishman*, 25 July 1903)

Lay nationalist writers like Sean O'Faolain and other *Bell* writers echoed this plea for mental freedom throughout the first post-independence generation. Modernisers who made explicit connections between mental freedom, innovation and economic and cultural progress had always existed in the movement but had tended to be shunted aside by those who, in effect, espoused a pious stasis and who got their way because of the depression of the 1930s and the isolation imposed by the Second World War. After 1945, this old concern about the tension between the puritans' project and modernisation was increasingly expressed *sotto voce* at home. Significantly, it was also expressed, more loudly and without fear, by sympathetic outsiders whose views seem to have influenced establishment opinion more effectively than those of internal commentators; the latter's criticisms were too easily dismissed as treason in the ranks.

It was an Irish-American priest who finally blew the whistle. Fr. John A. O'Brien edited a much-discussed collection of essays in 1954 with the alarming title, *The Vanishing Irish* (O'Brien 1954). The contributors launched what amounted to a polite but sustained and ultimately devastating attack on the intellectual assumptions of the Irish establishment. It was suggested in particular that sexual repression had created an emotional atmosphere which was damaging to family life and which made Irish people unwilling to live and marry in Ireland, particularly in rural areas. The intellectual vacuity of the official line was excoriated. Michael Sheehy, in a book entitled *Divided we Stand* (1955), tore apart the official position on partition for a newly attentive younger generation. In 1957, J. V. Kelleher, a well-known Irish-American, wrote in *Foreign Affairs* that a lack of intellectualism among Irish leaders, combined with an emigration-induced apathy among the general population, was almost literally killing the nation (Kelleher 1957). A hatred of intellect and of psychic freedom was finally coming to be recognised as a real threat to the entire nationalist project.[2]

Even the Catholic Church was not impervious to animadversions coming from Irish-American priests. The redoubtable John Charles McQuaid, Archbishop of Dublin 1939–72 and famed defender of orthodoxy, retained an American Jesuit in 1962 to inquire, using modern survey techniques, into attitudes of Dublin Catholics towards religion and clerical authority (Biever 1976; Garvin 1982).[3]

The portrait of Dublin Catholic political culture revealed by the survey was quite startling and, from the Church's point of view, alarming. Attitudes to the authority of priests and the Church varied little by class, region of birth or by age. Almost

90 per cent of the sample agreed, for example, that the Catholic Church was the greatest force for good in Ireland. Priests were accepted willingly and enthusiastically as the natural social, economic and political leaders of the country. Their status was so high, however, that the democratically elected leaders of Dáil Eireann were overshadowed. Cynicism about politicians and an accompanying suspicion about any laymen's attempts at political or cultural leadership were widespread. These attitudes had deep social and historical roots, as I have suggested. The post-Famine Church had done its work well. One respondent conceded that the clerics 'might make mistakes' occasionally, but they were not 'out for themselves' and he would rather be wrong with his priest than 'right with those damn crooks in Dublin'. When asked what side they would take in the event of a clash between Church and State, a stunning 87 per cent said they would back their Church (Biever 1976: 270–1, 306).

This was little more than a decade after a spectacular political crisis in which the Church had successfully vetoed a welfare scheme designed to assist expectant women in health matters. The politicians were helpless in the face of such a political climate, and most important legislation was cleared informally and secretly with the bishops in advance (Biever 1976: 397). The formally democratic Irish political process was heavily tinged with theocracy, because the people willed it to be so. The voters were children of God.

However, the survey was not uniformly reassuring to the Archbishop; even in 1962, incipient change was visible. Those few who had completed secondary education were far more willing to question clerical prerogatives and formed a small, isolated group, denied political power both by their clergy and by the mass of their fellow citizens. Whereas an extraordinary 88 per cent of the sample endorsed the proposition that the Church was the greatest source for good in the country, an almost equally massive 83 per cent of the educated group disagreed with it (Biever 1976: 226–7).

This boded ill for the future of the Catholic Church in Ireland; clerical fears of educated lay people were demonstrated to be well-founded by the survey. The division between the educated and uneducated segments of the population was enormous: while the rank and file of the Church's membership still looked to the Church for leadership, there was a 'solid core of what we may call the intellectual elite who flatly deny the contention . . .' The researcher concluded that there was a ferment of disillusionment among the intellectuals as to the efficacy of the Church in the performance of her functions' (Biever 1976: 227). Rather like the communist regimes of Eastern Europe in the 1980s, the Catholic Church in 1950s Ireland had begun to educate itself out of power; her own secondary schools were hatcheries of anti-clericals and sceptics.

In the 1960s, then, an undercurrent of anti-clericalism ran through the growing educated stratum of a relatively uneducated nation. Hindsight suggests that the resentment of Church power dated back much further, perhaps to the Mother and Child incident of 1951. It may be that the bishops, in sweeping aside a nascent liberal 'Christian Democrat' tendency in Catholic society in 1951, killed the prospects for an intellectual lay Catholicism, loyal to, if sometimes critical of, the Church. Certainly, in 1962, the better educated bitterly resented the Church's social power. The researcher, after all a Catholic priest himself, commented worriedly that the Irish priest was caught in a dilemma; he was confronted by a slowly growing, emergent educated future political class which required more sophisticated answers to contemporary problems than the platitudes with which an older generation had been satisfied, but he was confronted on the other hand by 'the suspicious gaze' of the many simple people in lower-class and rural areas 'who were hostile to change of any kind' (Biever 1976: 278). The researcher concluded that the church had attempted to solve the problem by brooking no rivals:

> ... the Catholic Church has progressively estranged the intellectual class, as our data conclusively indicated, and has deprived herself as well as Ireland of that vitality both so desperately needed by almost forcing the talented intellectual to seek his fortunes in some other country. (497, 503)

The will to continue the full campaign of cultural defence weakened in the 1950s and 1960s as the establishment itself ceased to believe in its desirability or efficacy. Fintan O'Toole, a prominent Irish commentator, argued, with some exaggeration, in the mid-1990s that the defeat of the official ideology had actually been quite easy; the growth of an international youth culture derived from cities swamped Irish official attempts to construct a pious and neo-Gaelic rural-based national culture.

> Nationalist ideology, Gaelic revivalism and religious reaction produced a culture whose real presiding goddesses were not Cathleen ni Houlihan and the Virgin Mary but A Gal from Kalamazoo and Our Lady Evelyn of the Follies. That [official] culture, with its contempt for cities, had nothing with which to absorb that which began to develop from the late 1960s onwards. It had no great over-arching myth into which the children of the suburbs, fed on sex and drugs and rock and roll, might be absorbed. It was, paradoxically, the critics of nationalist orthodoxy, chief among them Sean O'Faolain, and the exiles, both internal and external, from de Valera's Ireland who managed, in spite of everything, to create over time what Irish political nationalism had virtually destroyed – a vibrant and distinctive national culture. The problem for Irish conservatism was that this national culture was, and has remained, liberal, cosmopolitan and anti-clerical. (O'Toole 1996: 110)[4]

The change

Certainly, independent Ireland has changed more since 1960 than it did in the era between the end of the Civil War in 1923 and the retirement of de Valera in 1959. Social change is notoriously difficult to measure, but useful indices of such change are offered by such aggregate and crude measures as Gross National Product (GNP) and various indicators of educational levels.

Table 8.1 summarises the economic growth of the Republic of Ireland since 1953.[5] It should be noted that Irish economic growth between independence in 1922 and the retirement of de Valera in 1959 was low; GNP in 1959 was perhaps one and a half times as high as it was in 1922, and the Civil War and the 1939–45 period had both contributed to a general climate of stagnation. However, things have changed since the late 1950s, and, since 1987 in particular, the Republic has been going through what is by Irish standards and even by international standards, a boom period. A more flattering measure, Gross Domestic Product (GDP), would give an even more complimentary picture of Ireland's economic progress in recent years. A 1997 OECD report suggests that the Republic's GDP per head is now

Table 8.1 Average Annual GNP growth rates 1953–95

1953–60	1960–77	1979–86	1985–95
1.8%	3.1%	–0.3%	5.0%

Source: Kennedy 1988; *Irish Times* 23 December 1997; *Economist* 1997.

Table 8.2 Enrolment in third-level education, as a proportion of age cohort, selected years

1960	1980	1994
9%	18%	34%

Source: *Economist* 1997: Kennedy 1988.

actually higher, for the first time in possibly two centuries, than that of Britain. GNP growth in 1997 has been recorded as 7.5 per cent, and 1998 is tipped to be as high, or even higher – an OECD record. GNP may have doubled in the last 10 years. Certainly, Ireland's historically persistent image as the poor sister in the north European family of nations looks like needing some revision.

Educational attainment levels have also been transformed, as Table 8.2 indicates.

Education, long neglected and monopolised by religious organisations, became a boom industry in Ireland after 1967, and has had an indirect but pervasive effect on power relationships in the Republic. The old peasant deference to clerical authority, partly derived from a popular perception of priests as educated men who could be trusted because they were on your side, has faded.

Relative wealth and education have brought the usual consequences in the form of the spread of 'middle-class' values beyond the traditional middle class. A relative secularism and a tendency to follow one's own conscience in moral and civic matters, as distinct from following the advice of traditional moral mentors such as priests, characterises this new Irish social type. Relative wealth means personal independence and a lack of demand for patrons or powerful defenders such as clerics, local powerful men, politicians or publicists. Opinion surveys and referendum votes since the late 1960s have clearly indicated a slow but steady increase in the post-Catholic and '*à la carte* Catholic' segment of the population. It follows a class and urban-rural divide, and also displays an age dimension.

Following these changes in power relationships and culture has been a change in attitudes to the perennial national political question. Ireland was divided into two entities now known as Northern Ireland (NI) and the Republic of Ireland (RI) in 1920–23, in a period of great turmoil and subsequent bitterness. Irish partitioned independence was followed by a short civil war in the South and the echoes of these founding events have shaped the internal politics of both Irish states ever since. In NI, the Protestant two-thirds of the population defended successfully a continuing union with Britain, whereas the Catholic one-third contested that union and wished to join the independent South.

Rather similarly, for two generations in the southern Republic, an alliance of the Catholic Church and the new state promulgated an official 'Faith and Fatherland' popular ideology. This creed, enshrined in history books, literary texts, the Irish language and in Church teaching, was inculcated systematically into the minds of young people through the state-regulated and church-run school system. Nationality and the Catholic faith formed an apparently seamless garment. To be 'non-Catholic' was not quite the same as being 'non-Irish', but it was to be less definitely a member of the national club. Similarly, to be an atheist was to be disloyal. Again, to be a conspicuous adherent of the movement to revive the Irish language was to signal your ethnic credentials. Furthermore, anyone who spoke too clearly in defence of certain aspects of the partition settlement of 1920–23 was also seen as less than loyal to the national cause. Communists were, of course, quite outside the pale.

'Faith and Fatherland' nationalism achieved extraordinary heights. The cult of the martyrs of the 1916 Rising was quite extravagant. Patrick Pearse, the leader of the Rising, came to be regarded as a Christ-like figure who had given his life for Ireland as Jesus had given His for mankind. The Rising of Easter Monday 1916 was celebrated with military parades on Easter Sunday every year. It was not until 1974 that this possibly blasphemous symbolic conjunction of Church and State was abandoned.

In parallel to this, attitudes toward Northern Ireland gradually changed. Whereas loyalty to the ideal of a united Ireland persisted, the idea that somehow the local majority in NI should be coerced into unity with RI has weakened, although some double-think about this is still detectable. Here, television has been a great educator. Revulsion against the atrocities committed by the Provisional Irish Republican Army against civilians in both the North and South has led to a perception that the world-view of traditional insurrectionist nationalism is moribund. The collapse of the Soviet Union marked the disappearance of the guerrillas' most important external ally. The parallel conversion, by Irish government diplomacy, of Irish-America from pro-IRA sentimentality has also furthered this process of change.

The quasi-religious public and popular cult of Faith and Fatherland has been one of the more important casualties of the modernisation of Irish society since the 1950s. Ironically, it has been the Catholic Church as much as the State which has found the cult increasingly an embarrassment. Several events have weakened the old alliance of priest and patriot to the point of death. These include Vatican II, the IRA campaign in Northern Ireland, generational change through education, the growth of the mass media, economic change and 'Europe'.

Vatican II arguably delivered an unintentionally lethal blow to the kind of anti-liberal, anti-individualist counter-Reformation Catholicism which was symbolised in Ireland by the Archbishop of Dublin, John Charles McQuaid, in power between 1939 and 1972. It is evident that, even at the time of the Vatican Council in the early 1960s, McQuaid himself sensed this to be so. Rome itself, it appeared, had declared the Counter-Reformation to be over. Irish bishops publicly welcomed the changes ushered in by Vatican II, but their welcoming voices commonly sounded distinctly hollow.

Similarly, the renewed IRA campaign against British rule in NI after 1969, in the name of a traditional and officially approved aspiration to an all-Ireland independent Republic, had the ironic result of encouraging a demilitarisation of the existing southern Republic. It also caused a revulsion against the IRA's murderous methods and fostered a revisionist mood in southern society. The Republic, after 25 years of the barbarous activities of the IRA and its loyalist enemies in the North, is probably far more pro-partition now than it was then.

Generational change has also brought with it profound changes. Few people now alive in the Republic actually remember British rule. Most do not even remember the country's short period as a dominion within the British Commonwealth. The Empire is dead, and Irish anti-imperialism has died with it. Unlike Northern Ireland, the Republic has come to think of itself as a small European democracy which happens to be culturally and geographically close to Britain. Mass education of a kind not available to previous generations has accelerated the detraditionalisation of Irish political culture.

Television, as elsewhere, has been a powerful engine of cultural change. The Americanisation of popular culture so evident in twentieth-century Europe occurred at a particularly rapid rate in the English-speaking western fringe of Western Europe after World War II. Television played a central role in this process. North and South in Ireland have begun to share the same international popular culture, as each part of the island also shares it with Britain.

As outlined above, economic change has been very great. Ireland is now possibly four times as rich per head as it was at the time of Independence. A peasant country, with a large proportion of its population living at subsistence level, has been transformed into a relatively rich country. Again, membership of the European Community has effectively ended the old economic dominance of Britain. Trade with mainland Europe and the rest of the world now dwarfs trade with the neighbouring island.

In 1922, at the time of Irish Independence, about 55 per cent of the new country's population lived off farming; the equivalent proportion now is not far above 10 per cent. Furthermore, the proportion of small subsistence farms has fallen, and there is a general tendency for large, commercial farming to win out over traditional methods. In effect, the Republic has done without the classic phase of heavy industrialisation and has gone from a traditional rural society to being post-industrial with no intervening period; a classic 'stage-skipping' exercise. This has in turn entailed massive problems of cultural adjustment. A secular patriotism, which does not rely on tribal and religious identities, has evolved in the Republic of Ireland in the last few decades. There are those who dislike this new agnostic and liberal nationalism, but they are in full retreat.

This process is by no means complete, but it seems that the Irish, a politically rather adept people, are well up to completing it in their own good time.

Conclusion

The Irish experience vividly illustrates a lesson that many political leaders have had to learn in the twentieth century: that there are clear limits and considerable costs attached to any ambitious project of social engineering through political means. Prohibition in the United States generated a gangland underworld that has haunted the country ever since. Similarly, Soviet communism has robbed the Russian people of the kinds of political and economic habits deemed necessary to construct a modern civic order.

In Ireland, the attempt by priests and patriots to construct a political order morally superior to that of a century ago had the consequence of repressing much Irish social and cultural energy following independence. A quantifiable aspect of the price paid for this endeavour was very probably the sluggish economic growth of the first decades after the World War II. It was only when the power of the old revolutionaries and their ecclesiastical allies started to wane in the 1960s that economic growth started its surge. Ireland had to recover from its Catholic revolution.

Endnotes

1 See my 'The Politics of Denial and Cultural Defence: the Referendums of 1983 and 1986 in Context,' Irish Review, No. 3 (1988) 1–7, at 2–4; on blended ideologies, see Robert Dahl, Polyarchy, New Haven: Free Press, 1971, 443; see also generally, Terence Brown, Ireland: A Social and Cultural History, 1922–79, London: Fontana, 1981; Paul Blanshard, The Irish and Catholic Power, London: Derek Verschoyle, 1954; Tom Garvin, 'Priests and Patriots: Irish Seperatism and the Fear of the Modern, 1890–1914,' Irish Historical Studies, XXV, No. 97 (May 1986), 67–81, and ibid., Nationalist Revolutionaries in Ireland, 1858–1927, Oxford: Clarendon, 1987, 56–77 and passim.

2 Michael Sheehy, Divided We Stand, London: Faber, 1955; J. V. Kelleher, 'Ireland ... And Where Does She Stand?,' Foreign Affairs, 1957, 485–495; cf. Brown, 241–243.

3 B. F. Biever, Religion, Culture and Values: a Cross-Cultural Analysis of Motivational Factors in Native Irish and American Irish Catholicism, New York: Arno Press, 1976; see also my 'Change and the Political System,' in Frank Litton, Unequal Achievement, Dublin: Institute of Public Administration, 1982, 21–40.

4 Fintan O'Toole, The Ex-Isle of Erin, Dublin: New Island, 1996, 110. For a general analysis of attitudinal change toward politics in Ireland, see my 'Hibernian Endgame? Nationalism in a Divided Ireland,' in Richard Caplan and John Feffer, Europe's New Nationalism, New York and Oxford: Oxford University Press, 1996, 184–194.

5 Sources for Tables 1 and 2, World Development Report, various years; Kieran A. Kennedy et al., The Economic Development of Ireland in the Twentieth Century, Routledge, 1988, passim. For 1997 GNP estimate and 1998 forecast, Irish Times, 23 December, 1997. See in general, 'Europe's Shining Light,' The Economist, May 17–23, 1997, 15–16, 23–29.

Chapter 9

Ireland and the growth of international governance

Brigid Laffan and Rory O'Donnell

Introduction

The contemporary international system is characterised by an increasing inter-connectedness and interdependence which is driven by capital flows, technology, investment patterns, growing linkages between societies and more rapid dissemination of ideas. Internationalisation has been accompanied by a proliferation of regional and global organisations established to regulate international economic exchange, security, and issues such as the environment, that cannot be contained within the boundaries of states. The European Union (EU) represents the world's most extensive and intensive form of regionalism. No other system of regional co-operation is so heavily rooted in a dense pattern of co-operative institutions which has produced a loosely coupled albeit patchy form of European governance. Membership of the European Union alters the external environment of the traditional nation state and the internal dynamic of public policy-making. For Ireland, membership of the EU is different in character and in its consequences to participation in all other international organisations. It is bound up with the decision to open the economy in the search for prosperity and welfare.

Ireland, together with the United Kingdom and Denmark, joined the European Union on 1 January 1973 as part of the first enlargement of the Union. Ireland's desire for membership was closely tied up with British membership in two senses. Ireland's continuing dependence on the British market, for a large proportion of its external trade, meant that Ireland could not have remained outside without suffering serious economic consequences. In addition, membership of the Union offered a way out of excessive dependence on Britain. It offered the prospect of a shift from dependence to interdependence. It marked a reversal of protectionist economic policies, Ireland's changed relationship with Britain and represented the final nail in the coffin of the kind of Ireland that De Valera would have wanted. De Valera's nation-and state-building programme was rooted in an Ireland of political and cultural distinctiveness; his preferred image of the Irish was that of a god-fearing rural people who eschewed the excesses of materialism. For Ireland, participation in the EU was directly linked to the national project of modernisation. Economic growth was necessary to alleviate the political and social consequences of low incomes, emigration, high unemployment and low productivity.

Following the reassessment of Ireland's economic policy in 1958, when a decision was taken to pursue external-led economic growth financed by multinational investment, membership of the large European market with its common policy for agriculture became highly desirable. Although Ireland was a member of the Organisation for European Economic Co-operation (OEEC) established in 1948 to distribute Marshall Aid, it did not participate in the emerging European trading blocs, the European Economic Community (EEC – 1958), and the European Free Trade Association (EFTA – 1960). Ireland's relative isolation in the early postwar period was underlined by non-membership of the North Atlantic Treaty Organisation (NATO) and late membership of the United Nations in 1955. Membership of the International Monetary Fund (IMF) and the World Bank in 1957 and the GATT in 1967 was a harbinger of Ireland's growing involvement in the institutions governing the global economy.

This paper concentrates on the impact of internationalisation on: the economy and macro-economic management; management of the interface between Irish Government and international governance structures; and Irish identity.[1]

The internationalisation of the Irish economy

In studying the politics of change in Ireland it is necessary to take note of interactions between internationalisation/international governance, the cycle of the world economy and particular developments in Irish society and policy. To facilitate this, we begin with a thumbnail sketch of economic developments in Ireland since 1960. The switch to an outward-orientated strategy was prompted by the severe balance of payments difficulties, recession and emigration of the 1950s. The switch coincided with, and was encouraged by, the emergence of economic growth, which continued until 1973. Ireland's entry into the EEC in 1973 coincided with a major slowdown in economic growth in all OECD countries. However, Ireland's recovery from the recession of 1974–75 was very strong. Largely driven by increased public spending and borrowing, the Irish economy was buoyant during most of the 1970s. In 1979, Ireland abandoned its 150-year-old one-to-one link to Sterling and joined the European Monetary System. Ireland had, perhaps, the worst economic performance in Europe during most of the 1980s, as a result of international recession, reinforced by a dramatic domestic adjustment to reduce public finance and balance of payments deficits and reduce inflation (NESC 1989). Since 1987, overall economic performance has been much stronger, with growth well above the European and OECD averages, movement of the balance of payments into a strong surplus and steady reduction in the debt/GNP ratio. Since 1992, economic growth has been extremely strong, with unprecedented levels of employment creation, which has given rise to terms such as the 'Celtic Tiger' being applied.

The developments in the Irish economy, policy and society since 1960 can be seen as a process of learning how to manage internationalisation and the emergence of international governance. Ireland's decision in the late 1950s and early 1960s to switch from protectionism to outward orientation was a highly conscious one. It was intended to achieve an exporting economy by modernising and re-orienting the indigenous economy and attracting inward investment. Meticulous studies were undertaken and new public organisations and policies were created to address the perceived weaknesses. The process was shaped by major treaties – the Anglo-Irish Free Trade Area Agreement and accession to the EEC – which prompted reflection on the choice to internationalise. Yet Irish development quickly became dependent on inward investment, as indigenous industry withered in the face of international competition. Growth and international comparison created increased aspirations, distributional conflict, new social needs and intensified political competition. The approaches adopted by government and economic actors reflected insufficient awareness of international competition. Inevitable adversities were allowed to become divisive and produced delayed and insufficient responses. The sum total of societal demands on Irish output were resolved by public borrowing. Although Ireland handled certain aspects of EC membership relatively successfully – the CAP and Structural Funds – these were allowed to hide the wider policy and behavioural requirements of internationalisation. Overall, there was insufficient appreciation of the interdependence of the economy – between the indigenous economy and the international economy, between the public and the private sectors, and between the economic and the political. Organisational and institutional arrangements capable of identifying and mediating these mechanisms and pressures were not in place, and seemed beyond the capability of Ireland's political, administrative and interest-group system. By the mid-1980s, Ireland's economic, social and political strategy was in ruins, and its hope of prospering in the international economy was in considerable doubt.

Yet from within this traumatic, but dynamic, experience there emerged a new perspective on Ireland's position in European integration and a globalising economy. This was embodied in the social partnership approach to economic and social management, innovative approaches in several policy areas, a resurgent enterprise sector, attuned to the radical changes in international business, and a new cultural confidence to adopt and adapt international influences. Our central argument is that the process of internationalisation has involved an evolution from deliberate strategy, through radical disruption, disorientation and loss of direction, to a new shared understanding of the constraints and possibilities of international governance and internationalisation.

Inward investment

In assessing the impact of inward investment on Ireland we consider its interaction with the indigenous economy, its regional pattern, and its impact on organisation patterns.

Until about the end of the 1960s, new foreign investment was largely in technologically mature and often labour-intensive industries, such as clothing, footwear, textiles, plastics and light engineering. From the late 1960s, foreign investment in Ireland increasingly involved newer, more technologically advanced products, such as electrical and electronic products, machinery, pharmaceuticals, and medical instruments and equipment. Its impact on the Irish economy and Irish society was shaped by that pattern. An ongoing concern was the fact that transnational corporations (TNCs) located only certain stages of production in Ireland, retaining high value-added functions at headquarters, or in other advanced countries. Indeed, during the 1970s, the weakness of *linkages* from foreign-owned enterprises to the indigenous economy became a major subject of research and policy concern (O'Malley 1981). It was feared that the only significant impact of the TNCs on Ireland was the hiring of labour and the relaxation of the balance of payments constraint. This impression was reinforced by evidence that employment in each plant tended to decline after a number of years (O'Malley and Scott 1980). The extent and persistence of differences between foreign-owned and indigenous enterprises – in technology, export orientation, product quality, scale – prompted many to describe Ireland as a 'dual economy' (O'Malley 1981).

Inward investment in manufacturing had regional effects which were significant in the internationalisation of Irish society. Ireland's indigenous industrialisation behind protective tariffs was heavily concentrated in four main urban areas: Dublin, Cork, Limerick and Waterford. In the 1960s and 1970s, a high proportion of inward investment was located in smaller towns and rural areas. O'Farrell (1980) found that as much as 59 per cent of the new foreign industrial firms established in the period 1960 to 1973 were set up in the less developed 'designated areas' in the West. At the same time, the decline of traditional, indigenous industry reduced manufacturing employment in the main urban areas (see below). While overall manufacturing employment increased by almost 33 per cent between 1961 and 1981, it fell by 9.6 per cent in the Dublin area and Dublin's share of the total dropped from 47 per cent to 32 per cent (O'Malley 1992). In part, this reflected Irish policy which, pursuing dispersed development, offered higher government grants to TNCs willing to locate in less developed regions. It seems also to reflect the preferences of TNCs during the 1960s and 1970s. As a consequence, the social, political, cultural and organisational effects of the internationalisation of the economy were relatively widespread, rather than concentrated in leading urban areas.[2]

Recent developments in the Irish economy and society suggest that there may have been a larger effect of the TNCs on Irish organisation than has been recognised to date. While formal linkages between the TNCs and indigenous enterprises – such as subcontracting – were certainly slow to develop, it seems likely that other processes of linkage or diffusion were occurring. One of these would seem to be the impact of the TNCs on Irish management and organisation. It seems possible that while Irish observers were looking for commercial linkages, and not finding as many as they wanted, an organisational revolution was taking place behind their backs. In our view the internationalisation of the Irish economy has coincided with a profound transformation of the organisational capability and consciousness of Irish business, Irish policy and, indeed, Irish society – although this has yet to be systematically studied or documented. The role of emigration and return migration in facilitating technical and organisational change should also be considered.

The difficulties of indigenous development and the debate on Irish 'failure'

While Ireland achieved a significant internationalisation and structural adjustment of the economy since 1960, the role of indigenous enterprises in that achievement was disappointing. By default, Ireland's economic structure came to rely heavily on inward investment. Buoyant domestic growth in the 1960s and 1970s – funded by foreign borrowing in the 1970s – postponed the day of reckoning for parts of indigenous manufacturing industry. However, the 1980s – combining international recession, fiscal correction and dis-inflation – introduced a major shakeout in indigenous enterprises and employment. On moving to free trade, many of Ireland's relatively large manufacturing firms were in sectors such as textiles, clothing, footwear, leather, chemicals, motor vehicles and parts, electrical engineering, shipbuilding, bread, biscuits, flour and confectionery and other food industries. After the removal of tariff protection, import penetration was rapid and, in this highly competitive international environment, these industries suffered secular decline in which the larger Irish producers were eliminated. The drastic removal of these industries, and their replacement by foreign-owned firms in high-technology segments of chemicals, pharmaceuticals and electrical machinery, constituted a much more significant inter-industry adjustment than was experienced by other countries participating in European integration (NESC 1989). It created an enormous increase in unemployment, and is the major source of the continuing problem of long-term unemployment and poverty.

The severity of this experience in the 1980s altered perceptions of the Irish economy. Expectations of medium and long-term prosperity became extremely weak, which encouraged rent-seeking and profit-taking behaviour. This was evident in the extent of capital flight in the 1980s and the tendency for various government incentives to produce rent-seeking financial manipulation rather than increased business initiative. The emergence of the so-called 'black hole', and the coincidence of rapidly growing exports with falling living standards and employment, produced fears that the modern Irish economy was fundamentally fictitious – a view captured graphically in the title of Fintan O'Toole's book *Black Hole, Green Card: The Disappearence of Ireland* (1994). The failure, once again, of indigenous development gave rise to a number of major studies of Ireland's 'economic failure' – in which internationalisation, and its relation to domestic structures, politics and culture, was a central theme.

Crotty argued that Ireland should be compared with Third World countries and developed an account in which capitalist colonialism played a central role. In the twentieth century, the social and political structures established under colonialism used the state in ways which favoured entrenched elites (Crotty 1986). Likewise, O'Hearn traced Ireland's long run failure to its outward-looking free-market strategy, which made Ireland a 'classic case of "dependent" relations: slow growth and inequality caused by foreign penetration' (O'Hearn 1989). Although supportive of inward investment, O'Malley (1989), argued that Ireland, as a late-developing country, faced, and still faces, significant barriers to entry created by the scale, market power or technological lead of established firms in larger, more developed, economies.

In an important historical account, Lee enriched his earlier argument about lack of entrepreneurship (Lee 1968), tracing Ireland's twentieth-century experience to the predominance of a 'possessor ethic', as opposed to a 'performer ethic', in the country's institutions, intellect, character and identity (Lee 1989). Political structures, in particular the nature of party politics and the failure of politics to represent and mediate conflicting interests, were emphasised by Girvin (1989). Although not focusing specifically on economic performance, others analysed the relationship between national political mobilisation and the development of Irish Catholicism (Garvin 1981; Inglis 1987). Indeed, it was suggested that those factors could have an influence on economic life: directly, through their influence on state policy and, indirectly, through shaping cultural characteristics (such as the authoritarian family pattern), which were inimical to economic modernisation (Breen *et al.* 1990). Kennedy *et al.* (1988) identified a set of proximate causes of Ireland's failure at the level of policy and public administration: failure to grasp the implications of the small size of the economy, absence of a long-term perspective, and neglect of the human resource dimension.

Finally, Mjoset's (1992) work for NESC drew heavily on all these studies, to present an interpretation of Irish development which embodied the dynamic interaction of economic and social structures, global political factors, and cultural and attitudinal patterns. Mjoset added the argument that Ireland's 'basic vicious circle starts from two facts: the weak national system of innovation and population decline via emigration. The mechanism whereby these two features reinforce each other must be sought in social structure. These mechanisms are highlighted by studying contrasts which emerge from the comparison with the other . . . countries' (1992: 7–8).

In retrospect, many of these perceptions of the Irish economy seem somewhat overstated. Some of them reflect the fact that – because of its openness and high share of inward investment – Ireland was, perhaps, the first country in which conventional national accounting categories became insufficient. Others reflect the fact that deadweight, displacement and rent-seeking are particularly prevalent in a stagnant economy with weak expectations. In the light of developments since 1987, it seems that these large-scale studies of Ireland's 'failure' were somewhat coloured by the extreme difficulties of the 1980s.

A new perspective on internationalisation

It is notable that those studies which saw Ireland's engagement in European integration, the international economy and international governance as the source of ongoing economic failure, were never seen as offering a guide to practical action.

Indeed, the significant development in ideas and policy in the late 1980s was one that involved a new recognition of the link between domestic policy (and action by non-state actors) and international governance. Far from accepting the analysis of Crotty or O'Hearn, there emerged a view that internationalisation, and international governance, while they had exposed critical weaknesses in Ireland, were no longer the *cause* of those weaknesses. Indeed, even deeper international governance and internationalisation, when properly understood and managed, came to be seem as the route to success (NESC 1989; O'Donnell 1991a, 1993).

The turnaround achieved in the late 1980s involved, among other things, an intense reflection on the experience of European integration and internationalisation, and the emergence of a new, and widely shared, understanding of the constraints and possibilities of international governance. That new perspective had sectoral, developmental, technological, social, political and macro-economic dimensions. We briefly summarise these here and focus on one, in particular, in the next section.

While Ireland's membership of the EC allowed the country achieve one of its agricultural policy aims – access to a large, high-priced market – attention turned to problems in agriculture which remained despite, or because of, the Common Agricultural Policy (CAP) (Kennedy *et al.* 1988; NESC 1989, 1992). The disappointing development of the food industry, and other problems in agriculture, reflected a range of industrial, agricultural and structural constraints which had not been successfully removed by domestic policy. The loss of so many indigenous businesses was traced to failure of industrial policy and the uneven growth of domestic demand (NESC 1982, 1989; O'Donnell 1991b). There was greater recognition of the constraints which interdependence, particularly the EMS, places on domestic monetary and fiscal policy. Indeed, the NESC summarised its detailed study of Ireland's experience in the EC with the general lesson that 'membership of the Community does not reduce the need for clear Irish policy aims and methods. In particular, membership of the Community does not diminish the need for a national ability to identify solutions to national problems – even where those solutions require Community policies and action' (NESC 1989: 218).

It was noted that the effects of integration can take considerable time to work themselves out, adjustments to membership of the EC being experienced in the 1980s as well as the 1970s. Indeed, it came to be recognised that internationalisation is an ongoing process which throws ever greater sections of the economy and society into international competition (NESC 1996).

The political dimension of European economic integration was more deeply and, importantly, more *widely* understood in the late 1980s. This was reinforced by the Single European Act (SEA), the analysis of which undermined the element of opposition to European integration which had developed within Fianna Fáil during the early 1980s, and restored the recognition of the link between the economic and political goals of the EC, which had been the norm since Lemass's unambiguous statements in the early 1960s. Economic actors came to recognise what Irish officials had long understood: that small states generally benefit from the formal, legal, supranational elements of integration, whereas larger and more powerful states can work intergovernmental negotiations to much greater effect (Keatinge 1991).

This widely shared new perspective on international governance and internationalisation supported a more positive, if tentative, assessment of Ireland's chance of escaping more thoroughly from the vicious circles of the past (O'Donnell 1993). Note was made of the emergence of the type of autonomous civil society, which Mjoset identified as an important factor in all the successful small European countries which he compared to Ireland. The possibility was raised that changes in technology and the international economy could reduce the significance of some of Ireland's historical disadvantages and increase the economic relevance of some of Ireland's strengths. Finally, it was argued that some of the limitations of the party political system and interest-group mediation might be overcome by the development of 'political exchange' involving the social partners and government in 1987. We now turn to this aspect of Ireland's adaptation to internationalisation.

Managing Internationalisation through social partnership

Ireland's progress in learning how to manage internationalisation is nowhere more evident than in the system of social partnership, in place since 1987. In the context of deep despair in Irish society in the mid-1980s, the social partners – acting in the tripartite National Economic and Social Council – hammered out an agreed strategy to escape from the vicious circle of real stagnation, rising taxes and exploding debt. While the NESC is an advisory body – in which employers, trade unions, farmers and senior civil servants analyse policy issues – the NESC *Strategy for Development* (1986) formed the basis upon which a new government and the social partners quickly negotiated the Programme for National Recovery to run from 1987 to 1990. This was to be the first of four agreements which have recently brought Ireland to more than a decade of negotiated economic and social governance. Following the influence of *A Strategy for Development* (1986), the negotiation of each subsequent social partnership programme has been preceded by an NESC *Strategy* report, setting out the shared perspective of the social partners on the achievements and limits of the last programme and the parameters within which a new programme should be negotiated (NESC 1990, 1993, 1996).

The *Programme for National Recovery, 1987–1990* (PNR) involved agreement between employers, trade unions, farming interests and government on wage levels in both the private and public sectors for a three-year period. Moderate wage growth was seen as essential to international competitiveness and to achieving control of the public finances. However, the PNR, and its successors, involved far more than centralised wage bargaining. They involved agreement on a wide range of economic and social policies – including tax reform, the evolution of welfare payments, trends in health spending, structural adjustments and Ireland's adherence to the narrow band of the ERM. On the macro-economic front, each partner agreed that they would not generate inflationary pressures that would warrant devaluation and would not seek devaluation when external problems arose. The PNR also established a new Central Review Committee (CRC) to monitor implementation of the programme and ensure ongoing dialogue between government and the social partners on key economic and social policy issues.

The PNR enlisted trade union support for a radical correction of the public finances. In return, the government accepted that the value of social welfare payments would be maintained. In addition, it undertook to introduce reforms in income tax that were of benefit to trade union members. Moreover, the agreement set out the general direction of government policy in a number of areas, the broad parameters having been agreed between the social partners.

The three subsequent agreements – the *Programme For Economic and Social Progress 1990–1993* (PESP), the *Programme for Competitiveness and Work 1994–1996* (PCW) and *Partnership 2000, 1997–2000*, – had a broadly similar form. Each has covered a three-year period, and set out agreed pay increases for the public and private sector. They also contained agreements on a variety of policy areas, including commitments to social equality and tax reform. While the macroeconomic strategy has been adhered to consistently since 1987, subsequent agreements contained policy initiatives that are worthy of note. The PESP initiated an experiment in which local partnerships seek innovative approaches to long-term unemployment. A recent OECD evaluation of Ireland's local economic development policies considered that the local partnership approach constituted an experiment in economic regeneration and participative democracy which is, potentially, of international significance (Sabel 1996). Commercialisation, and limited privatisation, of Ireland's state-owned enterprises has proceeded in the decade of partnership. The most recent agreement, Partnership 2000, contains a significant measure of agreement on action to modernise the public service. This enlists the social partners in support of the Strategic Management Initiative developed in the past two years. Partnership 2000 marks some progress in addressing the issue of enterprise-level partnership. In addition, a partnership approach has been adopted in several policy areas, and was reflected in a range of Task Forces and Forums examining issues concerning education, poverty, the traveller community and people with disabilities. Indeed, an important feature of the recent Irish approach is the attempt to widen partnership beyond the traditional social partners (trade unions, business and agricultural interests). Partnership 2000 was negotiated in a new way, involving representatives of the unemployed, women's groups and others addressing social exclusion (NESF 1997).

The social partnership approach produced the much-needed recovery from the disastrous early and mid-1980s and has underpinned a sustained period of growth since then. In the decade 1986–96, Irish GDP has grown by an average of 4.9 per cent a year, compared to an OECD average of 2.4 per cent. Employment has grown by 1.8 per cent per year, compared to an OECD average of 1.0 per cent and an EU average of 0.3 per cent. More recently, growth of output and employment has reached unprecedented levels. From 1993 to 1996, Irish national output has risen by 7.5 per cent a year, and employment by a remarkable 4.0 per cent per year. The debt/GDP ratio, which reached 117 per cent in 1986, has fallen steadily, to 76 per cent in 1996. Inflation has remained significantly below the EU average and, having reduced inflation in the 1980s, Ireland did not need a second bite of the cherry (and a second deep recession), as the UK did. Low and predictable inflation has underpinned the three-year wage agreements which have, in turn, freed both management and trade union energies for issues such as corporate strategy, technical change, training in the workplace, working practices and other important influences on international competitiveness.

Indeed, the explicit rationale for the social partnership approach is one which sees it as the optimal approach to achieving international competitiveness, given Ireland's political and industrial relations structures and participation in European integration. The conduct of policy since 1987 allows us to identify some of the core elements of the emerging Irish model of economic and social governance (NESC 1996). The first element is an overall orientation, which begins from the belief that the widest participation in social life, economic activity and policy-making are inseparable and fundamental requirements for the well-being of Irish society. This is combined with an unambiguous recognition and acceptance of Ireland's participation in the international economy and the European Union. This implies that the competitiveness of the Irish economy is a precondition for the pursuit of all other economic and social goals. The second element of the emerging Irish model is the fact that the achievement of a consistent approach to macroeconomic policy, incomes and structural adjustment has been strongly associated with negotiated programmes. These align the social partners to consistent and competitive actions and provide a framework within which government can adopt a strategic perspective on important policy issues. Involvement in the EU and an internationalising political economy, requires national governments to manage the interface between the domestic and the foreign. We now turn to this aspect of Ireland's experience.

Managing the Brussels machine

The government and civil service

Membership of the European Union commits a state to active participation in a set of institutions and decision-making processes beyond its own boundaries. A member state of the Union is affected by the regulatory reach of the EU and the range of policies and expenditure programmes emanating from Brussels. The legislative output of the EU is directly applicable in the domestic legal system and is presumed to be constitutional. Irish public agencies must work within the dual framework established by the EU and the national constitution. Irish nationals have rights established by EC law which they can pursue though the Irish courts and at the European Court of Justice in Luxembourg. In addition to its extensive regulatory competence covering almost all areas of public policy, the Union budget finances infrastructure development, fisheries protection, farm incomes, research and development, conservation programmes, social policy and education. Membership of the Union dissolves the distinction between the domestic and the foreign by creating an intermediary form of policy and politics (EU politics) which is both domestic and foreign. Following membership of the EU, Irish public-policy making and politics became embedded in a wider arena of policy-making at the European level. The allocation of public goods is no longer confined to politics within Ireland.

The salience of the EU for its member states, including Ireland, accelerated following the Single European Act in 1986 which launched the '1992' process, an intensive process of market creation which brought the EU into the nooks and crannies of domestic regulation. This was accompanied by the enhancement of the Union's cohesion policies directed towards Europe's poorer states, including Ireland. In 1991, the Union signed the Treaty on European Union (TEU) which made provision for a single currency and for deeper co-operation on foreign policy and judicial co-operation. In 1997, the member states signed the Treaty of Amsterdam which further expanded the policy remit of the Union.

It was fortunate for Ireland that it could adapt to the growing intensity of European governance in a gradual and incremental manner, because its membership in 1973 preceded the growth of EU regulation and institutionalisation. Irish government ministers, civil servants, officials in the state-sponsored sector, and representatives of interest groups participate in thousands of meetings at ministerial and official levels in the Council and in the Commission. Committees and working parties are a core element of the Union's governance structures. Agenda items and their accompanying files wind their way from the Commission and its committees, to the European Parliament and the Council of Ministers, the decision-making bodies. The European Council acts are an overarching source of political authority in the system. Items on the Council and EP agendas are processed through the administrative and political hierarchy from working parties and parliamentary committees to full meetings of the Council of Ministers and plenary sessions of the Parliament.

The Council is the part of the Union's institutional system where national governments and the European process become intertwined. It is in the Council that national ministers and civil servants mould EU policy. Participants in the Council system are there to represent their national governments as delegated officials but also seek collective solutions to common problems. They straddle the boundary between the domestic and the European, no longer servants only of their states. The Council meets in many guises, including Foreign ministers, Finance ministers, Agricultural ministers and many others. Each Council and the working groups that prepare Council business develop a corporate identity of their own because of the intensity and iterative nature of EU negotiations. The demands of EU membership are particularly onerous for the ministers for Foreign Affairs, Finance, Industry, Enterprise and Employment and Agriculture. These five ministries are most involved in managing the interface between Brussels and Ireland. Ministers responsible for Justice, Fisheries, the Environment, Transport and the Budget have regular involvement in Council deliberations. Other government ministers are involved in meetings about once or twice a year. With the establishment of the European Council in 1975, the Taoiseach participates in meetings with his counterparts from the other member states between two and four times each year.

Irish officials track the movement of dossiers through the system and participate actively in the negotiations and bargaining that characterises the EU's policy style. Ireland's permanent representation in Brussels is its largest overseas embassy with staff drawn from the foreign Ministry (40 per cent of staff) and the home departments (60 per cent of staff). Officials from all government departments attend Commission advisory groups and Council working parties. They are instructed delegates working to a negotiating brief agreed in Dublin with the active inolvement of the Permanent Representation in Brussels. Official trips to Brussels are part and parcel of the working environment of an Irish civil servant. In the train from *Gare Centrale* to Brussels airport, they mingle with colleagues from other government departments and from other member states. The daily flights between Dublin and Brussels are more like a club than an inter-city flight because those flying usually know each other so well.

The development of a new type of policy and politics, which is neither domestic nor international, has had an impact on the respective roles of the Foreign Ministry and the domestic ministries. The Department of Foreign Affairs, and the minister in charge of that department, has assumed added significance in the ministerial pecking order and is now more involved in domestic issues. Likewise, domestic ministries have had to adapt to extensive external involvement. The process could be likened to a domestication of foreign policy and the internationalisation of domestic policy. The Department of Foreign Affairs has responsibility for monitoring the development of EU policy across the range to ensure that there is sufficient coherence in Ireland's EU policy. In addition, it maintains a watching brief over the development of the EU itself. The Taoiseach's department is also heavily involved because of the importance of European Council meetings, although it relies for most of its briefing material on the Foreign Ministry. The Department of Finance is centrally involved because of the significance of structural funds, the EU budget and the Single Currency project. The importance of the CAP endows the Department of Agriculture with a strong presence in Ireland's EU policy. The Department of Enterprise and Employment is responsible for major areas of EU regulation. All other domestic ministries participate in those areas of EU policy for which they have domestic jurisdiction.

The parliament

Ireland's membership of the EU posed particular challenges for the Oireachtas and for Irish political parties. The two large parties, Fianna Fáil and Fine Gael, had little international involvement prior to 1973, in contrast to the Irish Labour Party. The clientelist nature of Irish constituency politics and the weakness of the committee system in the Oireachtas militated against extensive involvement by the Irish Parliament in EU affairs. Since 1973, the Executive has been largely unfettered in its management of Ireland's EU policy. Successive Irish governments, unlike their counterparts in Denmark, for example, have been free to pursue policies on Europe secure in parliamentary majorities in the Oireachtas. The presentation of periodic reports on developments in Europe, and statements after each European Council, were ritualistic in character, rather than occasions for probing Executive policies. Parliamentary questions on EU matters relate largely to constituency issues.

Participation in the EU has, however, contributed in no small measure to changes in Irish parliamentary culture. The establishment in 1974 of the Joint Committee on Secondary Legislation to oversee the implementation in Ireland of secondary legislation arising from EC law was a precursor of a move to parliamentary committees in the Oireachtas. The Committee was subsumed into the Foreign Affairs Committee when it was established in May 1993. The establishment of a Foreign Affairs Committee brought Irish parliamentary practice into line with other parliaments in Western Europe. A separate Joint Committee on European Affairs was re-established in March 1995, because the work of the Foreign Affairs Committee left it with inadequate time for the scrutiny of European law. The Foreign Affairs Committee with 31 members is the largest parliamentary committee; the Joint Committee on European Affairs has 17 members. The record of both Committees is mixed. Neither has adequate research and administrative back-up to develop independent thinking on foreign and European issues. The Committees are heavily dependent on briefing papers from the Department of Foreign Affairs and on external consultants. Attendance at the Committees is patchy, given the constituency duties of Irish parliamentarians. That said, the Committees have contributed to greater openness on foreign policy matters. The meetings are usually held in public and successive ministers and officials have attended and given evidence. A small coterie of deputies and senators has become engaged in foreign policy matters. The involvement of the European Affairs Committee in the Conference of Parliamentary Committees on European Affairs (COSAC) has exposed Irish parliamentarians to practices in other member states. The Committees have also provided a focus for the attentive public in this domain.

The mobilisation of groups

From the outset, economic interests that would be affected by EU policies were quick to mobilise and establish a presence in Brussels. The social partners – employers and trade unions – joined their respective Brussels peak organisations. In addition, Irish business interests established a separate office, known as the Irish Business Bureau. The Bureau participates in working groups of UNICE, the industry federation, makes representations to the Commission on EC law and policies, engages in grantsmanship, and facilitates the flow of information to interested parties in Ireland with a range of newsletters that are widely circulated and of a high standard. The trade union movement does not maintain an office in Brussels, but senior officials of the Irish Trade Union Confederation (ITUC) actively participate in the activities of the European Confederation of Trade Unions (ETUC) and on Commission advisory committees. The agricultural groups were amongst the first to be represented in Brussels with their own office and with membership of the agricultural peak organisations.

Mobilisation is not limited to economic interest groups. With the expansion of the remit of the Union, women's groups, environmentalists, local authorities, anti-poverty groups, the Council for Voluntary Organisations, consumer groups, citizens' groups and welfare-rights groups participate in the Brussels arena of politics. They are linked to transnational networks such as the European Anti-Poverty Network and the European Social Action Network. They are drawn into transnational politics by the lure of EU finance, the deliberate creation of networks by the Commission, the desire to influence the direction of EU regulation and the growing salience of the EU in all facets of life. Revitalised community groups, a marked feature of Irish politics since the mid-1980s, look to EU involvement for money, policy strategies and channels of influence over the Irish government. Validation by the Commission can be an important resource in dealing with the government at home. Lobbying tactics and strategies are traded with like-minded groups in other member states. Opposition to national policy can be mobilised outside and not just within the state. The controversial siting of a visitors' centre at Mullaghmore in the Burren illustrates the manner in which groups can mobilise at the local, national and EU levels. The Mullaghmore site proved controversial at the local level with the emergence of considerable opposition to this centre on environmental grounds. The local group (the Burren Action Group), which opposed the centre, lobbied through Irish and international environmental groups (An Taisce), the World Wildlife Fund and the World Conservation Union. The EU Commission, because it was funding the proposed visitors' centre, came under intense lobbying. It was forced to ensure an adequate Environmental Impact Assessment be carried out on the project. Politics is no longer contained within the national state. Groups in Ireland can play nested games at the national level and connected games in the Brussels arena.

Institution building and policy diffusion

Ireland's adaptation to the demands of EU membership has been highly path-dependent. It did not entail major changes in Ireland's administrative culture or its system of public policy. Servicing the Brussels machine was grafted onto the existing machinery of government. There is, however, evidence of institution building and policy change in a number of areas. Irish gender-equality legislation owes much to EC laws in this field in the mid-1970s. The Irish Employment Equality Act (1977) made provision for the establishment of an Employment Equality Agency to oversee the implementation of Irish and EC equality legislation and to promote equality practices. The EEA is embedded in a European network of equality agencies. It participates in numerous transnational conferences, attends public hearings at the European Parliament, services the European Communities Standing Liaison Group for Equal Opportunities (now known as the Advisory Committee on Equal Opportunities) and carries out research for the Commission in Ireland. The Chair and Chief Executive of the Agency look to Europe to strengthen their position with the national government. Together with like-minded colleagues in other member states they seek to push the boundaries of EU gender legislation as far as possible.

Another example of institution building was the establishment in 1989 of a Health and Safety Authority. A marked feature of the EU's internal market was an emphasis on health and safety in the workplace. There was general agreement among the member states that divergent health and safety standards should not be a source of competitive advantage. Since the mid-1980s the EU greatly intensified its regulation in this sphere. Traditionally, the Department of Labour had responsibility for developing and implementing Irish safety law. The establishment of the agency in 1989 was a response to the intensification of Brussels legislation and the need to modernise the enforcement of national and EU law. Like the EEA, the Health and Safety Agency is locked into an EU system of advisory committees and working groups which gives its work an important European dimension.

Local economic development provides an interesting example of the interaction between Irish public policy and EU policy preferences. In 1988, following the reform of the structural funds, the Commission displayed a distinct preference for regional policies that were based on partnership between the EU, national, regional and local levels of government. Ireland was ill-prepared for this change because of the weakness of its local government and its highly centralised nature of public policy-making. In response to Brussels demands, a number of regional consultative committees were established to have an input into Ireland's national development plan, which formed the basis of Brussels funding between 1988–93. This was followed by a second development plan in 1993, which included a separate chapter on local development. The renewed emphasis on local development owed its origins to innovative projects such as the EU project (Leader) on rural development, the proliferation of urban and rural community groups which received validation from the Presidency of Mary Robinson, and the search for new strategies for combating long-term unemployment. The vibrancy of community groups in Ireland owes something to the availability of EU project finance and its innovative approach to development. The EU mattered in terms of principles of governance, notably partnership, and finance.

Ireland's policy style in Europe

The high level of support among the Irish public for Ireland's EU membership and the absence of splits in the political parties on European issues, facilitated an easy fit between Ireland and the Union. Ireland's policy style in Europe is influenced by its size, political and administrative resources, state tradition and culture. By and large, Ireland has adapted to the political and administrative demands of multi-levelled governance in the Union, although the character of its involvement is influenced by the small size of the Irish bureaucracy and resource shortages over the last 10 years. The sheer demand of servicing the Brussels machine has made it more, not less, difficult to tackle issues of structural reform in central government.

European public policy-making is managed much like domestic policy-making within the same standard working procedures. The style is pragmatic, with a marked emphasis on those areas of EU policy that are regarded as vital to Ireland – agriculture, the budget, structural funds, and EU regulations that might affect Ireland's competitive position. Interdepartmental co-ordination is more informal and less paper-driven than systems in the other member states. There are few standing interdepartmental committees, apart from the European Communities Committee, which involves senior civil servants and the Minister of State for European Affairs. This Committee meets, on average, once a month; its equivalent in most other member states meets weekly and is buttressed by an array of standing inter-ministerial committees. The practice in Ireland is to establish ad hoc Cabinet and inter-departmental committees to manage discrete negotiations or the Presidency of the council when the need arises. Administrative departments are left to manage areas that fall within their jurisdiction, unless a particular issue has cross-departmental implications. For example, the management of the Community Support Framework, which channels Brussels structural funds to Ireland, involves significant interdepartmental and vertical co-ordination with sub-national government.

This pragmatic, incremental, style owes much to the intimacy of the senior echelons of the Irish civil service, the ease of personal contact, and Ireland's small size. Interests can be identified and aggregated with relative ease. Limited resources are heavily focused on those areas that are accorded a high priority on the domestic political agenda. The civil service relies for technical support and analysis on the semi-state sector. The policy communities involved in discrete areas of EU policy have widened over the last 10 years because of the growing salience of EU regulation and finance. The management of the structural funds which was contained within the narrow confines of central government and the large state-sponsored bodies has evolved to include diffuse interests, including local authorities, community groups, environmental groups, and social partners, all in search of a slice of the Brussels pie. EU monies created a new kind of politics which encouraged people to look both below and beyond the state. Access to EU monies gave community groups additional authority and leverage *vis à vis* central government. On the other hand, the availability of EU finances has reinforced clientelism, a central feature of the Irish political culture (O'Toole 1998).

An evaluation of Ireland's adaptation to the demands of the Union's policy process must be somewhat impressionistic, given that so many Irish politicians and civil servants have participated in the EU's policy process across the range of public policy. Some of them, such as Garrett FitzGerald, Brian Lenihan, Dick Spring or Rurai Quinn, displayed an aptitude for the Union's style of policy-making, were clearly at ease in the Council chamber, and revelled in the multicultural and multinational environment of the EU. At the administrative level, Ireland has been served by distinguished diplomats and senior civil servants who contributed not only to representing Ireland interests, but who helped build up the EU as an arena of public policy-making. Irish participants in the Brussels process have a reputation as good networkers, a useful skill in a highly fragmented and complex policy process. Because of Ireland's economic benefits from the EU, successive governments have felt the need to contribute to the business of the Union where possible, notably by running good Presidencies of the Council.

The Irish civil service has been restricted in managing EU business because of resource problems in government. Fiscal deficits forced cutbacks in the number of civil servants for many years in the 1980s, with the result that all departments and individual units came under considerable pressure and had to stretch existing resources still further. All of the smaller EU member states – Belgium, Denmark, Finland, Greece, Portugal and Sweden – have twice the number of overseas missions and twice as many diplomats as Ireland. Yet this small service has had to adapt to the significant expansion in the work of the EU since the mid-1980s – while resources remained static. Equally, the numbers of civil servants working on Europe in the domestic ministries remains limited. This has meant that Irish civil servants service a wider range of committees than their counterparts in other member states and are in turn responsible for the implementation of laws once passed. The enormous expansion in EU regulation which followed the Single Act led to problems of implementation. At the beginning of the 1990s, Ireland's implementation record, which had been relatively good, began to deteriorate. It took a number of years to improve the transposition of EU legislation. Late implementation can cost the government money if Irish nationals use the courts to seek judicial redress. For example, late implementation of a gender-equality directive in social security in the 1980s led to successful legal challenges by a number of Irish women through the Irish and European legal systems.

The lack of resources has meant that the Irish system is largely reactive. The focus is on influencing Commission proposals as they wind their way through the Council hierarchy, entering reservations to those aspects of the proposal that are not viewed with favour, seeking alliances with like-minded states, ensuring derogations where appropriate in the legislation, and changing the wording of a proposal to suit Irish circumstances. Irish negotiators seek to get the tactics of negotiations right by tacking on to other member states rather than devoting energy to position papers which would attempt to fundamentally alter the Commission's original proposal. Garrett FitzGerald's memoirs provide an illustrative example of how one gets the tactics of EU negotiations right. The Council in question was addressing better access for Iberian products under the EU's Mediterranean policy, something of little interest to Ireland. The only Irish issue was an early onion crop from Castlegregory, Co. Kerry, which needed an extra fortnight of protection each year beyond what was proposed by the Commission, to enable growers to sell their crop before competing onions would be allowed into Ireland from Spain. Dr FitzGerald, then Foreign Minister, describes how:

> Throughout the long and tedious debate I remained silent on this issue, calculating that my best chance of securing the extra fortnight was to wait until the final package was ready and then to whisper in the ear of the President . . . a last-minute request. He would, I felt, be so grateful to me for having refrained from adding to his troubles over two difficult days that he would be prepared to slip our onion fortnight into the package at the last moment, without anyone even noticing. My manoeuvre succeeded. Castlegregory was saved without a word being spoken by me at the Council meeting. (FitzGerald 1992: 143)

By being reasonably *communautaire* on most agenda issues, the Irish are prepared to 'go it alone' on issues that are deemed vital.

A cohesive and professional administrative culture, added to an ease of personal relations, has meant that Irish officials and politicians manage the day-to-day interface with the Brussels machine relatively well. On issues such as agricultural prices or flows from the structural funds, the Irish are adept at EU negotiations and grantsmanship. Since the development of cohesion policy, Ireland has consistently benefited from the highest per-capita transfer from the EU budget. Officials in central government and the development agencies have built up close ties with the relevant Commission directorates and are regarded as accomplished at implementing EU grants within agreed timeframes and, by and large, on worthwhile projects.

But not all the effects of EU membership have been beneficial. It has been argued that the huge sums of money flowing to the agricultural industry created large food companies in need of political patronage (O'Toole 1998). As a result of serious allegations of malpractice in the beef industry, the Government established a Committee of Inquiry (The Beef Tribunal), which reported in 1994. The Tribunal found that there had been serious irregularities in a number of meat plants; moreover, weaknesses in the management of the EU's intervention scheme by the Department of Agriculture were exposed. As a result of the Inquiry, the EU Commission decided to recover a sum of £71 million from Ireland because of its weak control systems. The Irish Government strengthened the legislative and administrative framework at national level to ensure that fraud and malpractice in the beef industry would be reduced (Desmond 1996). The Inquiry showed that the control systems in Ireland were not sufficient to guard against fraud and corruption.

Irish identity

An important issue is the impact of internationalisation and international governance on Irish identity and culture. The decades of internationalisation and growing participation in international governance, described above, were also decades of profound and rapid social and cultural change. In this section we briefly describe that change and how it might be related to internationalisation.

The change in Irish culture and identity since 1960 might be described as a move from a relatively homogeneous, closed, Catholic culture since Independence, to an open, pluralist, culture today. That change was not so much a change from one fixed identity to another, as a move from a fixed identity – a strong Catholic nationalism defined by opposition to England – to multiple identities. As Fintan O'Toole has argued, in the 1990s, the only stable characteristic of Irish culture is that it has no stable characteristics. In seeking the relation between cultural change and internationalisation, in can fairly be said that in the 1990s, Irish culture has a distinct global dimension and Irish identity has become complex and multiple. The global dimension of the culture is evident in the strong presence of cultural influences from abroad in Irish life, and in the influence of Irish culture in other countries. The emergence of a complex and multiple identity can be seen in the fact that Irishness is no longer seen as a description only of those living in Ireland, while most Irish people living in Ireland seem to combine a strong sense of Irish identity with other identities. This strongly suggests that the opening of the economy and the society, and the international engagement of public policy, is a major cause of the change in culture and identity.

While that is widely accepted, it glosses over a number of issues which are critical to an understanding of Ireland and, indeed, of internationalisation and globalisation. Opinions are sharply divided on how desirable and profound these changes in culture and identity are. The brief factual account of the change may seem to suggest that Ireland benefited from a replacement of its own culture and identity with that of American capitalism and European modernity – a view which some see as denigrating Irishness and elevating foreignness. Views differ on the relative influence of global forces and Irish factors in shaping the culture which has emerged. Has Ireland been swamped by a bland, cosmopolitan consumerism, or has internationalisation allowed a flowering of Irish capabilities?

To get beyond an offensive internationalism and a reactionary localism, we need to re-examine both the Ireland of the mid-twentieth century and the globalisation of the past decade. The fiction of a uniformly shared culture has its uses in nation-building, state-building and solidarity. However, there are times and places where this fiction becomes more tenuous than useful (Rosaldo 1993). If this is true of all cultures, it seems to apply with particular force to the Ireland of the mid-twentieth century. Fintan O'Toole argues that several factors allowed Irish culture and identity to seem particularly uniform and stable, among them the stability of its 'opposite', Britain, and the peculiar way emigration operated. We can now see that uniformity and stability was imposed on those who remained in Ireland, while a significant part of the nation experienced a kind of forced internationalisation. In reality, Ireland, viewed as the life-world of a people rather than the image of the nation-state, was much less uniform and stable in the 1930s, 40s and 50s than it pretended to be, or than we tend to see it as from vantage-point of the 'liberal' 1990s. O'Toole argues that a particular aspect of the change in culture and identity has been incorporation of the Irish diaspora. One of the most striking features of the Robinson Presidency, was Mary Robinson's invocation of the Irish diaspora, of a non-territorial concept of what it is to be Irish. At her inauguration, while accepting that her primary role was to represent the Irish state, she went on to say that:

> the state is not the only model of community with which Irish people can and do identify. Beyond our state there is a vast community of Irish emigrants extending not only across our neighbouring island . . . but also throughout the continents of North America, Australia, and of course Europe itself. There are more than 70 million people on this globe who claim Irish descent. I will be proud to represent them. (Robinson 1990)

President Robinson wanted to value and cherish the Irish diaspora because she felt that an appreciation of the diaspora could enlighten Irish society in the values of diversity, tolerance and fair-mindness and that it remains 'a precious reminder of the many strands of identity which compose our story' (Robinson 1995). This has reinforced the emergence of a multiple, rather than unitary, identity, and of an open, rather than closed, culture. To that extent, however, Ireland has partly *become* internationalised, and partly *re-discovered* that it has been internationalised for a very long time.

Beneath the image of the uniform, closed, nation of mid-century, there lay a scattered, fragmented people. This fact changes our view of the starting-point of the recent rapid journey to international identity. We can also revise our view of the journey and its destination. In studying the development of societies in the international context, there are advantages of an 'interactive outlook', which sees change as the product of interaction between indigenous structures and policies, and international forces (Evans and Stephens 1988). This approach has been applied to both Irish economy/politics (O'Donnell 1993; Laffan, Keatinge, O'Donnell 1991) and to Irish culture (O'Toole 1996; Kiberd 1995). O'Toole notes the fact that the 'international' culture, large parts of which Ireland has imported in the past two decades, is partly shaped by Irish experience (O'Toole 1997). The impact of the 'periphery' in the formation of the 'modern' is documented and analysed by Kiberd in *Inventing Ireland* (1995). Consequently, the 'adoption' of a fairly international culture, and the move to multiple identities, is not, as some fear, a domination or a re-colonisation.

Ireland and the Irish people continue the journey of re-invention at the close of the twentieth century. They straddle many boundaries, notably the Anglo-Saxon world, the American world, Europe and, to a lesser extent, the Third World, where there are still large numbers of Irish missionaries and aid workers. Contemporary Ireland lies between these worlds and has a presence in all.

Membership of the European Union has had a major impact on the external identity of the Irish state and the Irish state elite. The EU was central to the search for economic and social modernisation. It was a project for Ireland's future which also vindicated one of Ireland's strongest traditions – nationalism. It appealed to both new and old concerns (O'Toole 1998). Although material considerations played a pivotal role in the decision to seek accession membership was a powerful symbol of Ireland's place in the European order as an independent small state with a voice at the table. The EU was necessary to consolidate the economic foundations of political independence, and nationalistic arguments were deployed to legitimise involvement in the Union. The 1996 Government White Paper on Foreign Policy concluded that:

> Irish people increasingly see the European Union not simply as an organisation
> to which Ireland belongs, but as an integral part of our future. We see ourselves
> increasingly, as Europeans. (Government of Ireland 1996: 59)

Irish nationalism is at ease with the immersion of the Irish state in the multi-levelled governance structures of the Union. The easy fit between Ireland and the EU should not, however, be read as an assumption of a 'new' European identity by the Irish.

Ireland's links with Europe are complex and deeply rooted. Continental Europe was Christian Europe for Irish monks from the 6th to the 10th centuries, a place of refuge for the 'Wild Geese', a source of assistance, albeit ineffective, in the continuing battles with the British and a place of exile for those Irish writers and artists who battled against the homogeneous, closed, Catholic culture. Membership of the EU has been part of a re-discovery of these older links. Contemporary Irish culture in both music and literature has a high standing on the Continent. In 1996, for example, there was a major festival of contemporary Irish art in France, *L'imaginaire Irlandais* and Irish writers received major exposure at the Frankfurt Bookfair in the same year.

Membership of the European Union enabled Ireland to move out of the shadow of Great Britain, while maintaining intimate relations at a political and societal level with its nearest neighbour. Figures on Irish citizens living abroad clearly shows that the English-speaking world continues to attract Irish people. Of the three million Irish citizens living outside Ireland, two million are in Britain, half a million in the US, sizeable numbers in Australia (213,000), Canada (74,000); EU countries other than Britain, boast just 36,000 (Ireland 1996: 284). Cultural and societal links between Ireland and the UK are particularly close because of geographical proximity, the common travel area and the intensity of interpersonal contact. Most parts of Ireland receive British television and UK newspapers and British retailers have a major presence in everyday life. However, with the important exception of Northern Ireland, Ireland no longer defines itself as the 'other' to Britishness.

The links between Ireland and the US are no less complex and deeply rooted. As a emigrant society, millions of Irish poor strove to participate in the American dream. They left their traces on American politics, music, the judicial system, the police and the arts. Conversely, today a strong American influence can be detected throughtout Irish society. American multinational business exposed Irish managers and workers to American management styles and practices. The presence of foreign, usually American, companies in Irish cities and towns fostered economic wealth and changing lifestyles. As an English-speaking society, Ireland is very open to the spread of American popular culture. American television programmes make up a large part of the non-Irish material shown on the national television station and dominate the network stations.

Successive Irish governments have also sought to leverage the many millions of people with Irish descent in the US. This began in the 1970s, when the Irish started to lobby the White House and Irish-Americans on Capitol Hill to support their policies on Northern Ireland. This process, referred to as the 'greening' of the White House, was remarkably successful: the US is now an important participant in the peace process in Northern Ireland. More broadly, Irish development agencies began to cultivate close relationships with successful Irish-American businesspeople. Consequently, in politics, economy and culture, emigration has become a source of opportunity rather than loss.

Conclusions

Developments in the Irish economy, policy and society since 1960 can be seen as a process of learning how to manage internationalisation and the emergence of international governance. Although Ireland handled certain aspects of EC membership relatively successfully, these were allowed to hide the wider policy and behavioural requirements of internationalisation. Irish development quickly became dependent on inward investment, as indigenous industry withered in the face of international competition. Mediation of the new pressures seemed beyond the capability of Ireland's political, administrative and interest-group system. By the mid-1980s, Ireland's economic, social and political strategy was in ruins, and its hope of prospering in the international economy was in considerable peril. Yet from within this traumatic, but dynamic, experience there emerged a new perspective on Ireland's position in European integration and a globalising economy. This was embodied in the social partnership approach to economic and social management and in innovative approaches in several policy areas. Overall, the process of economic international-isation has involved an evolution from deliberate strategy, through radical disrup-tion, disorientation and loss of direction, to a new shared understanding of the constraints and possibilities of international governance and internationalisation.

The internationalisation of the Irish polity has been much smoother but less profound than the process of economic internationalisation. The adaptation of central government and public administration to the EU was highly path-dependent. Procedures and processes for managing the interface with Brussels were crafted onto existing administrative arrangements and were moulded by Irish administra-tive culture. The wider political system – parliament and parties – has not experienced the same level of Europeanisation. This is in stark contrast to the intensive involve-ment of interest groups in the Brussels arena. Irish policy makers fit with relative ease into the multilevelled policy processes that characterise the EU. The ability of the Irish to network and a keen sense of negotiating tactics have ensured that policy outcomes in Brussels, in most areas, were in tune with Irish preferences. However, with the intensification of European integration, Ireland's rather informal approach towards Brussels may not be sufficient to ensure an Irish 'voice' on major issues in the future.

There is no doubt that Ireland's internationalisation is closely connected with the profound change in culture and identity over the past three decades. Ireland moved from a closed Catholic and rural culture to an open, liberal and urban one. At the same time, the Irish identity evolved from a unitary and territorial one to multiple identities. These transformations are not adequately characterised as the replace-ment of one, Irish, culture by either American consumerism or European pluralism. In reality, Ireland was less closed in the past than usually supposed and had a hand in shaping European, British and American cultures. Ireland has partly *become* inter-nationalised, and partly *re-discovered* that it has been internationalised for a very long time.

Endnotes

1 Research funding from the Royal Irish Academy is gratefully acknowledged.
2 In recent years, the locational pattern of inward investment has shifted. Cork has emerged as a centre of chemical and phar-maceutical production. The strong wave of inward investment in computer manu-facture, software and finance in the 1990s has located mainly in Dublin.

Chapter 10

Peace processes and communalism in Northern Ireland

Joseph Ruane and Jennifer Todd

Introduction

Northern Ireland in the 1960s showed many outward signs of political stability and growing economic prosperity. The Unionist party appeared firmly in control of the state; the new premier, Terence O'Neill, felt sufficiently confident to make mild gestures towards political and cultural reform. Catholics had moderated their opposition to the state and the Nationalist Party was seeking an accommodation with it. The economy was expanding, with growing inward investment, major developments in infrastructure and expanding social services. But within a decade, militant nationalists were in armed revolt, the Stormont government had been abolished and the economy was in crisis. In this chapter we chart the major structural trends in Northern Ireland during this period, drawing attention to communal, class, ideological and political responses to the crisis. We then ask whether the changes of the recent period have been sufficiently far reaching to allow a stable compromise settlement between the communities.

The changing economic structure and its political effects

The economy of Northern Ireland has undergone a long process of restructuring in the decades since partition. The traditional industrial economy based on linen, shipbuilding and engineering has disappeared. The workforce at Harland and Wolff had halved from over 20,000 in the 1950s to 10,000 in 1970; by 1988 it employed less than 5,000 workers, and these were heavily subsidised by the British government (Bardon 1992: 614, 641; Rowthorn and Wayne 1988: 82). In the 1960s, this decline was partially compensated by the attraction of new multinational industries, largely textiles. By the 1980s, however, the textile industry had collapsed and there was little new inward investment. The unemployment rate soared: from a post-war low of 4.2 per cent in 1974 to 9.1 per cent in 1979, to 18.6 per cent in 1986 (Ruane and Todd 1996: 159).

The decline in manufacturing has been accompanied by a growth in the service sector, particularly in state services. This began with the expansion in public spending after World War II, and increased after the advent of direct rule. Since 1972 there has been rapid growth in opportunities in the civil service, further education, community and social work, while the policy of 'Ulsterisation' – reliance on locally recruited security forces rather than the British Army – has led to a vast increase in the numbers of the security forces and security-related personnel; by 1985 there were almost 20,000 employed in the local security forces and an additional 10,000 in security-related employment (Rowthorn and Wayne 1988: 112). Public-sector employment increased from just under 25 per cent of total employment in 1970 to around 39 per cent by 1992 (Smyth 1993: 124–5). Growth was maintained even under Margaret Thatcher's Conservative administrations, largely out of fear of the civil disruption and militancy that cuts might provoke (Gaffikin and Morrissey 1990).

The change in the structure of the economy had a differential impact on the two communities. The decline in the traditional industrial economy eroded the Protestant economic position, weakening the indigenous Protestant bourgeoisie and hitting the skilled male Protestant working class which dominated that sector. On the other hand, Protestants found alternative employment in the rapidly expanding, and almost exclusively Protestant, security sector – the Royal Ulster Constabulary (RUC), Ulster Defence Regiment (UDR), police and army reserve, and the prison service. Government fair-employment policies also had an impact, although progress was slow. The first Fair Employment Act (FEA) of 1976 was relatively ineffective, though it helped strengthen Catholic employment in the civil service and public sector where Catholic employment had been very limited. Pressure came from other sources in the 1980s, in particular from the MacBride Principles campaign in the US (Jay and Wilford 1991). A second, much stronger, FEA was passed in 1989. By the 1990s Catholics were making up much of their previous disadvantage in the professional and managerial sectors (FEC 1995). Analysis of the 1991 census showed that Catholics – whose traditional middle class had serviced their own community as doctors, lawyers, teachers and shopkeepers – had now moved decisively into the universal middle class (Gallagher *et al.* 1995: 83–4). At the same time, Catholics continued to be under-represented even in this sector and were much more likely to be unemployed: the unemployment rate of Catholic males was more than double that of Protestant males (Gallagher *et al.* 1995: 84).

The difficulty of achieving parity was exacerbated by changes in the demographic balance. The Catholic population had remained at about a third of the population between 1911 and 1961, but then rose steadily to approximately 42 per cent in 1991 (Kennedy 1994: 9). Much of this increase was due to a sharp decline in Catholic emigration, in part because of the lack of opportunities abroad, in part because of better conditions at home with the post-1969 reforms. The growth in the Catholic population – and therefore in the expected participation of each community in the workforce – made fair employment, in the words of the chairman of the Fair Employment Commission, a 'moving target' (Cormack *et al.* 1993: 18).

The restructuring of Northern Ireland's economy had important political consequences. Increasing dependence on the British subvention confirmed unionists in their belief that there was no alternative to the union; an independent Ulster (briefly considered in response to the establishment of direct rule) was now dismissed as an option. Economic dependence also encouraged many Catholics to moderate their nationalism and to focus their immediate concerns on equality within Northern Ireland rather than on Irish reunification. In the 1980s, unity was a pressing issue only for a fifth of Catholics – predominantly young, male, Sinn Féin supporters. Another third, however, had a united Ireland as a medium-term goal, and another third again had it as a long-term aspiration (Ruane and Todd 1996: 66–70).

Increasing class tensions within each community are reflected in the political domain. The main effect has been in party political support. Within the unionist community, the Ulster Unionist Party (UUP) and the Democratic Unionist Party (DUP) are now divided more in terms of class and right/left ideology than in terms of attitudes to the union. Among nationalists, the Social Democratic and Labour Party (SDLP) continues to enjoy cross-class support but has lost ground among the working class to Sinn Féin (SF) (Evans and Duffy 1997: 69–70). On the other hand, there appears to have been little effect on attitudes to the constitution. For example, potentially the most volatile group on constitutional issues – middle-class Catholics – have retained their nationalist preferences (Duffy and Evans 1997: 127–9).

Changing attitudes, values and ideologies

Attitudes, values and ideologies in Northern Ireland have changed in line with international developments. Northern Ireland is directly affected by global cross-currents of ideas, while its dominant ideologies – unionism and nationalism – are part of wider British and Irish families of ideas. As the latter have changed, so too, though more slowly and unevenly, have their relatives in Northern Ireland. 'Pluralist', 'post-modernist' and 'post-nationalist' themes have found their way into the public culture of Northern Ireland, though selectively and differently for each community in accordance with its particular needs and concerns. Unionism in the 1950s and 1960s continued to identify with traditional imperial notions of Britishness, combining these with self-consciously modernising themes – the notions of progress and modernisation shared throughout the American-led 'free world' (Todd 1987). The end of empire, decline of British global power, and Britain's entry into Europe posed a challenge to unionist ideology, one that became even more pressing with the British government's direct involvement in Northern Ireland after 1969. Unionist ideology presupposed a common British and unionist identity and interest in the face of the nationalist threat. British pressure to reform placed that understanding under strain; the proroguing of Stormont in 1972 delivered it a fatal blow.

Some unionists – particularly those who supported the Alliance Party – responded by adopting the pluralist norms of a new multi-ethnic Britain. Others clung to the view that the British had misunderstood them and that the identity of unionist and British interests would eventually become clear to the government (Eames 1992:

29). The trauma of the Anglo-Irish Agreement of 1985 spurred unionist intellectuals to reconstruct the intellectual basis of unionism in a way more suited to contemporary political principles. A core theme of the 'new unionism' that emerged from the late 1980s was the need to bring Northern Ireland into line with the requirements of a modern, multi-ethnic and multi-cultural state (Aughey 1989, Porter 1996).

Nationalism in Northern Ireland continued to be part of the wider tradition of Irish nationalism, looking to it for its justification and legitimation. However Northern and Southern nationalisms necessarily took on different emphases. Southern nationalism was engaged in building a state to meet the needs and interests of its 26 counties' population; Northern nationalism was forced into an oppositional role in a state whose legitimacy it refused to accept. The emergence of modernising currents within Southern nationalism during the 1950s and 1960s increased the sense of growing divergence between the two streams (McKeown 1986: 19–22).

Northern nationalism, however, developed its own modernising themes and used them to strengthen its critique of the unionist state (McAllister 1975). Nationalists harnessed the new international emphasis on civil, human and minority rights to their purpose, with major impact in the civil rights movement. The subsequent deepening of conflict and resurgence of armed republicanism led the SDLP, John Hume in particular, to infuse the language of constitutional nationalism with pluralist themes – the acceptance of difference, equality rather than dominance and agreement on the island rather than Irish unity. This new Northern nationalism dovetailed neatly with the liberal nationalism now dominant in the South, underpinning the close relationship between successive Irish governments and the SDLP, and preparing the way for the New Ireland Forum of 1983–4, the Anglo Irish Agreement of 1985 and, most recently, the peace process.

Republicans and loyalists also took up the new ideological currents. In the 1970s and 1980s, Sinn Féin combined traditionalist militant opposition to the state with contemporary anti-imperialist discourse; in the 1990s, it drew on some of the central themes of reconstructed nationalism – in particular the goal of a settlement which could win 'the agreement and allegiance' of all concerned. Loyalists in the Progressive Unionist Party (PUP) and Ulster Democratic Party (UDP) by the 1990s had moved away from the closed, religiously-infused ideology which had been dominant in loyalist politics to secular and socialist views which left some room for negotiation with nationalists.

Cultural change was also evident in the beliefs and practices of the wider population. Northern Ireland was becoming more secular: in 1991, a third of the population (predominantly Protestants but including 11 per cent of Catholics) rarely attended church (Bruce and Alderdice 1993: 7). Western trends towards 'post-nationalism' were echoed in Northern Ireland in the distancing of many Catholics from an explicit nationalist identity: in the 1990s, surveys showed that only about half of Catholics (and in some years no more than 40 per cent) considered themselves nationalists. The trends were also reflected, though more ambiguously, in the disparity between the 95 per cent of Protestants who are committed to the union and the 75 per cent who consider themselves 'unionists' (Breen 1996: 37). At first sight these reconstructions and moderations of unionist and nationalist ideology offer hope for a compromise settlement. On the other hand, there is ample evidence of continued, indeed growing, polarisation in constitutional preference and party-political support. One symptom of this is the decline in the vote of the main cross-communal party, the Alliance Party, from over 14 per cent in 1977 to under 7 per cent in the 1990s. The incorporation of themes from liberalism and pluralism have given reconstructed nationalism and unionism a more subtle and modern ring. Yet these same reconstructed ideologies are no less effective in articulating opposition than the irredentist nationalism or supremacist unionism of the past (see Ruane and Todd 1996, Ruane and Todd 1998).

Political changes and their effects

The political crisis in Northern Ireland had deep structural roots in conditions of communal opposition and inequality (Ruane and Todd 1996). It erupted in the late 1960s because of the changing balance of communal power. The civil rights move-ment and subsequent disturbances revealed that change and finally proved that the Unionist-controlled state was no longer capable of managing communal opposition. The British government's proroguing of Stormont in 1972 and its commitment to a more inclusive system of governance – this time based on the participation of both Protestants and Catholics – was a pragmatic acceptance of the new reality. A new inclusive devolved government, however, was precluded by the very communal opposition that had generated the crisis. The history of failed political initiatives in Northern Ireland is instructive. It shows how the possibility of settlement depended on far-reaching changes in British and Irish policies and institutions.

The first steps towards a new devolved settlement were quickly put in place. The 1972–74 Conservative administration proposed a new form of devolution with a power-sharing executive combined with a weak Council of Ireland. The executive took office in January 1974; the Council of Ireland, agreed in principle, was to follow. The power-sharing executive, however, divided unionists and enraged working-class loyalists. The sharing of power with the enemies of the state was rejected, but there was also a class dimension. Protestant control of the state had permitted the Unionist Party to enact policies which benefited Protestants of all classes (Bew, Gibbon and Patterson 1979); its abolition removed that crucial mechanism for securing cross-class Protestant unity. In the power-sharing executive, a middle-class dominated Unionist Party would compromise with a middle-class dominated SDLP, thus radically curtailing the influence and benefits for which working-class Protestants might hope. Unionist and loyalist anger was further fuelled by the pro-posed Council of Ireland, seen as a stalking horse for Irish unity. The power-sharing executive was brought down in May 1974 by the loyalist Ulster Workers Council (UWC) strike. It showed the political power of grass-roots loyalists, although it would take two decades before viable independent loyalist parties were to emerge. Even more crucially, it showed that the Protestant community as a whole, not simply political elites within it, would have to be persuaded to compromise.

The Labour administrations of 1974–79 took only part of these lessons. In failing to defend the power-sharing executive, the Labour government had rewarded loyalist intransigence; in subsequent years it worked on the assumption that the unionist majority could not be forced into a settlement. But it was also committed to the principle that any new form of government must have nationalist as well as unionist support. In the political stalemate that followed, government policy concentrated on showing the benefits of 'good government' (particularly through expansion of the public service) and strong security ('Ulsterisation' of the security forces, criminalisation of the IRA and harsher security policies) while awaiting the gradual emergence of a more accommodationist politics (Rees 1985). Predictably, neither unionism nor loyalism changed its opposition to power-sharing. The only middle ground to emerge was the Alliance Party, whose vote was at its height in these years – 14.4 per cent in the district council elections of 1977 and 11.8 per cent in the 1979 Westminster general election. Meanwhile government policies politicised the divisions within the Catholic community. The new security measures alienated not only republicans but entire working-class Catholic neighbourhoods, which were further hit by the crisis in the economy. The Catholic male unemployment rate rose sharply in absolute terms, and also increased relative to Protestants. The SDLP had been embittered by the government's failure to support the power-sharing executive and now concentrated on building support in the Republic and in the United States. Its fear of losing the support of an increasingly alienated Catholic working class ruled out any moves towards political compromise with unionism.

Events in the late 1970s and early 1980s showed the difficulty of stabilising Northern Ireland without more radical political initiatives. Harsh security policies led not to the collapse of the IRA, but to resistance both inside and outside the prisons. This culminated in the hunger strikes of 1981 which in turn mobilised the Catholic population and encouraged Sinn Féin to enter the political process. In the 1983 general election Sinn Féin achieved over 40 per cent of the nationalist vote, alarming the SDLP and the Irish government and pushing them towards a common front (FitzGerald 1991: chapters 15–17). Unionist resistance to compromise with nationalism intensified and the political middle ground narrowed further with a sharp fall in the Alliance Party vote. The increasing polarisation within Northern Ireland, however, prompted new strategies from the Irish government which were to have major political effects. The New Ireland Forum of 1983–84 was set up, designed to achieve a common position of constitutional nationalists on the island which was then used in negotiations with the British government. The outcome was the Anglo-Irish Agreement (AIA) of 1985, a purely intergovernmental agreement which recognised the right of the Irish government to act as guarantor of Northern nationalist interests, giving it a 'more than consultative' role in the government of Northern Ireland, and participation in a permanent Anglo-Irish secretariat in Northern Ireland. The Irish government's primary policy concern in negotiating the Agreement was the stability of the state in the South against a potential republican threat. However its increasing involvement in Northern affairs moved the North higher on the government's political agenda and gave further impetus to the convergence of Northern and Southern nationalism. For Northern nationalists, the Agreement was a major advance. It offered symbolic recognition of their Irish identity and a new channel of influence on policy. Reforms followed in flags and emblems, fair employment, recognition of Irish culture, and there was increased pressure to reroute particularly contentious Orange marches (FitzGerald 1991: 573ff).

The Agreement was a severe blow to unionists (Ruane and Todd 1996: 113–5). More worrying than the formal powers it gave the Irish state was the policy direction in which it pointed and its confirmation of the continued strengthening of the nationalist position, both in Northern Ireland and on the island. One consequence was increased loyalist paramilitary violence and a focusing of popular unionist feeling on the unionist right to march. Protestant alienation became a theme in public comment and research, while Catholics were described as increasingly self-confident (Bruce 1994; Dunn and Morgan 1994; Pollak 1993). The AIA, however, and the failure to break it by mass protests, gave an incentive to unionists and loyalists to engage in negotiations. By 1991 they were involved in talks with the SDLP, the Alliance Party and the British and Irish governments. In fact the two Northern communities remained very far apart, as the failure of the Brooke/Mayhew talks of 1991–93 revealed. But the talks also marked a new stage in the search for a solution to the conflict: an acceptance by unionists of the role of the Irish government in the process, and the acceptance by all sides that there were three strands to any resolution: agreement within Northern Ireland, between North and South, and between Ireland and Britain. This was a decisive move beyond any narrowly 'internal' model of the conflict or of its possible resolution.

The violence continued throughout this period. Sinn Féin rejected the Agreement and continued to defend the IRA's campaign. However the Agreement also had an important impact on republicans. It suggested that a 'rolling' Irish dimension might be possible, that from small beginnings the Irish state could come to play an increasingly important role in Northern Ireland. There were other factors also – the effect on public opinion of the IRA's campaign, particularly atrocities such as the Remembrance Day bomb at Enniskillen in November 1987, 'war-weariness' among republican supporters and, later, a fear that the other parties might reach an agreed settlement from which republicans would be excluded. Leading republicans began to explore an alternative option to 'armed struggle'.

By the early 1990s republicans had moved to a position where they were willing to test the view that they could make more progress to the goal of Irish unity by a peaceful, but strong and united, nationalism than by an isolated armed struggle. By 1993 the conditions for a republican cessation of violence were moving into place – assurances, public and private, from the Irish government, Irish-Americans (with favourable signs from the White House) and more ambiguously from the British government, that in the event of an IRA ceasefire, Sinn Féin would be included in the talks process and republican issues would be included on the political agenda. The announcement of the ceasefire on 31 August 1994 was quickly followed by gestures on the part of the Irish government and the Irish public that symbolised the reintegration of republicans into the 'nationalist family'.

A combined loyalist ceasefire was declared just weeks after the IRA ceasefire. Its adroit handling by the Progressive Unionist Party (PUP) and Ulster Democratic Party (UDP) proved a propaganda coup for the parties and gave them an immediate and positive public profile. The Ulster Unionist Party (UUP) and Democratic Unionist Party (DUP) were more suspicious. They were unconvinced of the genuineness of the IRA ceasefire, and, in any case, unwilling to negotiate with republicans. The UUP at that time held the balance of power in the British parliament, and used it to counter British government concessions to republicans.

In this context, the two governments published their joint proposals for a settlement – the Frameworks Documents – in March 1995. The proposals, particularly those in the Joint British–Irish Framework Document, suggested still wider-ranging North–South relations. Nationalists and republicans interpreted them as laying the economic and administrative groundwork for future Irish unity, should a majority in Northern Ireland come to want it. The proposals met strong opposition from the UUP and the DUP.

The British government, anxious to keep unionist support, stressed the right of unionists to veto the documents if they so chose, and also insisted that republicans could not enter talks until they had first decommissioned their weapons. Republicans refused. In the hiatus that followed, communal conflict in the North intensified, particularly over Orange marches, and relations between the British and Irish governments became more strained. Continual stalling on republican inclusion in talks by the British government finally strengthened the militants within the movement. The ceasefire ended with the massive IRA bomb at Canary Wharf on 9 February 1996; other bombs followed. The British government broke off formal contact with republicans but informal contacts continued, culminating in a renewed IRA ceasefire in July 1997.

The calling of the second ceasefire reflected the republican view that the wider political context was now more favourable to political negotiation. Bill Clinton had been re-elected in the US; the Labour Party had just won a massive victory in the UK; Fianna Fáil had been returned to government in the Republic. The new Labour Prime Minister, Tony Blair, had promised a renewed talks process aiming at a May 1998 agreement, to which SF would be admitted in the event of a ceasefire.

The talks opened in October 1997 with the participation of the two governments, the SDLP, SF, the Alliance Party, the UUP, the PUP and the UDP. The refusal of the DUP and the United Kingdom Unionist Party (UKUP) to participate meant that only two-thirds of the unionist population were represented at the talks. The talks, chaired by US senator George Mitchell, Finnish ex-prime minister Harry Holkieri, and Canadian General John de Chastelain, had a three-stranded agenda – internal Northern Irish, North/South, and East/West (ie British–Irish) relationships. Initially, progress was slow and fringe paramilitary groups continued to be active on both sides, with loyalist groups the most lethal: eight Catholics were killed between December 1997 and January 1998. But on 10 April 1998, agreement between the parties was reached, to be put to referendum in both parts of Ireland in May 1998.

The present talks were made possible by the new structures and role for the Irish government initially outlined in the Anglo-Irish Agreement and developed in the 1991–93 talks and peace process. But these structures and alliances gave opposing incentives to the Northern Irish parties: the unionists' aim was to reduce the role of the Irish government, nationalists, and republicans, aims (in line with the proposals of the Framework Document) to increase North/South integration. The eventual agreement did not represent a change in the views of either side. It was in part a compromise where each side got some, but not all, of what it wanted. But it was also in part a triumph of 'creative drafting', where ambiguous wording allowed opposing interpretations, and where conflict over the powers and remit of institutions was postponed rather than resolved. In the next section we look at the conflicting interests of the political parties in the talks process and the extent to which the Multi-Party Agreement offers a stable settlement of these conflicts.

The political parties, the talks process and the Multi-Party Agreement of 10 April 1998

The political parties

The peace process was made possible by a political realignment within Irish nationalism. Once republicans adopted a peaceful strategy, constitutional nationalists, republicans, the Irish state and leading Irish-Americans would make common cause. In fact the diversity of political position and interest would remain, but a degree of unity was achieved on aims and methods – if not on priorities and urgency – which gave greater coherence to Northern nationalist demands and greater resources to achieve them. In the talks process, this nationalist alliance held despite tensions.

The unionist position is less consolidated. The position of the British government is ambiguous, although unionists have some reason to believe that Tony Blair may be committed to a (constitutionally reconstructed) Union not just in Great Britain but also in Northern Ireland and perhaps even in the two islands. Within Northern Ireland, unionists present a picture of division. The UUP chose to enter the talks; the small UKUP remained outside. The main loyalist party, the DUP, was equally hostile to the talks, while the new fringe loyalist parties, the PUP and UDP, supported them. The parties at the talks supported and those outside the talks opposed the Multi-Party Agreement. With the exception of the small loyalist parties (whose support for a negotiated settlement appears to be a matter of principle) the differences are primarily tactical: whether the union can be better defended from within the agreed institutions or by opposing them.

Differences in tactics are not simply different ways of defending the union, they are also strategies of electoral competition. Nor is party competition confined to unionists. Whether and how the institutions agreed on 10 April 1998 will function depends not simply on the political strength of each communal bloc, but on the relative strength of the parties within each bloc.

Recent elections – the Forum election of 1996, the UK General Election of May 1997 and subsequent local government election – offer a guide to current party support. The nationalist vote overall has increased and in the general election rose to over 40 per cent for the first time. The SDLP has kept its share of the overall vote, ranging from a low of 20.7 per cent in the local to a high of 24.1 per cent in the General Election. Within the nationalist bloc, however, Sinn Féin has benefited electorally from the peace process, increasing its share of the nationalist vote to nearly 45 per cent in the recent local government election. It now wins about 16 per cent of the overall vote, with two Westminster seats, one of these retaken from the SDLP.

The overall vote for unionist parties (UUP, DUP, UDP, PUP, UKUP) has declined. The UUP remains the largest party: its vote has declined slightly, ranging from a low of 24.2 per cent in the Forum to a high of 32.7 per cent in the General Election. The DUP vote has steadied after a sharp decline in the late 1980s although in the May 1997 elections, at no more than 15 per cent of the overall vote, it was overtaken by Sinn Féin and lost one Westminster MP. The Alliance Party's vote remains low, ranging from about 6.5 per cent in the Forum and local elections to 8 per cent in the General Election.

These electoral trends represent changes in the structure and attitudes of the communities. The demographic increase in the Catholic population has translated into an increased nationalist vote more quickly than most commentators expected. There is every reason to expect this trend to continue. The increasing political influence that nationalism has won over the past decade gives an incentive for more Catholic voters to vote nationalist. Within this constituency, recent research suggests that Sinn Féin has consolidated its support among younger voters – those who came to maturity since it entered electoral politics in 1981. This strategically important group has also become more willing to compromise on political and constitutional issues (Evans and Duffy 1997: 72, 76–7. Evans and O'Leary 1997. For contrary evidence, see Dowds and Devine 1997).

Within the unionist population, the UUP, under David Trimble's leadership, has consolidated its share of the vote and won the reputation of being as strong on the Union as the DUP. DUP supporters are now distinguished from UUP supporters less on grounds of unionist ideology than on their distinctive generational and class profile: they tend to be young and working class (Evans and Duffy 1997). In contrast to nationalists, there is less evidence among unionists of willingness to compromise with nationalists (Evans and O'Leary 1997). The young are more likely than the old to understand the viewpoint of Catholics and to have more moderate political attitudes, but only marginally more likely to compromise on constitutional issues (Dowds and Devine 1997). There has been, therefore, no direct popular pressure on the unionist parties to compromise; indeed the pressure is in the opposite direction.

On the nationalist side, these trends constrain party strategy. Sinn Féin's increasing electoral strength suggests strong support for its pursuit of radical long-term objectives by peaceful means. This lends support to the peace strategy within the republican movement. Since its main electoral competitor has less far-reaching goals, Sinn Féin has some leeway to compromise, although this is limited by the need to keep militant republican support for the ceasefire. The SDLP's support base is more divided. Around half would be relatively content in a reformed Northern Ireland; around half want more far-reaching constitutional change. The former would be happy if their representatives worked in a new power-sharing Assembly with the UUP in an effective governing coalition; the latter might switch allegiance to Sinn Féin if it seemed more effective in securing change.

Within the unionist bloc, the UUP's possibility of compromise is still more seriously constrained. The DUP has succeeded in keeping its vote despite competition from the socially more radical and politically more open PUP and UDP. To survive it must maintain at once its strong radical and strong unionist profile. It has done this by remaining outside the talks process and denouncing the agreement as putting the union at risk, forcing the UUP to vindicate both its participation in the talks and its commitment to the agreement by taking hardline positions and interpretations. The fringe loyalist parties serve two important functions for the UUP in this respect. First, their paramilitary connections leave their commitment to the union beyond doubt; they therefore vindicate the UUP's claim that participation in the agreed institutions will not endanger the union. Second, as representatives of other strands of unionism, they convey the impression that a broad range of unionist opinion is represented in the agreement.

The effect of electoral competition has been that tendencies towards communal opposition outweigh those towards cross-community compromise. If Sinn Féin won a little room to move away from its most extreme demands, the SDLP had to toughen its stance in negotiations to guard its vote against Sinn Féin encroachment and the UUP's room for compromise was still more constrained. These tendencies created formidable obstacles to reaching an agreed settlement at the talks. Agreement was eventually reached on a three-stranded package but this was at the cost of postponing rather than resolving many of the issues in conflict.

The Multi-Party Talks and Agreement

Strand 1 of the talks process dealt with internal Northern Ireland issues. Here there were two main areas of disagreement – the 'equality agenda' and a devolved Assembly for Northern Ireland. Sinn Féin's core demands included an 'ethos of equality' and 'total demilitarisation' in Northern Ireland: radical changes in employment legislation, the public culture, the security forces and release of prisoners convicted of terrorist offences. The SDLP placed less priority on equality than did Sinn Féin. The UUP, in contrast, strongly resisted any far-reaching reform of the security forces, and made any reform of policing or prisons contingent on decommissioning of paramilitary weapons. While the talks were in process, the British government initiated new fair employment legislation and a parades commission (already the subject of conflict) to deal with contentious marches. In the agreement itself, the British government pledged quite strong egalitarian policies supporting the Irish language, a commission – with a strong reforming remit – to report on reform of the police, a review of criminal justice procedures and an incorporation of the European Convention on Human Rights into Northern Ireland law. The governments also promised release of appropriate categories of prisoners within two years. In return there was a commitment by all parties to work for decommissioning within two years. This signified quite a strong equality agenda, but one dependent on the make-up and functioning of the Policing Commission and on a strongly reforming policy by the British government. These provisions have already been criticised by unionists (both those who oppose and those who support the agreement) and conflict on these issues is set to continue.

Strand 1 also dealt with the question of a devolved assembly. All parties, with the exception of Sinn Féin, agreed on the desirability of a devolved assembly, but the UUP and the SDLP disagreed on its structure and powers. The UUP preferred an assembly without legislative powers, with a committee system in which they would have no obligation to share collective responsibility with Sinn Féin. The SDLP preferred a strong assembly with legislative and executive powers; with this, they – as the constructive nationalist party – could hope for a strong showing in the assembly elections. The final agreement proposes an assembly with both legislative and executive powers and a committee system; there are safeguards for communally based interests on contentious issues, including the election of chief and deputy chief ministers. Other ministers are to be appointed in proportion to party strength in the assembly, but there is no collective responsibility; only some decisions (such as budgeting) require agreement among the executive as a whole. Ministers' pledge of office includes commitment to peaceful and democratic means and to principles of equality.

This complex compromise practically ensures that the UUP and SDLP will take the chief and deputy chief ministerial positions, while Sinn Féin and the DUP will have ministerial posts. Whether and how the institution will function remains less clear. Are the ministers impeachable, and by what process? The UUP has argued that Sinn Féin cannot take ministerial positions prior to decommissioning but it is unclear how this will be adjudicated. The DUP will use its positions in the assembly to try to roll back reforms. If the UUP and the SDLP gain resounding victories in the assembly elections, one would expect gradual movement towards a functioning power-sharing assembly. If Sinn Féin and the DUP have a strong showing in the assembly, continuing conflict within this institution can be expected.

Strand 2 of the talks dealt with the most contentious issue of all – relations between North and South. The central nationalist demand was for strong North–South bodies. Both the SDLP and Sinn Féin made it clear that anything less implied a settlement internal to Northern Ireland which they would not accept. Neither party had much room for manoeuvre. The SDLP was under pressure from Sinn Féin, while Sinn Féin had to work within limits set by its argument to the IRA that unity can be achieved peacefully by the dynamic effects of strong North–South bodies. The Irish government equally required strong North–South bodies to sell its proposed constitutional changes to its own backbenchers and to Southern public opinion. The UUP, in contrast, argued that North–South relations should be incorprated as part of East–West relations. It was adamant that strong North–South bodies which might lead to integration between North and South, and so erode the union, were completely unacceptable.

In the Agreement a North–South Council (which would incorporate implementation bodies) is constituted by Westminster and Dublin legislation but only begins to function after an initial period when the assembly agrees on its scope and mode of functioning. However during this initial 'shadow' period (not to exceed six months) the assembly does not have powers. The North–South bodies are to function by agreement and to be accountable to the assembly but ministers and implementation bodies have a level of autonomy of action. The functioning of the Council and implementation bodies and their degree of autonomy from assembly scrutiny remains to be fought out within the new institutions.

Strand 3 of the talks dealt with East–West relations. The final agreement includes promised amendments of articles 2 and 3 of the Irish constitution and repeal of the British Government of Ireland Act of 1920 and its replacement with an assertion of British sovereignty which makes it conditional on majority consent within Northern Ireland. It also incorporates a new British–Irish Agreement to replace the Anglo-Irish Agreement. In the new agreement the Irish government retains most of the powers that it had under the Anglo-Irish Agreement but there are symbolically important concessions to unionists in the admission of representatives of the Northern Assembly to intergovernmental discussions.

Finally, there is provision in the agreement for a British–Irish Council which includes representatives of the British and Irish governments, the Northern Ireland assembly and the devolved institutions in Scotland and Wales. The Council is legally enabled to set up modes of cooperation parallel to those of the North–South Council but is not required to do so.

The participants in the talks remained in deep opposition up until the final hours. That an agreement was reached at all is a tribute to the negotiating skills of the chairmen, particularly Senator George Mitchell, who drafted the final agreement, and to the commitment of the British and Irish governments. But the agreement is not yet a settlement that commands widespread legitimacy. Sinn Féin did not vote for the agreement although it was on balance positive and agreed to bring it to its party members. The UUP was divided on its merits and the DUP and UKUP opposed to it. As we have seen, central issues in dispute are postponed rather than resolved: policing and decommissioning, the speed of reform, the functioning of the Assembly, the degree of autonomy of North–South bodies. There are already conflicting pressures on the two governments from nationalists and unionists. In short, instability and conflict seem set to continue even when the new political institutions come into being. It is an urgent task for political leaders in Northern Ireland, Britain and the Republic to develop these structures and institutions in ways that can command the widest popular support and legitimacy. In the final section of this paper we outline some of the opportunities opened by the new agreement.

Towards an interim settlement

How is a stable settlement of the Northern Ireland conflict to be achieved? We believe a settlement must be based on more than the strategic considerations and compromises which we sketched in the last section. We have argued elsewhere for a dismantling of the conditions which give rise to communal conflict (Ruane and Todd 1996). That is a long-term process to which the Multi-Party Agreement can contribute. Here we draw out some of the implications of our analysis and suggest those aspects of the agreement which must be built on if stability and wider legitimacy are to be assured.

Despite the changes outlined earlier in this chapter, communal identities and interests in Northern Ireland remain starkly opposed. This is so whether one takes the overt interests of nationalists and unionists in Irish or British national sovereignty, or their underlying interests in autonomy, self-determination, equality and security. Each community has sought to secure its interests through the pursuit of power. The increasing instability of the balance of communal power has encouraged each community to mobilise the full range of its resources – political, cultural, economic, (para-) military – to shift the balance further in its favour. The struggle is, then, not simply about interests, but about the power to defend or advance interests (Ruane and Todd 1996). But the pursuit of power by each community compels the other to do likewise; the conflict therefore becomes self-sustaining (Wright 1987). The form of the state becomes central to this power struggle – a resource or tool for each community to use rather than a legitimate authority to which all can give allegiance (see Ruane and Todd 1996: 231). If power struggle continues, new political institutions will be used in precisely this way.

A critical step in diminishing conflict is the creation of a political order which all can recognise as legitimate. This requires that fundamental interests be distanced from communal power and guaranteed instead as rights by the legitimate political order. And this, in turn, requires sufficient disaggregation of the issues and interests in conflict to make the rights of each community compatible.

The Multi-Party Agreement goes some way to meeting these criteria. It pledges strong guarantees of rights in both Irish jurisdictions; it promises swift movement towards greater equality in Northern Ireland. It reasserts the right of majority consent to constitutional change. In this, it is following the dynamic of the peace process. The peace process aimed to bring the conflict to an end through a process of negotiation that would put in place a settlement capable of commanding widespread agreement and the allegiance of all its citizens. It arose in part from new currents in nationalist thinking (see above), in part from wider changes in the nature and meanings of state boundaries in the modern/postmodern world, in part from a principled commitment to equality born of the experience of inequality. Moreover, those nationalists engaged in the peace process went some way to disaggregating the issues in conflict. They came to accept the rights of unionists to shape the conditions under which they are governed; these rights are limited only by the equal rights of the substantial minority of nationalists living in Northern Ireland.

There are inherent difficulties – the imbrication even of normative ideals with power struggle – which became explicit in the course of the peace process. Nationalists could easily accept the aim of a consensual political order, for they stood to benefit from such change. For unionists, in contrast, the move towards a consensual political order stands to decrease their power resources. Further, unionist ideology, even in its reconstructed forms, has not come to accept the rights which nationalists claim. Unionists accept the right of Southern nationalists to shape the state in which they live, but accord no such rights to Northern nationalists. In their view the constitutional standing of Northern Ireland is to be fully and solely determined by its majority community, and even in Northern Ireland, nationalists are to participate and have power as a minority, not as full equals to the majority population. Protection of the union, not consensuality, remains the priority for the UUP.

In the talks process the two governments' primary concern was to reach an agreement. To secure UUP participation and agreement, normative primacy had to be given to the majoritarian principle that there can be no change in the constitutional status of Northern Ireland without the consent of a majority there. The consensual principle, that a legitimate settlement must win widespread agreement and allegiance was put in second place.

Very serious consequences follow from this approach. Formally, the unionist position – that the legitimacy of Northern Ireland is already established and must be recognised – is treated as equal to the nationalist view that negotiation towards consensus on the constitutional issue is necessary. Practically, because of the re-affirmation of the majoritarian guarantee, the unionist view is given priority. But this offers no route to the establishment of a constitutional order in Northern Ireland that can have general legitimacy.

On the unionist view, the legitimacy of Northern Ireland is a matter of majority will – the unionist majority founded the state in 1920 and have sustained it since. They argue that Northern Ireland is no different from other states in this respect, for all state boundaries have their origins in conflict and in the victory of one side over another. However, such boundaries achieve general legitimacy not because of such victories, but despite them: the defeated are expelled or reintegrated into the community of the victors; they are not left as discontents or outcasts, marked by the fact of defeat (Wright 1987). In a divided society, in contrast, the legitimacy of the state cannot be founded on the victory of one of the communities over the other. As in Northern Ireland, where this is attempted, the price is continuing conflict and instability. If general legitimacy is to be established this requires negotiation on the constitutional status of Northern Ireland as well as on arrangements within it; only consensus based on such negotiation will make the unionist victory of 1920 less and less relevant and create a state equally respected by all its citizens.

The second consequence of the linking of legitimacy to the views of the majority community is that it increases the salience of power. It is the principle of 'winner takes all' and cannot but encourage the nationalist community to adopt whatever means are available to it to become the majority community. Much more is involved here than the birth rate. Differential emigration makes the demographic balance dependent on factors which are the subject of political struggle – access to jobs, recognition of political and cultural rights and the degree of optimism and pessimism in each community about its future.

In our view, a settlement which fails to tackle the issue of general legitimacy is bound to be unstable. The best hope for an stable settlement lies in rediscovering and reinvigorating the consensual and normative aspects of the peace process – seeing the Multi-Party Agreement as a path towards such a consensual order rather than as a final settlement. But that means tackling the difficulties that beset the peace process in the earlier stages, primarily unionist scepticism and unwillingness to participate wholeheartedly in the process. Here the Multi-Party Agreement may provide incentives to both unionists and nationalists to participate wholeheartedly in forming a consensual order.

We argued above that nationalists partially moderated their views and entered into a peace process aimed at consensus because of the new political opportunities (AIA, Frameworks) and political alliances (Irish government/Irish-Americans) presently and potentially open to them. Such opportunities (in particular in North–South bodies) are increased in the new agreement. But equally such opportunities and alliances are now beginning to be provided for unionists. It is in this respect that the two governments must continue to be proactive in the peace process. Only by developing these opportunities, rather than simply relying on unionists and nationalists to work together in the new assembly, can wider change in the conditions which generate conflict occur.

First, a move beyond majoritarianism is necessary to guarantee the basic rights of each community to determine and to consent to their mode of government, subject only to the equal rights of others. A principle of consent has long been guaranteed by the governments, but its application is very uneven (see Todd 1995). In our view a full commitment to the principle of 'double consent' is needed – a recognition that both nationalist and unionist consent is necessary to legitimise political structures in Northern Ireland and on the island as a whole. This may simply be an ideal but it is one which touches the vital interests of both communities, as much of unionists in the event of a nationalist majority in Northern Ireland as of nationalists at present.

Second, institutions and structures which can guarantee unionists' fundamental interests, equally to those of nationalists, are necessary. Here the agreement offers real opportunities. For nationalists, their fundamental interests in equality and in a substantial influence in government and policy-making have been guaranteed by Irish government involvement, by British government policy pledges and by the promise of North–South bodies. But the new institutions will work only with unionist consent, and for this to be forthcoming unionists as a whole must see that their influence and their long-term security as a community is assured. This requires wider alliances and institutional openings for unionist influence beyond Northern Ireland, to balance those of nationalists. The British context is crucial, and here Tony Blair's commitment to constitutional reform in Britain and to the British–Irish Council seems to be an important step forward. But the Irish context is even more important, precisely because it is more dangerous from a unionist perspective.

Just as the AIA gave nationalists an input into affairs in Northern Ireland, so unionists need an institutional means of corresponding input into the affairs of the Republic. The Multi-Party Agreement goes some way towards this: in guaranteeing parallel minority rights in the Republic as in Northern Ireland and in the role of North–South bodies. As the reality of their increasing engagement with the South becomes clear to unionists, having an input into decision making there will become an imperative. It is in the development of such institutions that the openness of nationalists, particularly in the South, to unionist input will be truly tested.

In short, the central conclusion which arises from our argument in this chapter is that the conditions for political stability do not yet exist. Continuing political change is necessary to secure and sustain the agreement already reached. The dynamic character of the peace process will not end with the Multi-Party Agreement: continuing structural change is rather the prerequisite of more widely based agreement in a situation of such deep-set communal opposition.

Conclusion

In this chapter we have shown how wider socio-economic, cultural and political changes have laid the foundation for the peace process and the Multi-Party Agreement of 10 April 1998. However, the changes are still too limited to ensure a stable settlement. In the final sections of this chapter we have suggested that the agreement offers major opportunities for progress. However, further political change is necessary to maintain the dynamic of agreement against the strong tendencies to communal conflict.

Chapter 11

Northern Ireland: international and north/south issues

Adrian Guelke

Introduction

Persistence of parochialism and resistance to the influence of globalisation form striking features of the politics of Northern Ireland, so that the notion that the province is stuck in a time-warp remains one of the commonest observations made about its communal divisions. The point was eloquently expressed by Winston Churchill after the First World War:

> The mode and thought of men, the whole outlook on affairs, the grouping of parties, all have encountered violent and tremendous changes in the deluge of the world, but as the deluge subsides and the waters fall we see the dreary steeples of Fermanagh and Tyrone emerging once again. The integrity of their quarrel is one of the few institutions that have been unaltered by the cataclysm that has swept the world. (1941: 319)

None the less, during the 1990s internationalisation of the Northern Ireland problem came to be identified as a new factor in the situation. One context for such references was the establishment by the European Union of a special support package for the region in the wake of the 1994 paramilitary ceasefires (Wilson 1997: 7). Another, more significant basis was President Bill Clinton's triumphant visit to Northern Ireland on 30 November 1995 highlighting America's commitment to the peace process, a degree of involvement in the domestic affairs of the United Kingdom that would have been unthinkable during the Cold War (O'Clery 1996: 4). However, the concept of the internationalisation of the Northern Ireland conflict itself remains problematic for a number of reasons.

Firstly, from the perspective of the academic interpretation of the problem, far from there being a process of the internationalisation of the conflict, it has been internalised. Thus, one of the main themes of John Whyte's magisterial survey of the literature on the Northern Ireland problem is the growth of the dominance of internal-conflict interpretations of the conflict (1990: 202). That is to say, whereas before the onset of the current phase of the troubles in 1968 and in its early years there was a preponderance of literature that blamed either British imperialism or southern Irish irredentism for the conflict, by the 1980s there was a virtual consensus among academic analysts of the conflict that the root of the problem lay in communal antagonism between Protestants and Catholics within Northern Ireland. Of course, a belief that the principal antagonists were within Northern Ireland did not preclude according a role to external factors in influencing that battle. That at least is John Whyte's justification for including a number of works that specifically examined the role of external factors, including this author's, under the heading of internal-conflict interpretations (1990: 200).

Secondly, while, in particular, the extent of American intervention under Clinton is unprecedented, internationalisation is not new. In important respects, it can be traced back to the very start of the current phase of the troubles in 1968. This point will be elaborated below.

Thirdly, confusion arises over what is meant by internationalisation because of the existence of different international dimensions of the problem. Five broad areas can be identified:

1   the ostensible territorial dispute between two states, the United Kingdom and the Republic of Ireland, over Northern Ireland
2   the involvement of countries outside the British Isles in the conflict
3   the international affiliations of the parties to the conflict in Northern Ireland
4   the impact of the conflict on the outside world
5   the influence of international opinion on the conflict.

While there has been wide variation in which of these areas have seemed important at particular times, it is nevertheless possible to identify different phases of the internationalisation of the conflict. Three phases in the development of the international political system had a particularly important bearing on the conflict in Northern Ireland. They were:

1   the end of the colonial era, exposing the province's anomalous status in the post-colonial era
2   the establishment of the human rights agenda
3   the end of bipolarity, in the context of which the United Kingdom had played a crucial supporting role to the United States in the Western alliance.

Each of these areas and phases will be examined in turn.

A territorial dispute?

In formal terms there is a conflict between the claim of the Irish Republic's constitution that Northern Ireland is part of Ireland and the constantly reiterated position of the British government that Northern Ireland will remain part of the United Kingdom as long as a majority in Northern Ireland so wishes. That stance pre-dated the current troubles, though it took the slightly different form of a guarantee that Northern Ireland would not cease to be part of the United Kingdom without the consent of the parliament of Northern Ireland. The suspension of the Stormont parliament in 1972 resulted in the principle of consent being vested in the people rather than in the parliament. The formal stance of the Republic of Ireland was enshrined in Articles 2 and 3 of the country's 1937 constitution. Article 2 asserts that 'the national territory consists of the whole island of Ireland, its islands and territorial seas', while Article 3 acknowledges that in practice the jurisdiction of the Irish state is limited to 26 counties 'pending the re-integration of the national territory'. At various junctures, unionists have made great play of these Articles to press the charge of irredentism against the Republic.

But what is far more striking, particularly in comparative terms, has been the lack of enthusiasm which at times British and Irish governments and political parties have shown towards these formal commitments. Garret FitzGerald's indiscreet political memoirs provide a number of startling examples of the point. Two are particularly worth highlighting. Thus, he recounts the Irish government's concern at the beginning of 1975 at the possibility of a unilateral British withdrawal from Northern Ireland. FitzGerald – at the time Irish foreign minister – raised the matter with the American Secretary of State, Henry Kissinger.

> I said that I knew of his non-interventionist stance so far as Irish affairs were concerned and was not seeking any action by the United States at that time; but in the event
> – unlikely, I hoped – of a shift in British policy towards withdrawal from Northern Ireland in advance of an agreed political solution we would then seek US assistance in persuading Britain not to embark on a course of action that could be so fraught with dangers not just to Northern Ireland but to the whole of the island, and conceivably even – given the involvement of Libya, for example, with the IRA, and Cuba's long-distance role in Angola – to the wider peace of north-western Europe. He agreed that he would be open to an approach from us in the event of such a grave development. (1991: 259)

It does not seem to have occurred to FitzGerald quite how incongruous an argument he was advancing, considering his position as a representative of a neutral state and Britain's as America's leading ally in the Western alliance.

The second example comes from his account of his negotiations on the Anglo-Irish Agreement with the then British Prime Minister, Margaret Thatcher. FitzGerald saw amending Articles 2 and 3 of the Irish constitution as an important confidence-building measure. Admittedly, partly because this proposal was linked to others for the radical restructuring of government in Northern Ireland, this suggestion was met with less than whole-hearted enthusiasm from the British side; he gives the following account of a conversation he had with Thatcher on the issue of amending the two articles:

> Was there really a chance to amend our Constitution? she asked at the outset, following up our discussion of the previous night. Might we not fail because of distortions and false accusations? Perhaps we should not be running that particular risk. (1991: 516)

What these anecdotes underline is the priority that both governments gave to damage limitation in respect of their policies towards Northern Ireland and a tendency of both governments to see their country's commitment to Northern Ireland as an unwelcome burden.

However, the reversal of positions described by FitzGerald is not the norm in Anglo-Irish relations. Generally speaking, disagreement between the British and Irish governments stems from conflict between positions tilted towards unionism in the case of London and tilted towards nationalism in the case of Dublin. Thus, prior to the Good Friday Agreement the stated desire of the British Prime Minister, Tony Blair, was to see Articles 2 and 3 amended by the Republic as a confidence-building measure ahead of a negotiated settlement, while the Irish government's position remained that amendment of the Articles should take place in the context of the achievement of a negotiated settlement (*The Irish Times*, 17 May 1997). Further, for all the disdain shown by British and southern Irish opinion to their respective 'sides' in the Northern Ireland conflict, the possibility that the two countries could become magnetised by the conflict cannot be totally discounted. That potentiality is evident in the continued demonisation of the Sinn Féin leader, Gerry Adams, in sections of the British media and in the ferocity of southern Irish reaction on the issue of Orange marches through Catholic neighbourhoods in Northern Ireland. An important consequence of the institutionalisation of co-operation between the British and Irish governments through the mechanisms of the Anglo-Irish Agreement was that it substantially reduced the likelihood of a serious breach in relations between the two states over the issue of Northern Ireland.

External interventions

The involvement of countries outside the British Isles in the conflict needs to be divided into state-level interventions and transnational exchanges at a non-governmental level. State-level interventions can be further subdivided into direct engagement in the conflict through the supply of weapons to paramilitary organisations, and diplomatic activity directed at influencing, usually, the British government, sometimes the Irish government, and still more occasionally, parties within Northern Ireland. Only two states have been directly implicated in supplying weapons to paramilitary organisations. They are Libya and South Africa. Libyan involvement can be dated to June 1972 when the Libyan leader, Colonel Gadafy, made a speech in which he declared his willingness to support Irish revolutionaries. This was in the context of a far-reaching attack on British and American policies in the Middle East. There was a cool response to the speech in Britain with the Ministry of Defence noting that there was no evidence that arms from Libya had reached Ireland. However, in March 1973, the Irish navy intercepted the freighter, *Claudia*, capturing five tons of arms destined for the Provisional Irish Republican Army (IRA) which, it emerged, had been loaded on to the ship by Libyan soldiers at Tripoli.

Gadafy saw the conflict in Northern Ireland as an opportunity to put pressure on the British government over its approach to Middle Eastern issues. His simplistic view of the conflict as a popular struggle against British imperialism was shaken by the events of May 1974 when the power-sharing Executive was brought down by a general strike by Protestant workers. His response was to invite members of the Ulster Defence Association (UDA) to Tripoli. However, he continued to give some aid to the Provisional IRA until about 1977. The growth of trade between the Republic of Ireland and Libya (particularly imports of Irish beef) led to the establishment of diplomatic relations between the two countries; Gadafy eventually acceded to pressure from Dublin to end support for the Provisionals.

The revival of Libyan involvement in Northern Ireland took place in 1984. The context was the mysterious shooting dead of a policewoman outside the Libyan embassy in London. The assumption that she had been shot by someone in the embassy led to the expulsion of Libyan diplomats from Britain. (Subsequent investigations by the media suggest that this assumption was mistaken.) Gadafy's response to this humiliation was to issue a public invitation to the IRA to set up an office in Tripoli. After the Americans bombed Libya in April 1986 using air bases in Britain for the raid, Gadafy first said he would be resuming military aid to the IRA, then in an interview with the British newspaper, *The Observer*, said that he had already done so (1 March 1987).

The full significance of Gadafy's rhetoric became apparent at the end of October 1987 when the French navy intercepted a Panamanian-registered ship, the *Eksund*, with 150 tons of arms and ammunition, including 20 Soviet-made surface-to-air missiles, on board. The French authorities quickly determined that the shipment had been bound for the Provisional IRA and that Libya was the source of the weapons. They also acquired information about earlier shipments which had not been intercepted. According to the information they were given, there had been four earlier shipments to the Republic of Ireland. The first was in August 1985 and consisted of ten tons of weapons, including large quantities of AK47s and seven rocket-propelled grenade launchers. The remaining shipments took place after the American bombing raid. By far the largest was the last in October 1986, consisting of over 80 tons of arms, including ten SAM-7 missiles and at least a ton of Semtex. Apparently, it was the size of this shipment that alerted the authorities to what was happening and led to the interception of the *Eksund*.

The Irish government was shocked by the revelations. They coincided with a strong backlash against the Provisional IRA within the Republic as a result of an IRA bomb attack on a Remembrance Day ceremony in Enniskillen in November 1987 in which 11 civilians had been killed. In response, the Irish government mounted an extensive search for IRA arms in the Republic. Operation Mallard uncovered a considerable number of Provisional IRA arms caches. However, the quantity of weaponry recovered represented only a fraction of what had got through to the Provisional IRA, according to the French authorities. There were no further interceptions of arms from Libya after the *Eksund*. In 1992, in the context of seeking a de-escalation in its conflict with the international community over the investigation into the destruction of Pan Am Flight 103 over Lockerbie, Libya declared in a letter to the United Nations that it was severing its links with all groups and organisations that targeted civilians (O'Brien 1995: 256–7). The Libyan government later provided information to the British authorities on its previous links with the Provisional IRA.

The other country that provided weapons to paramilitary organisations was South Africa. The apartheid regime's intervention in Northern Ireland had its roots in the country's involvement in the civil war in Angola. After the supply of sophisticated fighter aircraft to the Angolan government by the Soviet Union in the mid-1980s, South Africa had lost air superiority over southern Angola. South African forces became vulnerable to air attack and that was reflected in heavy casualties among white army conscripts in late 1987. South Africa became desperate to acquire surface-to-air missile technology to counter the threat. This drew South Africa into involvement in Northern Ireland since the Northern Ireland firm of Short Brothers, with a largely Protestant workforce, had a division producing missiles. Through links with Loyalist paramilitary organisations, South Africa hoped to acquire the technology it was looking for. This all came to light in Paris in April 1989 when the French authorities arrested three members of a Loyalist paramilitary group, Ulster Resistance, in the company of a South African diplomat and in possession of a missile display model.

This case prompted further investigation of the South African connection, leading to revelations that the South African armaments corporation, Armscor, had sent a large shipment of arms to three Loyalist paramilitary organisations. The shipment had been sent through intermediaries in Israel and the Christian militias in Lebanon. The arms, which had been landed in Belfast in January 1988, had been disguised as ceramic tiles. The reaction of the British government to these disclosures was minimal; the expulsion of three South African diplomats from Britain. The links continued. In April 1992, agents of South African Military Intelligence were implicated with members of a Loyalist paramilitary organisation in what the British police took to be an attempt to assassinate a former member of the South African police force who was a threat to the South African authorities because of what he had revealed about security-force involvement in the murder of anti-apartheid activists (*The Independent*, 15 July 1992).

It is significant that direct intervention at state level in the violence in Northern Ireland has been limited to two pariah states. Rather more states have become diplomatically involved in the conflict. However, its extent has been limited by the fear of other states that the appearance of intervention against British interests might damage their relations with the United Kingdom. The Irish government has lobbied for support internationally when it has believed that the British government has been pursuing policies detrimental to the Catholic minority in Northern Ireland. The purpose of such lobbying has been to mobilise international opinion so as to put pressure on the British government to change course. That was particularly the case during the hunger strike crisis of 1980–81 when the Irish government was fearful of the destabilising consequences of the radicalisation of the Catholic minority in Northern Ireland. However, while other states were often sympathetic to the Irish viewpoint and shared their concern over the likely consequences of British policy, they remained reluctant to criticise the British government publicly, though on a few occasions the exasperation of foreign leaders did become evident (Hainsworth 1981: 14).

The American connection

By far the most important source of diplomatic pressure on the British government has been the United States. In the early years of the troubles, the United States took a strictly non-interventionist stance on the conflict in Northern Ireland. The view taken was that the problem was a domestic concern of the United Kingdom. It became clear that this stance would become difficult to sustain after Jimmy Carter became President and made human rights a foreign-policy priority of the United States, since that undercut the notion that the domestic affairs of states were matters outside the purview of foreign policy. After lobbying by prominent Irish-American politicians, Carter agreed to issue a statement on Northern Ireland. Although the statement of 30 August 1977 was in the end somewhat bland and carefully couched so as not to offend the British government, which was consulted over its content, it represented a significant change in the American government's position in that it treated the conflict in Northern Ireland as a legitimate concern of American foreign policy. Furthermore, in addition to its condemnation of political violence and its promise of American support in the event of a political settlement, it endorsed the principle that another state (the Irish Republic) should be involved in any settlement.

Worse for the British government followed in August 1979 when the American State Department suspended the sale of handguns to the Royal Ulster Constabulary (RUC) under the rubric that the United States would not permit the sale of arms to countries or institutions that had been found guilty of violating human rights. The context was a scandal over police interrogation methods in Northern Ireland that had attracted the attention of Amnesty International and the exploitation of President Carter's domestic political difficulties by the Irish-American lobby. However, in the end, these difficulties were also to provide the British government with a measure of respite from American pressure. Reagan's victory in the 1980 Presidential elections and the conservative tide in Congress reduced the influence of the Irish-American lobby. Almost as important in limiting American pressure on the British government during the 1980s was its acceptance of a role for the Irish government, culminating in the Anglo-Irish Agreement of November 1985. When it had seemed possible that the British government might reject such a role in the wake of the British Prime Minister's abrupt rejection in November 1984 of the options outlined in the report of the New Ireland Forum, Thatcher had come under pressure from Reagan to make amends, which she did when she addressed a joint session of Congress in February 1985 (Rutherford 1985).

The next phase of American governmental involvement in Northern Ireland came during the Clinton Presidency. In his quest for the Democratic nomination, Clinton had given qualified support to a set of proposals being urged on candidates by a new Irish-American grouping, Americans for a New Irish Agenda. The proposals included the appointment of a peace envoy to Northern Ireland, the grant of a visa to the Sinn Féin leader, Gerry Adams, and exerting diplomatic pressure on the British government over Northern Ireland. However, after his election as President, Clinton had disappointed the Irish-American lobby, many of whom had been recruited by Irish-Americans for Clinton/Gore, during the campaign itself. On the advice of the Irish government, he had resisted appointing a peace envoy. It was only after differences emerged between the British and Irish governments over the handling of the peace process that the two governments had launched with a joint declaration in December 1993 that Clinton authorised a departure from the practice of previous American government.

Clinton granted Gerry Adams a 48-hour visa to attend a one-day conference on Northern Ireland in New York at the beginning of February 1994. It was organised by the National Committee on American Foreign Policy, the chairman of which was a prominent Irish-American, Bill Flynn. Admitting Adams ran contrary to American policy towards individuals associated with ongoing terrorism. The decision was con-troversial within the Clinton Administration and involved the White House over-ruling other agencies of government. In the words of Niall O'Dowd, the founder of the weekly newspaper, *The Irish Voice*, the decision 'overturned a 50-year hegemony over Irish policy that the British government had exercised through the State Depart-ment' (Coogan 1995: 373). There was a furious reaction from the British govern-ment to the decision, which was reflected in extremely hostile commentary on the influence of the Irish-American lobby over the Clinton administration in the British press.

At one level the row between London and Washington was somewhat artificial. Both governments shared the same objective. This was to bring about a Provisional IRA ceasefire. The difference was over what tactics should be employed to bring it about. The British government's viewpoint, contrary to that of the Irish govern-ment, was that no rewards should be offered to Sinn Féin ahead of a ceasefire. However, the strength of British reaction to Clinton's decision on Adams's visa owed far more to concern about the loss of British influence in Washington than to fear that the decision would have a negative impact on the peace process. The fact that the Provisional IRA eventually called a ceasefire on 31 August 1994 and the prominent role of Irish-American groups in the deliberations within the Republican movement leading up to the ceasefire was widely seen as vindicating Clinton's decision on the visa.

An impasse over the issue of the decommissioning of weapons during 1995 held up progress towards all-party negotiations on Northern Ireland's future. The dead-lock threatened the survival of the ceasefire. It also threatened to wreck a trip President Clinton planned to make to Northern Ireland. In the week of the visit at the end of November, the British and Irish governments, at American prompting, finally agreed to a face-saving device to break the deadlock, the appointment of an international body given the task of coming up with a formula to bridge the gap in the positions of the parties on the issue. This development was widely presented as rescuing the peace process, contributing to the hero's reception that Clinton received in Northern Ireland.

However, for reasons that had to do with the precarious position of his govern-ment at Westminster, the then British Prime Minister, John Major, added a further pre-condition of elections to the formula that the international body had come up with for dealing with decommissioning. That contributed to the breakdown of the

Provisional IRA ceasefire in February 1996. The Clinton administration called for a restoration of the ceasefire, closed its doors to Sinn Féin leaders and supported the joint efforts of the British and Irish governments to revive the peace process. However, the role played by the Clinton administration in the run-up to the Provisional IRA's second ceasefire of 20 July 1997 was low-key, and the American connection did not loom large in explanations of the reasons for the new ceasefire. The decisive factors were seen as being the election of a new government in London and, to a lesser extent, the election of a new government in Dublin as well.

Diplomatic engagement with the issue of Northern Ireland by other countries has been too episodic to deserve more than passing mention, with the exception of the surprising attempt at mediation in the conflict by the new post-apartheid South African government. The South African government invited representatives of Sinn Féin and of all the parties taking part in the multi-party negotiations in Northern Ireland to South Africa for a weekend seminar in June 1997 on the lessons of the South African transition. All of the parties accepted the invitation, with the exception of the United Kingdom Unionist Party, though the other Unionist parties insisted on arrangements for the conference that kept them separated from the representatives of Sinn Féin, an ironic echo of the policy of apartheid.

Below state level, political groups in other countries outside the British Isles have had a small but not totally insignificant impact on the conflict. Unionists and Loyalists receive very little support from outside the British Isles. A few arms have been channelled to Loyalist paramilitary organisations through Canada, but in general the response of the outside world to the conflict has tended to reinforce Unionist perceptions of themselves as friendless. Much the most important source of support for the nationalist cause has been the Irish-American lobby in the United States, though through the course of the Troubles there has been considerable change in the nature and priorities of Irish-American groups involved in the conflict.

The Irish-American lobby

In the early years of the conflict, the most important Irish-American organisation involved in the conflict in Northern Ireland was Irish Northern Aid or, as it was better known, NORAID. NORAID was founded in 1970. Between its founding and 1991 – when it ceased to report remittances – it officially remitted approximately $3.5m to Ireland to a Sinn Féin-controlled charity that assisted the families of Republican prisoners. While this is a tiny amount in the context of political fundraising in the United States, it represented an important source of funds for the Provisionals. Through its newspaper, *The Irish People*, it promoted the cause of the Provisionals in the United States. A number of important figures in NORAID were implicated in gun-running to the IRA. NORAID's founder, Michael Flannery, admitted his involvement in a court case in 1982 but persuaded the jury to acquit him of the charge of conspiring to smuggle arms to the Provisional IRA on the grounds that he had been under the impression that the shipment had been sanctioned by the Central Intelligence Agency! (Richey 1985).

During the 1980s another grouping achieved greater prominence than NORAID. This was the Irish National Caucus (INC). It was founded in September 1974 to lobby in Washington for a number of Irish-American organisations, including NORAID. By the 1976 Presidential campaign, the main focus of the INC had become the violation of human rights in Northern Ireland. It achieved success when it persuaded the Democratic nominee, Jimmy Carter, to take up the issue in his campaign. In September 1977 the Ad Hoc Congressional Committee on Irish Affairs was established at the initiative of the INC. Pressure from the Ad Hoc Committee was instrumental in the State Department's decision to suspend the sale of handguns to the RUC to avert Congressional hearings over British policy in Northern Ireland. The INC itself achieved most success with a campaign over the issue of discrimination against Catholics in employment in Northern Ireland. In 1984, the INC co-ordinated the formulation of a set of nine employment principles, modelled on American affirmative action programmes, while also drawing on the Sullivan principles, a voluntary code of conduct governing American investment in South Africa. They were named the MacBride principles after a former Minister of External Affairs in the Irish Republic.

In November 1985, Massachusetts became the first state to adopt legislation requiring compliance with the MacBride principles. New York, New Jersey, Connecticut and Rhode Island followed suit in 1986 and 1987. In response, the British government enacted the Fair Employment (Northern Ireland) Act of 1989, extending the scope of its anti-discrimination measures, including empowering the Fair Employment Commission to issue affirmative action directions to employers with the goal of reducing imbalances in the employment of Protestants and Catholics. The British legislation had only a temporary effect in slowing the momentum of the MacBride principles campaign and there are efforts continuing in the United States to enact legislation at different levels to enforce compliance with the principles.

In 1981, a group of leading Irish-American politicians who had been instrumental in persuading President Carter to issue his statement on Northern Ireland in 1977 formed the Friends of Ireland. Its purpose was to promote the cause of moderate constitutional nationalism within Congress. It frequently challenged the positions taken up by the Ad Hoc Committee and the INC. In the first half of the 1980s the Friends of Ireland gave strong backing to an initiative of the Social Democratic and Labour Party (SDLP), the New Ireland Forum. The Friends welcomed the Anglo-Irish Agreement of November 1985 and helped to secure Congressional support for an package of aid to Ireland as a mark of approval for the Agreement.

However, arguably the most influential Irish-American grouping in recent years has been Americans for a New Irish Agenda. Its influence on Clinton was described above. Through the course of the Troubles, there has been a considerable evolution in Irish-American attitudes to the conflict. In its early years, a common assumption was that partition was the cause of the conflict and that all that was needed to end it was British withdrawal. With greater recognition of the complexity of the Northern Ireland problem, there has been a shift in emphasis away from the necessity of British withdrawal to that of the achievement of a negotiated settlement among the parties in Northern Ireland, with the goal of peace tending to displace that of unity. However, it remains the case that there is greater support for Sinn Féin among Irish-Americans taking an interest in the conflict, admittedly a small minority of the Irish-American population, than exists in Ireland itself. Support groups for the Republican cause exist in other countries besides the United States where there are significant numbers of Irish immigrants to be found. However, none has had a major impact on the conflict.

International affiliations and comparisons

Under the heading of the international affiliations of the parties can be placed the Republican movement's attempts to establish links with other nationalist movements that have been engaged in violent struggles and the efforts of the SDLP to gain support for constitutional nationalism through its membership of the Socialist International. Once again it is striking that Unionists and Loyalists have few such links. There has been limited co-operation between Loyalist groups and neo-fascist groups both in Britain and on the continent of Europe. However, only the British groups have been consistent supporters of the Loyalist cause and there has been equivocation on the Loyalist side even about these groups because of a lack of sympathy with their broader ideological objectives.

During the 1980s, the Provisionals strongly promoted comparison of the Northern Ireland conflict with the struggle by the African National Congress (ANC) against white minority rule in South Africa and the campaign of the Palestine Liberation Organisation (PLO) for a Palestinian state. The PLO played down links with the IRA as an obstacle to its diplomatic efforts to win the support of European governments, with Arafat denouncing stories of links as 'a big lie' (*The Irish Times*, 12 January 1980). Little emerged to suggest substantial links between the IRA and the ANC during the 1980s, despite the efforts of the apartheid regime to play up the issue to damage the ANC's reputation in Britain. However, in the 1990s, Mandela ran into criticism in Britain for expressing sympathy for the Republican cause (*The Irish Times*, 21 October 1992). That the ANC tended to view the conflict as an anti-colonial struggle was further underlined in 1995, when the Sinn Féin leader, Gerry Adams, visited South Africa and was warmly received. The Provisionals also sought to establish links with violent nationalist movements in other regions of Western Europe, the most important being the contacts they had with Basque and Corsican nationalists.

The direct impact of the conflict in Northern Ireland on the outside world has been slight, especially if that is understood to mean outside of the British Isles. The Provisionals have carried out a number of attacks on British military personnel abroad, particularly in Germany, and in 1979 the British ambassador to The Netherlands was assassinated by the IRA in The Hague. The spill-over of the conflict onto the UK mainland and into the Republic of Ireland has been much more serious. In the case of the Republic, much the most serious episode occurred in May 1974 during the Ulster Workers Council strike when Loyalist car bombs in Monaghan and Dublin killed 31 people. More than a hundred people have died on the UK mainland as a result of the activities of Republican groups, principally the Provisional IRA. Further, two Provisional IRA bombs in the City of London in 1992 and 1993 caused damage estimated as close to two billion pounds. But part of the explanation why there has been relatively little spill-over from the conflict into other countries has been the enormous indirect impact of the conflict internationally. Few of the world's conflicts have received as much attention in the mass media around the world as Northern Ireland has over the course of the Troubles. The paramilitaries have had little need to engage in activities outside Northern Ireland so as to attract attention to the existence of the conflict.

The influence of the attitudes of the outside world on the parties in Northern Ireland has been very significant. In sharp contrast to the IRA's border campaign between 1956 and 1962 which caused scarcely a ripple outside of Ireland, the current troubles, from their very outset in October 1968, attracted widespread attention, thanks in part to the innovation of the transmission of television pictures by satellite, which provided the basis for almost instant coverage of violent events. At the onset, opinion was sympathetic to the Catholic minority which was seen even in Britain to have been the victim of discrimination and oppression at the hands of the Protestant majority. The reaction of international opinion helped to shape the responses and strategies of the two communities. The siege mentality of the Protestant majority was strongly reinforced. Grass-roots Unionist opinion became fearful of any compromise, since it tended to see it as a slippery slope to a united Ireland. This was to undermine the efforts of moderate Unionist political leaders to reconstitute Northern Ireland as a political entity in a form capable of securing the allegiance of both communities. After the failure of power-sharing in 1974 discredited liberal Unionists, Unionists focused on the need for terrorism to be defeated, but Unionists remained divided on whether the best way forward lay in the total integration of Northern Ireland into the United Kingdom or the restoration of the autonomy the province had enjoyed prior to the imposition of direct rule in March 1972.

The sympathy that the Catholic minority received emphasised the advantages from the perspective of nationalists of the internationalisation of the conflict. This led to resistance to British policy in its first phase after August 1969 when British troops were sent to the province to aid the civil power. In particular, the objective of British policy of effecting the re-establishment of the province's autonomy after limited reform of the province's security apparatus had a radicalising impact on nationalists who feared that this would pave the way for the restoration of Unionist dominance and the neglect of their grievances for another 50 years. Their desire to internationalise the conflict to prevent such an eventuality led them to stress the lack of legitimacy of partition and therefore of Northern Ireland as a political entity, even though emphasis on the goal of a united Ireland inevitably made it more difficult for there to be a political accommodation between the two communities in Northern Ireland.

Shifts in international opinion

However, international opinion has not been static throughout the Troubles and in the final part of this chapter, its main phases and their consequent impact on the conflict will be traced briefly. The onset of Northern Ireland's current troubles coincided with the completion of a far-reaching revolution in the international political system – decolonisation. The end of formal colonial rule through much of the world, with the exception of Portugal's small overseas empire, had created the basis for the universalisation of a world order based on the principle of the sovereign equality of states. While the states that made up the international system were clearly unequal in economic terms and in terms of the military power at their disposal, all appeared equal in status as fully independent sovereign states. A corollary of acceptance of the legitimacy of the struggle against colonialism was that the sovereign territorial state would be the norm of the post-colonial era. In this context, Northern Ireland's status as conditionally part of a sovereign state seemed anomalous, though there were a variety of ways that the anomaly could be ended, including a united Ireland, the total integration of Northern Ireland into the United Kingdom and the creation of an independent Northern Ireland.

In practice, international opinion tended to favour a united Ireland far more strongly than other solutions to the anomaly. The imposition of direct rule from London in March 1972 simply served to strengthen perceptions of Northern Ireland as an undemocratic colonial entity, lending a measure of credibility to the Provisional IRA's claim to be engaged in a struggle against British imperialism. However, the nature of the Provisional IRA's campaign of violence tended to undercut support for the organisation as bearing a closer resemblance to marginalised terrorist groups in other European societies than to the mass movements associated with the struggle against colonial rule in the Third World. However, an important change in external perceptions of the Provisional IRA occurred in the context of the 1980 and 1981 crisis in the prisons. The mass support the Republican prisoners were able to attract weakened the portrayal of the IRA as terrorists akin to the Red Army Faction in Germany or the Red Brigades in Italy.

However, by this time the international agenda had changed and there had been a shift away from concern about unfinished business from the colonial era to the issue of human rights. From the perspective of the British government, this intensified its embarrassment over the continuation of the conflict, as well as forcing it to adopt strategies such as criminalisation that stressed the containment of political violence through the ordinary law, to minimise criticism of its rule in Northern Ireland. The issue of human rights provided a further basis for the internationalisation of the conflict, partly as a result of the monitoring of the conflict by non-governmental organisations such as Amnesty International, but also as a result of Britain's involvement in European institutions and the progress of European integration. In particular, in January 1978, the British government was convicted by the European Court of Human Rights of having authorised the employment of inhuman and degrading treatment of detainees at an early stage of the conflict. Following direct elections to the European Parliament from 1979, British policies in Northern Ireland became a focus of criticism in the parliament on human rights grounds.

One of the British government's motives for entering into the Anglo-Irish Agreement in November 1985, giving the Republic of Ireland a right to be consulted on the policies pursued by the British government in Northern Ireland, was to reduce its exposure to international criticism. However, criticism of British policies on human rights grounds have not ceased, though in general the association of the Republic with the conduct of British rule has served to make it appear more legitimate to the outside world (*At the Crossroads* 1996). Further, the interpretation of human rights has undergone change, so that criticism of the violation of human rights is no longer solely directed at governments, with the consequence that the paramilitaries have also come under attack for their violation of human rights.

The impact of the end of bipolarity on the Northern Ireland conflict has been indirect, as, despite concerns expressed by Garret FizGerald and others about the possible implications of the conflict for Western security, Soviet involvement was never a significant factor in the conflict and thus the ending of communism in Eastern Europe and the demise of the Soviet Union had no direct bearing on any of the combatants in Northern Ireland. However, the indirect effect has been considerable. The fall of the Berlin Wall was an important factor in President de Klerk's decision to liberalise the South African political system. The South African transition and the aftermath of the Gulf War were factors in the Middle East peace process, while the fact that the Provisionals had looked to the ANC and the PLO to legitimise their campaign of violence put them under pressure to develop a peace strategy so as to sustain the validity of their comparison of Northern Ireland with the situation in South Africa and the quest for a Palestinian state (Guelke 1996). The end of the Cold War also increased the readiness of the Clinton administration to intervene in the Northern Ireland problem, since the State Department was no longer able to deploy the argument that involvement in the Northern Ireland problem carried the unacceptable risk of alienating Britain, the United States' most important ally in the Western alliance. On the contrary, it could be argued that if American mediation proved successful in Northern Ireland, it would provide a boost to its role as a mediator in other conflicts around the world.

Further, the break-up of Yugoslavia and the successful completion of the South African transition have had a significant bearing on the interpretation of international norms that the parties in Northern Ireland have invoked to justify their conduct. Importantly, there has been a weakening of the international community's hostility towards secession, reflected in the recognition accorded to Slovenia and Eritrea, among others. The effect has been to reduce the rigidity of the territorial interpretation of self-determination, as well as giving greater legitimacy to the demands of minorities to be accorded better treatment within states. As a consequence, Northern Ireland's conditional status appears less anomalous. Further, in so far as the conflict between Unionism and nationalism comes to be seen in other than all-or-nothing terms, the prospects for political accommodation through an historic compromise between Unionism and nationalism are enhanced. The completion of South Africa's transition has ended a conflict in which a large part of the international community endorsed the use of political violence by the ANC directed at securing the political rights of a subordinate community. But there remains less reason for any substantial section of the international community to treat the use of political violence by other groups as legitimate, now that the battle against apartheid has been won.

Conclusion

The change in international circumstances provides a large part of the explanation for the success of Northern Ireland's peace process, culminating in agreement at the multi-party talks in Belfast on Good Friday, 10 April 1998. It remains to be seen if the agreement will provide the basis of a long-lasting settlement of the Northern Ireland problem. The obstacles remain formidable. The negotiations among the parties aroused considerable fears in Northern Ireland, particularly among Unionists, and that was reflected in a polarisation of opinion during the course of 1996 and 1997. Unionists remain divided on the agreement itself. Their divisions could ultimately make the agreement unworkable. The emergence of both Loyalist and Republican paramilitary groups opposed to the peace process means that the threat of political violence has not disappeared with the agreement. However, because parochialism has triumphed in the past does not necessarily mean that it is bound to do so forever.

Chapter 12

Conclusion: continuity, change and challenge

David E. Schmitt

The history of the Republic of Ireland since the late 1950s has been marked by profound change. The preceding chapters have described a process of economic growth and social transformation that has made Ireland a much more modern nation. From the standpoint of material well-being, most Irish citizens are far better off than they were prior to 1960. The rapid expansion of educational opportunities has produced a large middle class, and opportunities for women have increased. Membership in the European Union has drastically reduced economic dependence on the United Kingdom, and Ireland has acquired the capacity to thrive in a highly competitive international economy. The political and social changes produced by modernisation have led to a more open, pluralistic, outward-looking nation that is more respectful of individual choice.

As Tony Fahey pointed out in Chapter 3, however, there have been significant problems accompanying modernisation, such as higher rates of marital breakdown and unmarried parenthood. Furthermore, much of the period since 1959 has been marked by serious economic difficulties, such as the failure of many domestic companies and high rates of unemployment and inflation; poverty produced by economic change as well as by unequal access to quality education remains a problem. Thus, progress has not been uniform. Moreover, from the viewpoint of citizens holding traditional values, many important institutions such as the family have been undermined. The tension between tradition and modernity has been at the heart of some the most contentious political conflicts in Ireland such as the struggle over divorce and abortion.

For Northern Ireland the central issue since the late 1960s has been communal conflict that degenerated into an armed campaign by militant republicanism to drive the British out of Ireland and create a unified state. The conflict among the paramilitary organisations and the security forces has been the primary issue confronting Northern Ireland for nearly three decades. The Republic of Ireland has become a key player in the attempt to create a lasting peace in the North.

This chapter will analyse patterns of continuity and change in the Republic of Ireland as well as Northern Ireland. It will conclude with a brief assessment of ongoing challenges. This overview will draw primarily on the chapters of this book, highlighting some of the key themes, while presenting a few additional perspectives.

Irish traditionalism prior to 1960

At independence, Ireland possessed a quite traditional political culture, reminiscent of some of the world's less modern societies. It should be emphasised, however, that in certain respects Ireland in 1922 possessed many modern social, economic and political characteristics that supported the democratic political development of the country. Educational reforms in the nineteenth century virtually ended illiteracy, and land reform had replaced a system of exploited tenant farmers with farmers who largely owned their own land. Nineteenth-century political reforms created a citizenry familiar with democratic processes such as voting and free elections. An Irish administrative class holding professional and democratic values was especially important (Schmitt 1973: 25, 27, 28). As Jonathan Haughton pointed out (Chapter 2), moreover, the southern state at its inception was not at the level of poverty of many Third World nations, even though it was relatively poorer than many European nations.

Yet one of the most striking features of Irish political culture was the authoritarianism of both social institutions and popular attitudes. Authoritarianism refers to pronounced hierarchical patterns of decision making and the attitudes that support this pattern of behavior. Within families, fathers could wield autocratic authority over economic issues, although women played key roles in matters of education and marriage (O'Danachair 1962: 185–96). The principal source of authoritarian values for society as a whole was the Catholic Church. Education in southern Ireland was controlled by the Catholic Church and inculcated strong values of obedience. Deference to authority, compliance with regulations, and veneration of the Catholic religion and the elderly were among the principal values and themes in Irish education. The Church set the moral tone for southern Irish society through its demands for strict censorship and an adherence to a puritanical sexual morality. Additionally, the Catholic hierarchy occasionally intervened in political decisions, such as its central role in preventing a mother and child health care plan in the early 1950s (Whyte 1971; Kelleher 1957: 488). Yet the impact of the Church upon democratic political development was positive in many respects. The clergy played a key role in the development of Irish democratic nationalism through support of politicians such as Daniel O'Connell and of the broader movement for Catholic emancipation and democratic representation. The Church strongly supported the democratic institutions of the new Irish state (Schmitt 1973: chapter 4). It should also be noted that authoritarianism in Ireland has been muted by a cultural resistance to regimentation and a certain flexibility in the interpretation by citizens of laws and rules (Coakley 1993: 38).

Furthermore, the possible negative consequences of authoritarianism were softened by a personal style that helped overcome possible bureaucratic rigidities. An emphasis on connections based upon family or friendship as well as a friendly, affable personal style characteristic of Irish social interaction facilitated networking. This seemingly traditional approach is not necessarily at odds with modern forms of political, social and administrative organisation. Indeed, most students of modern political and administrative systems recognise informal organisation as a central part of effective planning, decision making and policy implementation. Brigid Laffen and Rory O'Donnel (Chapter 9) noted how the Irish skill at networking increases Ireland's influence within the European Union. The small size of the country and many of its institutions makes it much more likely that people will be known to one another and that social and professional networks will have a more enduring quality than might exist in larger political systems.

The personal style was characteristic of the operation of much of the administrative and especially the political processes of Irish society. Many observers have noted the importance of personal interventions by members of the Dáil on behalf of their constituents (Chubb 1992: 209–10; Sacks 1970: 45). A brokerage system where politicians operate as intermediaries included local councillors as well as members of party organisations and political clubs. A key point about these networks is that politicians were not so much patrons dispensing favours, as in less developed societies, than they were intermediaries (Bax 1970: 179–91). In sum, traditional values, behaviours and institutions such as the Catholic Church served Ireland well from the standpoint of many citizens. Ireland was a viable political democracy, and most Irish men and women displayed strong support for family, Church and country.

Tom Garvin (Chapter 8), however, portrayed the negative side of traditionalism from the standpoint of economic development and the desire of many of Ireland's educated citizenry for intellectual and social freedom. Political and Church leaders were wary of modernisation, seeing secular individualism as a byproduct of modern thinking. The focus on religious, rural and family values produced an 'ideology of cultural defence' that resulted in attempted social control through such measures as censorship and an educational system characterised by strict discipline. The economic aspect of this internal focus was the protectionist economic policies described by Jonathan Houghton (Chapter 2) that began in the 1930s and contributed significantly to economic stagnation. The pattern of emigration discussed by Tony Fahey and Jonathan Haughton (Chapters 2 and 3) drained Ireland of much talent critical to the economic transformation of society as emigrants sought economic opportunity and sometimes greater personal liberty in other countries. Also a comparatively low percentage of citizens completed secondary and third-level educational programmes, weakening the capacity of the economy to make significant gains in productivity. In short, the Irish society and economy did not serve well the aspirations of those who aspired to greater material well-being and personal freedom as well as the development of a new, modern Ireland.

Patterns of change and continuity

The economic and social transformation of the Republic of Ireland that began in the late 1950s resulted in large measure from a conscious decision by elites to modernise the country. These leaders and intellectuals rejected inward-looking values emphasising tradition and stability. As several chapters made clear, however, much change is attributable also to a modernising world economy characterised by high technology, new trading partnerships and mass media that challenged traditional values and institutions. Modernising elites were themselves influenced and inspired by these forces. The impetus for change thus had both internal and external roots. All major political parties became committed to economic development and the provision of state services to citizens.

Social and economic change

As Tony Fahey's analysis in Chapter 3 demonstrates, social resources have dramatically increased since the 1960s. The pattern of population decline that began in the last century appears to have been halted and population growth has occurred, even though the process has been uneven and the problem of emigration not fully reversed. Fahey also points out that the increase in active-age adults is likely to continue, thus reducing burdens on government for various social services. Advancements in the levels of education have been especially impressive. The decision in the 1960s to provide free universal secondary education as well as the expansion of third-level programmes has provided dramatically improved human resources for the Irish economic expansion. The percentage completing second-level education increased from 20 per cent in 1960 to more than 85 per cent in 1997, with 40 per cent of this age group proceeding to third-level education and training. It is not merely that much higher levels of education are attained but that education is becoming more relevant to a growing, modern economy. Increasing educational attainment and employment opportunities for qualified citizens have altered the class structure of Ireland, producing a large and growing group of skilled, professional and technical employees.

As Jonathan Houghton noted, the rise of real per capita GDP in the Republic of Ireland between 1960 and 1997 was greater than any other member of the European Union. The level of growth since 1992 has been especially spectacular, placing the Irish economy's per capita GDP in 1996 at 85 per cent of the European Union average and ahead of the United Kingdom. The strategies employed by the Irish government to promote growth revolved around three pillars: liberalisation of trade, the attraction of foreign investment, and education and training. By the 1990s Ireland had become one of the world's most open economies. Low taxes had induced many foreign companies to invest in Ireland, and Irish workers were regarded as among the most highly trained and capable in the European Union.

Yet Houghton also noted problems and limitations that require a more qualified understanding of the Celtic Tiger's success. Deficit financing produced the highest level of national debt in the European Union during the 1980s, slowing growth and impacting negatively on efforts to control inflation. More broadly, despite the impressive success of government programmes to create economic growth, it is apparent that the Irish government has only limited ability to control many economic variables.

As a small country it stands to benefit from free-trade policies, but it is also highly dependent upon the actions and experiences of the larger economies with which it has close relations. Unemployment and wage levels, for example, are in part determined by the conditions of the British labour market. It should also be emphasised that the growth of the Irish economy is explained by several variables such as the shift out of agriculture, a larger, better-trained labour force and improvements in technology and managerial techniques. Today, of course, the range of economic choices open to Irish political leaders is significantly constrained by membership in the European Union. Nevertheless, key elements of the Republic's economic successes are directly attributable to conscious planning and policy decisions by the Irish leadership class.

Changing values

As Niamh Hardiman and Christopher Whelan made clear in Chapter 4, the processes of modernisation do not produce a linear pattern of development among countries. Their chapter demonstrates the unique pattern of value change that has emerged in Ireland, a 'value pluralism' of traditional and modern attitudes that makes Ireland increasingly similar to other European nations along some dimensions while retaining distinctive features emanating from its cultural past.

One of the most dramatic changes has been the decline in support for the Catholic Church and its teachings. Secularisation has proceeded unevenly and incompletely along several fronts, diminishing traditional values of deference toward the Church, especially among the young and educated sectors of society. Indicators of this change include declining church attendance and more liberal attitudes on such issues as premarital sex. Among the most important indicators of change was the referendum on divorce of 1995 (that just barely passed) as well as somewhat more liberal attitudes on abortion, in limited instances, as indicated by polls and the referendum of 1995. Declining support for the Catholic Church is also reflected by polls which show an erosion of confidence in the Church, especially on matters other than spiritual issues, although support for the Church is higher than for other institutions such as the Dáil.

These changes help explain the declining role of the Catholic Church as a direct participant in the political process, although the Church was never involved in most governmental affairs. The removal in 1972 of the symbolic 'Special Position' of the Catholic Church clause of the Irish Constitution mirrors the altered role of the Church in Irish society. No longer routinely consulted even on sensitive issues, the Church has taken a role more typical of institutionalised religion in other democracies. Church leaders and politicians continue to respect one another's power and influence in their respective spheres, but the politicians have clearly gained greater autonomy.

The increase in secular attitudes and behaviour in Ireland has several causes. Modernisation that produced a large, educated middle class has been one factor. Perhaps in part due to reduced self-esteem and social isolation, the unemployed also attend church less frequently (Hornsby-Smith and Whelan 1994: 43). The modern mass media also tends to present more liberal attitudes. Unfortunately, respect for the Catholic Church also declined because of highly publicised scandals such as the sexual abuse of children by a small number of religious, and the Church hierarchy's mishandling of the problem.

Yet secularisation is far from complete. Although the level of attendance at church services has dropped, it still remains quite high by international standards. Several studies, including Chapter 4 in this volume, show that Irish men and women remain religious and continue to hold the Catholic Church in high regard. (MacGréil 1996: Chapter 6). It should also be noted that adherence to authoritarian values remains at higher levels than the rest of Europe, according to results of the 1990 European Values Survey. Analysis of these findings also suggests that authoritarian values are weaker among the young and more highly educated (Hardiman and Whelan 1994: 126–7).

John Coakley (Chapter 5) depicts an important transition in values of national identity among the small Protestant population of the Republic. Although they did not hold attitudes identical with those of Northern Protestants, most members of this ethnic group, constituting about 10 per cent of the population in 1910, had a British sense of identity and were hostile to Irish nationalism. By 1926, the Protestant population had declined by one-third as a result of the struggle for Irish independence and its aftermath. The emigration of Protestant military and civil-service personnel accounts for part of this decline. It can be further noted that government policies regarded by Protestants as excessively supportive of the Catholic and Gaelic culture also contributed to their sense of alienation. Coakley notes several causes for the continued decline of the Protestant community, such as a low birth rate and high levels of intermarriage, where children were typically raised as Catholics.

Protestants did not form a distinct political force in the new Irish state owing to a variety of circumstances, including their relatively small numbers and the nature of the electoral system. Coakley describes several processes by which Protestants have come to identify with the Irish state. He notes that since the 1950s, social separation in social clubs and other organisations has declined. He emphasises the contemporary ecumenical attitudes of the Catholic Church and the increasingly secular nature of Irish society and government policies. Today, Protestants identify with the Irish state and are on the whole accepted by Catholics, who see Protestants as essentially like themselves (MacGréil 1996: chapters 3, 7).

The changing role of women

In Chapter 6, Yvonne Galligan showed that women have made significant strides in acquiring a broader role in Irish society. Among the most important changes has been the dramatic increase in women in the workplace, including married women and mothers. Between 1971 and 1996 the percentage of women in the workplace increased from 26 to 38 per cent. The number of women in politics has also grown. For example, three women were members of the Dáil in 1969 compared with 20 in 1997, and representation has also increased on local politics and state boards.

Of particular importance has been the development of women's organisations lobbying for policy positions of interest to women. The National Women's Council of Ireland is viewed by the Irish government as the official representative of women's interests, and other women's organisations work toward specific goals, such as equality in family law. Yvonne Galligan, as well as Brigid Laffan and Rory O'Donnell (Chapter 9), note the importance of EU guidelines in the development of equal employment legislation and the establishment of the Employment Equality Agency.

On the other hand, the movement of women into positions of economic and political leadership is still disproportionate to their numbers in society as a whole. Galligan notes the conservative attitudes of some political parties as well as the disadvantages of time constraints women face in their roles as home-makers and mothers. Although attitudes on women's employment have become more liberal and are consistent with those in other European nations, there is still a perception among many that women's employment impacts negatively on children (Whelan and Fahey: 50–2). As Galligan explains, traditional attitudes among both women and men serve to limit the full participation of women in Irish society. Women, for example, have less confidence about their ability to influence politics. In short, attitudes toward women's roles are complex, but they have clearly become much more liberal in recent decades, with younger, more educated citizens holding more egalitarian views. Although the electoral outcomes were the result of complex events and motivations, the elections first of Mary Robinson and then of Mary McAleese to the presidency of the Republic are dramatic illustration of changing attitudes toward women.

Changing political processes and institutions

The broad institutional characteristics of the Irish political system remain fundamentally unchanged. Ireland is a parliamentary democracy with power concentrated in the office of the Taoiseach and cabinet which interact closely with government administrators in developing policy. To an unusual degree Ireland has relatively weak local governments, placing even further power in the hands of the country's political and administrative leadership. Yet there have been significant modifications in the processes by which some key decisions are made as well as significant changes in the composition of interest-group activity.

The declining political role of the Catholic Church has already been noted. Of great importance has been the development of a corporatist style of decision making on key economic decisions such as wage levels. These centralised pay agreements have been an important element in Ireland's ability to gain control of inflation as well as its capacity to avoid labour unrest. Niamh Hardiman in Chapter 7, however, points out that not all groups have equal influence in this process. Even though public opinion supports reducing the income gap between the highest and lowest income levels, the privileged groups appear to retain a strong advantage in the policy-making process. Local community and activist organisations operating in the interests of the poor and unemployed lack the organisational and other resources of groups such as business and powerful sectors of the labour movement. Also, agencies of the Catholic Church that take a strong position as advocates of the poor and disadvantaged now have less access and influence than they did earlier.

Although overall unemployment levels have declined to below 10 per cent, a figure under the EU average, long-term unemployment remains high. Ireland also has unusually high levels of income inequality, with poverty remaining higher than in most European countries. Despite reforms of the tax system, the burden of taxation continues to fall disproportionally on the middle- and lower-income groups. Among the causes of high levels of inequality, long-term unemployment and poverty are electoral and administrative processes. Politicians tend to discount poor voters and areas because of lower voter turnout, and political campaign contributions may have increased the influence of business interests. The Electoral Reform Act 1997 is a positive development in this regard. Yet the ad hoc, incremental nature of the policy-making process in Ireland makes a strong and expensive attack on the underlying causes of these inequities, such as unequal access to quality education, more difficult to resolve. In brief, Ireland has had impressive economic growth from which many have benefited, but significant problems of poverty, long-term unemployment and disparities in income as well as tax burdens continue to be a major challenge.

It should be noted that the Irish government has established numerous government programmes and organisations to further the goal of economic development. The Industrial Development Authority has been a particularly important organisation for encouraging investment. As Haughton pointed out, numerous other state-owned enterprises have, for the most part, performed effectively, contributing in many ways to the development of the Irish economy. One final change in institutional processes should be noted. Formal credentials have become much more important in determining one's chances for career success in the Irish Republic. Leaving certificate scores determine a student's access to university places, and credential-based employment decisions are now firmly established (Breen *et al.* 1990: 139). A personal style and emphasis on networking still characterise the Irish way of doing things in politics, administration and business, but formal standards and rules have become increasingly important as Ireland's economy and society has continued to modernise.

Internationalization

The international development with the most profound impact on the politics of Ireland has been Irish membership in the European Union. The Irish economy has benefited in many ways from EU membership. Funding from the EU has supported economic and social development projects, and access to the large EU market has been an important part of diminished dependence on Britain. As Brigid Laffan and Rory O'Donnell point out in Chapter 9, the implementation of Ireland's overall strategy of internationalisation was marked by great disruption and loss of direction, evidenced by the economic difficulties of the 1980s. But the rapid economic growth of the early 1990s demonstrates that the Republic has learned how to manage internationalisation effectively. EU policies have mandated progressive measures in such areas as employment safety and have had a significant impact on the details of domestic regulations.

Additionally, the institutions and processes of government in the Republic have been modified by EU membership. Members of the Irish government are assigned to or travel frequently to Brussels, with Irish government ministers and administrators taking an active role on EU bodies. The major concern of Irish politicians and administrators in EU affairs is to protect and promote Irish interests. The relatively small size of the Irish administrative system, however, makes this a formidable task. Not all issues can be monitored completely, and representatives of the Republic must prioritise carefully in order to be effective. As a small nation, the Irish Republic has little independent impact upon the overall European economy, and will be powerfully constrained by the probable adoption of a common currency and further coordination of foreign and judicial affairs. Yet it has been effective in spheres it considers vital and has built a reputation for effectiveness in such areas as managing well its Presidencies of the Council.

There is an unusually strong sense of pride in their country among Irish citizens, and especially among the more educated sectors of society the shift has been more from local to national identity rather than identity toward Europe (Hardiman and Whelan 1994: 130–2). Yet the analysis by Laffan and O'Donnell demonstrates that a strong sense of Irishness is compatible with multiple identities, including an increasing sense of being European. Another growing embodiment of this multi-faceted and changing identity is a renewed emphasis upon the Irish diaspora and the link with people of Irish heritage in many countries. Irish-American businessmen and women, for example, have been an important source of investment in the Irish economy, while American politicians played an important role in backing the peace process in Northern Ireland.

Continuity and change in Northern Ireland

The defining characteristic of Northern Irish society is the deep social and political cleavage between the Protestant and Catholic communities. With a majority of two-thirds of the population at the founding of the Northern Irish political system, unionists were able to politically dominate the provincial government. Control of the political system was seen as a vehicle for defending unionism against nationalist desires for unification as well as a means to preserve economic advantage. The Northern Ireland civil rights movement of the 1960s emerged primarily as a reaction to inequalities under the Stormont government and sought equality for nationalists within the system.

Jonathan Haughton (Chapter 2), as well as Joseph Ruane and Jennifer Todd (Chapter 10), describe key economic characteristics of Northern Ireland that have important political implications. Although its per capita GDP is now lower than the level in the Republic, Northern Ireland does register higher on certain measures of economic well-being. Nevertheless, it confronts significant economic difficulties and limitations. It is heavily dependent upon subsidies from the British government that in 1993–4 constituted 24 per cent of its GDP. This dependence strengthens unionist resolve to stay tied to the United Kingdom and weakens the desire of nationalists for unification between the Republic and Northern Ireland. As the government of the Republic does not have the resources to support the Northern Irish economy, both groups would face a decline in their standard of living if Ireland were united. Northern Ireland has witnessed a significant decline in its traditional industries such as shipbuilding, to the particular detriment of the Protestant working class. To some extent a thriving security industry has created opportunity for Protestant workers, but both the dependence on UK subsidies and jobs in the security industry add to unionist fears of a united Ireland. Although significant gains in Catholic employment and upward mobility have been made, Catholics face higher unemployment rates than Protestants, and some employment gains have been offset by population growth and reduced levels of emigration. Unemployment among Catholic males is twice that of Protestant men.

Ruane and Todd note a trend toward secularisation in Northern Ireland. For example, in 1991 a third of the population seldom attended Church. This cultural secularisation is echoed in a shift in ideological emphasis in the political parties toward more moderate positions on religious and ethnic issues. The Progressive Unionist Party and Ulster Democratic Party, representing militant loyalism, have shifted from religious symbols to secular and socialist views. The SDLP has emphasised pluralism and the need to respect the interests and identities of both communities, an approach mirroring contemporary nationalism in the Republic. In recent years, Sinn Féin has recognised the need to win the support of both communities for any settlement. Pluralist themes have also become more important in the thinking of unionist intellectuals (Porter 1996).

A more secular Republic of Ireland might appear to be less threatening to unionists concerned about possible loss of their culture and liberty within a traditional Catholic state. Yet being a part of the United Kingdom for most unionists represents an important part of their identity. Neither secularisation within the Republic nor more modern ideological views in Northern Ireland appear to have resulted in less polarisation on party preference or constitutional position. Indeed, Ruane and Todd argue that these more modern ideas within unionism and nationalism are equally powerful in opposing the goals of the other side.

The struggles of the 1970s and 1980s were marked by reforms, harsh security measures, and violence involving both republican and loyalist groups. A major attempt at a political solution during this period was the short-lived power-sharing government that was brought down in 1974 by a loyalist workers' strike. Partly in frustration at British failure to support more strongly the power-sharing government, John Hume and the Social Democratic and Labour Party (SDLP) turned increasingly to the United States and the Republic of Ireland to gain support. The role of the Republic has been especially crucial in altering the dynamics of power in the conflict. Working closely with successive Irish governments, the SDLP has acquired the concerned and active assistance of an increasingly respected country in advancing the moderate nationalist cause, including the effort to find a peaceful resolution to the conflict.

The Anglo-Irish Agreement of 1985 was a major innovation that gave the Republic a consultative role and real voice in Northern affairs. The increasing power for the minority community represented by this Agreement as well as the symbolically significant involvement of the Republic in Northern Ireland was one of the forces encouraging a more moderate approach by republican leaders. Rejected by unionists, the Anglo-Irish Agreement nevertheless laid the groundwork for the development of a more comprehensive peace process in which unionists could seek a return to having a direct voice in Northern Irish politics. As Adrian Guelke pointed out in Chapter 11, the AIA also provided a stable institutional basis for cooperation between the British and Irish governments on the issue of Northern Ireland. It thus facilitated the Agreement reached on 10 April 1998.

In his analysis of the international aspects of the conflict, Guelke described several important aspects of American involvement. Support for the republican movement came from organisations such as Irish Northern Aid (NORAID). But the main American thrust has favoured peaceful constitutional resolution of the conflict. Irish-American politicians, influenced themselves by members of the Irish government and the SDLP, placed increasingly successful pressure on the executive branch to support the cause of reform in behalf of moderate Irish nationalism. Democratic presidents were particularly susceptible to this influence, and pressure by the United States government on the British government increased, especially after the end of the Cold War. In the late 1990s, positive cooperation among the British, Irish and American governments has been an important contribution to the peace processes.

The three strands of the Agreement reached in the talks process include a democratic assembly for Northern Ireland, a North–South Ministerial Council as well as a British–Irish Council to be composed of representatives of the British and Irish governments as well as the devolved legislative bodies of Northern Ireland, Scotland and Wales. Among the most contentious of the issues have been the composition and powers of the devolved assembly for Northern Ireland and the powers of North–South institutions. As Ruane and Todd demonstrate, the room for manoeuvre of the Northern Irish participants has been highly constrained. The more moderate politicians face a continuing threat of losing support to more extreme elements.

Ruane and Todd note that each of the parties has been concerned not solely with their interests but with sources of power that protect and enhance those interests. Thus, the loss of the majority-rule principle for many unionists means losing the ability to protect their cultural and political heritage. North–South links to the SDLP are a means of protecting the vital interests and cultural aspirations of the nationalist community and for Sinn Féin an interim step toward eventual unification.

Adrian Guelke points out that one of the limitations of the peace process is that much of the impetus for a settlement has come from outside Northern Ireland, and not all groups in the North are equally committed to the need for significant change. With paramilitary groups on each side capable of resorting to violence, the leaders of the United Kingdom and Irish governments and other international participants cannot compel change. But the two sovereign governments have the power and resources to set parameters, offer inducements and encourage concessions. The Agreement reached on 10 April 1998 illustrates the importance of this kind of leadership. Few would predict with confidence the long-term outcome, yet the potential for the development of viable political institutions, whether during this or some future phase of the peace process, is perhaps greater than at any time since the 1960s.

Change and challenge

From the standpoint of the conceptual framework employed by William Crotty in his introductory chapter, the Republic of Ireland has made significant progress since 1959. It has achieved greater economic self-sufficiency and higher levels of economic well-being for its citizens. 'Civil society', the infrastructure of groups and organisations enhancing, among other things, political representation, has been broadened to include such groups as women's organisations and community organisations representing the poor. Under the category of 'pluralism, tolerance and religious freedom', the right of citizens to obtain a divorce and the removal of the symbolic 'special position' constitutional clause concerning the Catholic Church illustrate movement in this direction. From the standpoint of 'national autonomy, territorial integrity and political independence' it can be noted that, owing mainly to membership in the EU, the Republic of Ireland has acquired much greater independence from the British economy and has learned to manage internationalisation well.

Of course, progress has been uneven and incomplete in all of these areas, and there are many Irish democrats who argue that much of this change has negative implications or has come at too high a price. Change inevitably produces some degree of alienation among those holding traditional values. The intensity of resistance by some is understandable considering their strong convictions against matters such as divorce and abortion, and in democracies it is right and proper that individuals on all sides freely express and work toward their goals. Both the advocates of change and the proponents of tradition support the political system and the processes of democracy. Although the differing interpretation of change as 'progress or decline' is likely to produce additional conflict in the future, such conflict will almost certainly be within the confines of democratic norms.

The major challenge for the people of Ireland as a whole, of course, is to achieve a workable resolution to violence in the North, however evolutionary such progress might have to be. Given the polarisation of the northern communities and the technological ease by which fringe groups can mount violent attacks, the long-term outlook must remain uncertain. A resolution will not be achieved until competition between the unionist and nationalist communities of Northern Ireland becomes institutionalised within the framework of democratic processes and structures that function effectively over time. For the Republic of Ireland there may be no greater or more important challenge than the need to help resolve the violent conflict in the North, however halting and incomplete that process might have to be. Among other things, deflected attention from economic and social problems and the loss of time and energy in political, administrative and judicial systems all impede the capacity of the state to perform effectively.

In summation, the Republic of Ireland has undergone substantial change since 1959. The lives of most of its citizens have improved in a material sense, and Irish men and women have a strong and justifiable pride in their country. Educational opportunities have improved dramatically, and there is greater tolerance for the range of opinion and belief characteristic of a modern society. The Republic is more independent economically of the United Kingdom and has become an economic success story of the late twentieth century. Much of this development has been the result of imaginative planning by the country's political, administrative, economic and intellectual elites. Coupled with the energetic participation of Irish citizens, these strategies have produced remarkable growth.

Yet much of this change has also been the result of processes of globalisation and world-wide economic interdependence. That the Republic of Ireland has embraced internationalism enthusiastically has given it a distinct advantage in the competitive world arena. The decision to join the European Union resulted not only in significant funding for some of its developmental efforts but, more importantly, gave Ireland economic access to a powerful economic union that has altered the structure of international economics. By improving educational opportunity and by aggressively seeking investment for its economic development, the Republic of Ireland has positioned itself to benefit from continued fast-paced technological change. To be sure, significant problems and inequities remain, and new difficulties will inevitably arise. Furthermore, many economic forces determining the Republic's fate are beyond its control. Yet the dramatic successes of the Republic thus far suggest that it has a strong potential to manage change effectively well into the twenty-first century.

Select bibliography

Adams, Gerry (1995) *Free Ireland: Towards A Lasting Peace* (Dingle: Brandon).

Adams, Gerry (1997) *Selected Writings* (Dingle: Brandon).

ADM (1997) *Partnerships: Making a Difference in People's Lives: A Report on Progress Up To December 1996* (Dublin: ADM).

Akenson, Donald Harman (1991) *Small Differences: Irish Catholics and Irish Protestants, 1815–1922: an international perspective* (Dublin: Gill and Macmillan).

Allardt, Erik, and Starck, Christian (1981) *Språkgränser och samhällsstruktur: Finlands-svenskarna i ett jämförande perspektiv* (Stockholm: Almqvist & Wiksell).

Almond, Gabriel A. and Sidney Verba (1965) *The Civic Culture* (Boston: Little, Brown).

Almond, Gabriel A. and Sidney Verba (eds) (1989) *The Civic Culture Revisited* (Newbury Park, CA: Sage).

Andrews C. S. (1982) *Man of No Property* (Dublin and Cork: Mercier).

At the Crossroads: Human Rights and the Northern Ireland Peace Process (1996) (New York: Lawyers Committee for Human Rights).

Atkinson, A. B. 1997. 'Poverty in Ireland and anti-poverty strategy: a European perspective', in Alan W. Gray (ed.) *International Perspectives on the Irish Economy* (Dublin: Indecon Economic Consultants).

Atkinson, A. B. and G. V. Mogensen (eds) (1993) *Welfare and Work Incentives: a North European Perspective* (Oxford: Clarendon Press).

Atkinson, A. B., L. Rainwater and T. M. Smeeding (1995) *Income Distribution in OECD Countries: Evidence from the Luxembourg Income Study* (Paris: OECD).

Aughey, Arthur (1989) *Under Siege: Ulster Unionism and the Anglo-Irish Agreement* (Belfast: Blackstaff).

Bardon, Jonathon (1992) *A History of Ulster* (Belfast: Blackstaff).

Barrett, Alan, Tim Callan and Brian Nolan (1997) *The Earnings Distribution and Returns to Education in Ireland, 1987–1994* (London: Centre for Economic Policy Research, Discussion Paper No. 1679).

Bax, Mart (1970) 'Patronage Irish Style: Irish Politicians and Brokers', *Sociologische Gids*, 17, pp. 179–91.

Beckett, J. C. (1976) *The Anglo-Irish Tradition* (London: Faber).

Bendix, R. (1967) 'Tradition and modernity reconsidered', *Comparative Studies in Society and History*, Vol. 9, pp. 292–346.

Beresford, David (1987) *Ten Men Dead* (London: HarperCollins).

Berger, P. (1973) *The Social Reality of Religion* (Harmondsworth: Penguin).

Bew, Paul and Gordon Gillespie (1996) *The Northern Ireland Peace Process 1993–1996: A Chronology* (London: Serif).

Bew, Paul, Peter Gibbon and Henry Patterson (1996) *Northern Ireland 1921–1996: Political Forces and Social Classes* (London: Serif).

Biever, B. F. (1976) *Religion, Culture and Values: a Cross-Cultural Analysis of Motivational Factors in Native Irish and American Irish Catholicism* (New York: Arno Press).

Biggs-Davison, John, and George Chowdharay-Best (1984) *The Cross of St Patrick: The Catholic Unionist Tradition in Ireland* (Bourne End: Kensal Press).

Blanshard, Paul (1954) *The Irish and Catholic Power* (London: Derek Verschoyle).

Blaschke, Jochen (ed.) (1980) *Handbuch der europäischen Volksgruppen* (Frankfurt-am-Main: Syndikat).

Block, F. (1990) 'Political choice and the multiple "logics" of capital', in S. Zukin and P. DiMaggio (eds) *Structures of Capital: the Social Organization of the Economy* (Cambridge: Cambridge University Press).

Bowen, Desmond (1995) *History and the Shaping of Irish Protestantism* (New York: Peter Lane).

Bowen, Kurt (1983) *Protestants in a Catholic State: Ireland's Privileged Minority* (Toronto: McGill-Queen's University Press).

Boyce, D. G. (1996) *The Irish Question and British Politics, 1868–1996* (second edition) (London: Macmillan).

Boyle, Kevin and Tom Hadden (1994) *Northern Ireland: The Choice* (Harmondsworth: Penguin Books).

Breen, Richard and Christopher Whelan (1993) 'From ascription to achievement? Origins, education, and entry to the labour force in the Republic of Ireland during the twentieth century'. *Acta Sociologica*. 36, pp. 3–17.

Breen, Richard and Christopher Whelan (1996) *Resources, Deprivation and Poverty* (Oxford: Clarendon Press).

Breen, R., A. Heath and C. T. Whelan (forthcoming), 'Educational inequality in Northern Ireland and the Republic of Ireland', in R. Breen, A. Heath and C. T. Whelan, *Ireland, North and South* (Oxford: Oxford University Press).

Breen, R., D. F. Hannan and R. O'Leary (1995) 'Returns to education: taking account of employers' perceptions and use of educational credentials', *European Sociological Review* 11, 1.

Breen, Richard and Christopher T. Whelan (1996) *Social Mobility and Social Class in Ireland* (Dublin: Gill and Macmillan).

Breen, Richard, (1996) 'Who wants a United Ireland? Constitutional preferences among Catholics and Protestants' in R. Breen, P. Devine and L. Dowds (eds), *Social Attitudes in Northern Ireland: The fifth report* (Belfast: Appletree) pp. 33–48.

Breen, Richard, Damian F. Hannan, David B. Rottman and Christopher T. Whelan (1990) *Understanding Contemporary Ireland: State, Class and Development in the Republic of Ireland* (Dublin: Gill and Macmillan).

Breen, Richard, Damien Hannan, David Rottmann and Christopher T. Whelan (1990) *Understanding Contemporary Ireland: State, Class and Development in the Republic of Ireland* (London: Macmillan).

Brown, Alice and Yvonne Galligan (1998) 'Why so few seats in parliament for Irish and Scottish women: what women say', *Comparative Politics* (forthcoming).

Brown, Terence (1985) *Ireland: A Social and Cultural History 1922–1985* (London: Fontana Press/HarperCollins).

Bruce, Steve (1994) *The Edge of the Union: The Ulster Loyalist Political Vision* (Oxford: Oxford University Press).

Bruce, Steve and Fiona Alderdice (1993) 'Religious belief and behaviour', in P. Stringer and G. Robinson (eds) *Social Attitudes in Northern Ireland: The third report* (Belfast: Blackstaff) pp. 5–20.

Buckland, Patrick (1972) *Irish Unionism 1: the Anglo-Irish and the New Ireland, 1885–1922* (Dublin: Gill and Macmillan).

Buckland, Patrick (1981) *A History of Northern Ireland* (Dublin: Gill and Macmillan).

Cairns, E. (1991) 'Is Northern Ireland a conservative society?', in P. Stringer and G. Robinson (eds), *Social Attitudes in Northern Ireland. 1990–91 Edition* (Belfast: Blackstaff).

Callan T., B. Nolan, B. J. Whelan, C. T. Whelan and J. Williams (1996) *Poverty in the 1990s: Evidence from the 1994 Living in Ireland Survey* (Dublin: Oak Tree Press).

Census of Ireland (1861–1991) *Census of the Population of Ireland [Irish Free State, Eire]* (Dublin: Stationery Office).

Chubb, Basil (1992) *The Government and Politics of Ireland* (third edition) (Harlow: Longman).

Churchill, Winston S. (1941) *The Aftermath: being a sequel to The World Crisis* (London: Macmillan).

Clancy, P. (1996) *Access to College: Patterns of Continuity and Change* (Dublin: HEA).

Clark, C. and J. Healy (1997) *Pathways to a Basic Income* (Dublin: CORI Justice Commission).

Coakley, John (1980) 'Independence movements and national minorities: some parallels in the European experience', *European Journal of Political Research*, 8, pp. 215–47.

Coakley, John (1993) 'Society and political culture', in John Coakley and Michael Gallagher (eds) *Politics in the Republic of Ireland* (Dublin: Folens and PSAI Press), pp. 25–48.

Coakley, John and Michael Gallagher (1996) *1922: The Birth of Irish Democracy* (Dublin: Gill and Macmillan).

Cochrane, Feargal (1997) *Unionist Politics* (Cork: Cork University Press).

Coleman, D. A. (forthcoming) 'Demography and migration in Ireland, north and south', in R. Breen, A. Heath and C. T. Whelan, *Ireland, North and South* (Oxford: Oxford University Press).

Commission of the European Communities (1987) *Women and Men of Europe* (Brussels: Commission of the European Communities).

Commission on Taxation (1982) *First Report: Direct Taxation* (Dublin).

Commission on the Status of Women (1972) *Report to the Minister for Finance*, [Prl.2760] (Dublin: Stationery Office).

Community Platform (1997) *Achieving Social Partnership* (Dublin).

Connolly, Linda (1996) 'The women's movement in Ireland, 1970–1995: a social movement analysis', *Irish Journal of Feminist Studies*, 1:1, pp. 43–77.

Coogan, Tim Pat (1987) *Disillusioned Decades: Ireland 1966–87* (Dublin: Gill and Macmillan).

Coogan, Tim Pat (1995) *The IRA* (revised edn) (London: HarperCollins).

Coogan, Tim Pat (1997a) *On the Blanket* (Boulder: Roberts Rinehart).

Coogan, Tim Pat (1997b) *The Troubles* (Boulder: Roberts Rinehart).

Cooke, Dennis (1996) *Persecuting Zeal: A Portrait of Ian Paisley* (Dingle: Brandon).

CORI (1996) *Part-Time Job Opportunities: Progress Report* (Dublin: CORI Institute for Action and Research on Work and Employment).

CORI (1997) *Planning For Progress: Tackling Poverty, Unemployment and Exclusion Socio-Economic Review* (Dublin: CORI Justice Commission).

Corish, M. (1996) 'Aspects of the secularisation of Irish society' in Eoin G. Cassidy (ed.) *Faith and Culture in the Irish Context* (Dublin: Veritas Publications).

Cormack, R. J., A. M. Gallagher and R. D. Osborne (1993) *Fair Enough? Religion and the 1991 population census* (Belfast: Fair Employment Commission).

Cox, B. and J. Hughes (1989) 'Industrial relations in the public sector', in T. Murphy (ed.) *Industrial Relations in Ireland* (Dublin: UCD).

Coyle, C. (1996) 'Local and regional administrative structures and rural poverty', in Curtin *et al.* (eds) *Poverty in Rural Ireland: A Political Economy Perspective* (Dublin: Oak Tree Press).

Crotty, Molly (1997) *British Policy in Northern Ireland: The Anglo-Irish Agreement of 1985* (London: London School of Economics).

Crotty, R. (1986) *Ireland in Crisis: A Study of Capitalist Colonial Underdevelopment* (Dingle: Brandon Book Publishers).

CSO (Central Statistics Office) (1995) *Population and Labour Force Projections 1996–2026* (Dublin: Stationery Office).

CSO (1996) *Census 96*, Vol. 3 (Dublin: Stationery Office).

CSO (1997a) 'Population and migration estimates, April 1997', *Statistical Release*, 29 October 1997 (Cork: Central Statistics Office).

CSO (1997b) *Statistical Release: Women in the Workforce* (Cork: Central Statistics Office) 22 September 1977.

Culliton, J. *et al.* (1992) *A Time for a Change: Industrial Policy for the 1990s* (Dublin: The Stationery Office).

Cunningham, Michael (1997) 'The political language of John Hume', *Irish Political Studies* 12, pp. 13–22.

Curtin, C., T. Haase and H. Tovey (eds) (1996) *Poverty in Rural Ireland: A Political Economy Perspective* (Dublin: Oak Tree Press).

Dahl, Robert E. (1971) *Polyarchy* (New Haven: Yale University Press).

d'Alton, Ian (1973) 'Southern Irish Unionism: a study of Cork unionists, 1884–1914, *Transactions of the Royal Historical Society* 5th series, 23, pp. 71–88.

d'Alton, Ian (1978) 'A contrast in crises; Southern Irish Protestantism 1820–43 and 1885–1910' A. C. Hepburn (ed.) *Minorities in History* (London: Edward Arnold).

d'Alton, Ian (1980) *Protestant Society and Politics in Cork* (Cork: Cork University Press).

Daly, Mary (1984) *Dublin: the Deposed Capital. A Social and Economic History 1860–1914* (Cork: Cork University Press).

Darby, John (ed.) (1983) *Northern Ireland: Background to the Conflict* (Syracuse: Syracuse University Press).

Department of Education (1995) *Charting our Education Future* (Dublin: Stationery Office).

Diamond, Larry and Marc F. Plattner (eds) (1993) *Capitalism, Socialism, and Democracy Revisited* (Baltimore: Johns Hopkins University Press).

Diamond, Larry and Marc F. Plattner (eds) (1996) *The Global Resurgence of Democracy* (second edn) (Baltimore: Johns Hopkins University Press).

Dillon, M. (1993) *Debating Divorce: Moral Conflict in Ireland* (Kentucky: University of Kentucky Press).

DiPalma, Giuseppe (1990) *To Craft Democracies* (Berkeley: University of California Press).

Dooley, Terence (1990) 'Monaghan Protestants in a time of crisis, 1919–22, in R. V. Comerford, Mary Cullen, Jacqueline R. Hill and Colm Lennon, eds, *Religion, conflict and coexistence in Ireland: essays presented to Monsignor Patrick J Corish* (Dublin: Gill and Macmillan).

Dougherty, John C. (1991) 'A Comparison of Productivity and Economic Growth in the G-7 Countries,' PhD thesis, Harvard University.

Dowd, Lizanne, Paula Devine and Richard Breen (1997) *Social Attitudes in Northern Ireland: The sixth report* (Belfast: Appletree Press).

Dowd, Lizanne and Paula Devine (1997) 'Unleashing the apathy of a lost generation? Community relations among young people in Northern Ireland' in L. Dowd, P. Devine and R. Breen (eds), *Social Attitudes in Northern Ireland: The sixth report* (Belfast: Appletree Press).

DuBois, Paul (1908) *Contemporary Ireland* (Dublin: Maunsel & Company).

Duffy, Mary and Geoffrey Evans (1997) 'Class, community polarisation and politics', in L. Dowds, P. Devine and R. Breen (eds), *Social Attitudes in Northern Ireland: The sixth report* (Belfast: Appletree Press) pp. 102–37.

Dunn, Seamus and Valerie Morgan (1994) *Protestant Alienation in Northern Ireland: A preliminary survey* (Coleraine: Centre for the Study of Conflict).

Eames, Robin (1992) *Chains to be Broken: A Personal Reflection on Northern Ireland and its People* (London: Weidenfeld and Nicolson).

Eckstein, H. (1960) *Pressure Group Politics: the Case of the British Medical Association* (London: Stanford University Press).

Economist Intelligence Unit (1997) *Ireland: Country Profile 1996–1997* (London: EIU).

EEA (Employment Equality Agency) (1995) *Women in Figures* (Dublin: EEA).

Elster, Jon and Rune Slagstad (eds) (1993) *Constitutionalism and Democracy* (Cambridge: Cambridge University Press).

EOCNI (Equal Opportunities Commission for Northern Ireland) (1993) *Where do Women Figure?* (Belfast: Equal Opportunities Commission for Northern Ireland).

EOCNI (Equal Opportunities Commission for Northern Ireland) (1996) *Women and Men in Northern Ireland* (Belfast: Equal Opportunities Commission for Northern Ireland).

European Commission (1996) *The Economic and Financial Situation in Ireland: Ireland in the Transition to EMU* (Brussels: ECSC-EC-EAEC).

Evans, Geoffrey and Brendan O'Leary (1997) 'Frameworked futures: Intransigence and flexibility in the Northern Ireland elections of May 30 1996', *Irish Political Studies* 12, pp. 23–47.

Evans, Geoffrey and Mary Duffy (1997) 'Beyond the sectarian divide: the social bases and political consequences of unionist and nationalist party competition in Northern Ireland', *British Journal of Political Science*, 27, pp. 47–81.

Evans, P. and T. D. Stephens (1988) 'Development and the world economy', in N. Smelser (ed.) *Handbook of Sociology* (London: Sage).

Fahey, Tony (1994) 'Catholicism and Industrial Society in Ireland', in J. H. Goldthorpe and C. T. Whelan (eds), *The Development of Industrial Society in Ireland* (Oxford: Oxford University Press) pp. 241–64.

Fahey, Tony (forthcoming) 'Religion and sexual culture in Ireland', in L. Hall, G. Hekma and F. Eder (eds), *Sexual Cultures in Europe: Volume II, Studies in Sexuality* (Manchester: Manchester University Press).

Fahey, Tony, and John FitzGerald (1997) *Welfare Implications of Demographic Trends* (Dublin: Oak Tree Press).

Fahey, T. and M. Lyons (1995), *Marital Breakdown and Family Law in Ireland: A Sociological Study* (Dublin: Oak Tree Press).

Fair, Ray C. (1978) 'The effect of economic events on votes for President', *Review of Economics and Statistics*, 60, pp. 159–73.

Fair, Ray C. (1996) 'Econometrics and presidential Elections', *Journal of Economic Perspectives*, 10 (3), pp. 89–102.

Fawcett, Liz (1992) 'The recruitment of women to local politics in Ireland: a case study', *Irish Political Studies*, 7, pp. 41–55.

FEC (Fair Employment Commission) (1995) *A Profile of the Northern Ireland Workforce. Summary of the 1994 Monitoring Returns* (Belfast: Fair Employment Commission).

FEC (Fair Employment Commission), E. E. Davis and R. Sinnott (1979) *Attitudes in the Republic of Ireland Relevant to the Northern Ireland Problem* (Dublin: Economic and Social Research Institute).

Feingold, W. F. (1975) 'The tenants' movement to capture the Irish poor law boards, 1877–1886', *Albion*, 7 pp. 216–31.

Finance, Department of (1997) *Economic Review and Outlook* (Dublin: Government of Ireland).

FitzGerald, G. (1992) *All in A Life* (Dublin: Gill and Macmillan).

Fitzsimons, Yvonne (1991) 'Women's interest representation in the Republic of Ireland: the Council for the Status of Women', *Irish Political Studies* 6, pp. 37–52.

Ford, Alan, James McGuire and Kenneth Milne (eds) (1995) *As by Law Established: the Church of Ireland Since the Reformation* (Dublin: Lilliput Press).

Foreign Affairs, Department of (1996) *Challenges and Opportunities Abroad: White Paper on Foreign Policy* (Dublin: Government of Ireland).

Forfás (1996) *Shaping Our Future. A Strategy for Enterprise in Ireland in the 21st Century* (Dublin: Forfás).

Foster, Charles R. (ed.) (1980) *Nations Without a State: Ethnic Minorities in Western Europe* (New York, NY: Praeger).

Gaffikin, Frank and Mike Morrissey (1990) *Northern Ireland: The Thatcher Years* (London: Zed Books).

Gallagher, A. M., R. D. Osborne and R. J. Cormack (1995) *Fair Shares? Employment, Unemployment and Economic Status* (Belfast: Fair Employment Commission).

Gallagher, M. and M. Laver (eds) (1993) *How Ireland Voted 1992* (Dublin: Folens/PSAI Press).

Galligan, Yvonne (1993) 'Women in Irish Politics' in John Coakley and Michael Gallagher (eds) *Politics in the Republic of Ireland* (second edition) (Dublin: Folens/PSAI Press) pp. 207–26.

Galligan, Yvonne (1993) 'Gender and party politics in Ireland' in Pippa Norris and Joni Lovenduski (eds) *Gender and Party Politics* (London: Sage).

Galligan, Yvonne (1997) 'Implementing the Beijing Commitments in Ireland.' Paper prepared for presentation at the 17th World Congress of the International Political Science Association, Seoul, 17–21 August 1997.

Galligan, Yvonne (1998) *Women and Contemporary Politics in Ireland: from the Margins to the Mainstream* (London: Cassell).

Galligan, Yvonne and Rick Wilford (1998a) 'Women's political representation' in Yvonne Galligan, Eilís Ward and Rick Wilford (eds) *Contesting Politics: Women in Ireland, North and South* (Boulder, Co: Westview Press).

Galligan, Yvonne and Rick Wilford (1998b) 'Gender and party politics in the Republic of Ireland' in Yvonne Galligan, Eilís Ward and Rick Wilford (eds) *Contesting Politics: Women in Ireland, North and South* (Boulder, Co: Westview Press).

Gardiner, Frances (1992) 'Political interest and participation of Irish women 1022–1992: the unfinished revolution', *Canadian Journal of Irish Studies*, 18:1, pp. 15–39.

Gardiner, Frances (1993) 'Women in the election' in Michael Gallagher and Michael Laver (eds) *How Ireland Voted 1992* (Dublin: Folens, and Limerick: PSAI Press).

Gardiner, Frances (1998) 'Irish women in the European Union' in Yvonne Galligan, Eilís Ward and Rick Wilford (eds) *Contesting Politics: Women in Ireland, North and South* (Boulder, Co: Westview Press).

Garvan, T. (1981) *The Evolution of Nationalist Politics* (Dublin: Gill and Macmillan).

Garvin, Tom (1982) 'Change and the political system' in Frank Litton, *Unequal Achievement* (Dublin: Institute of Public Administration), pp. 21–40.

Garvin Tom (1986) 'Priests and patriots: Irish separatism and the fear of the modern, 1890–1914', *Irish Historical Studies*, XXV, No. 97 (May).

Garvin, Tom (1988) 'The politics of denial and cultural defence: the referendums of 1983 and 1986 in context', *Irish Review*, No. 3, pp. 1–7, 2–4.

Garvin, Tom (1993) 'Democratic politics in independent Ireland' in John Coakley and Michael Gallagher (eds) *Politics in the Republic of Ireland* (Dublin: Folens/PSAI Press) pp. 250–61.

Garvin, Tom (1996a) 'Hibernian endgame? Nationalism in a divided Ireland' in Richard Caplan and John Feffer, *Europe's New Nationalism* (New York and Oxford: Oxford University Press) pp. 184–94.

Garvin, Tom (1996b) *1922: The Birth of Irish Democracy* (Dublin: Gill and Macmillan).

Girvin, B. (1989) *Between Two Worlds: Politics and Economy of Industrial Society in Ireland* (Dublin: Gill and Macmillan).

Girvin, B. (1996) 'The Irish Divorce Referendum, November 1995', *Irish Political Studies*, 11, pp. 174–81.

Girvin, B. (1997) 'Political culture, political independence and economic success in Ireland', *Irish Political Studies*, Vol. 12, pp. 48–77.

Girvin, B. (forthcoming) 'Irish political culture: Between tradition and modernity' in Roger Eatwell (ed.) *European Political Culture* (London: Routledge).

Goldthorpe, J. (1994) 'The theory of industrialism and the Irish case' in J. H. Goldthorpe and C. T. Whelan (eds) *The Development of Industrial Society in Ireland* (Oxford: Oxford University Press).

Goldthorpe, J. H. and C. T. Whelan (eds) (1994) *The Development of Industrial Society in Ireland* (Oxford: Oxford University Press).

Government of Ireland (1996) *Challenges and Opportunities Abroad: White Paper on Foreign Policy* Pn.2133 (Dublin: Government Publications).

Guelke, Adrian (1996) 'The Influence of the South African Transition on the Northern Ireland Peace Process', *The South African Journal of International Affairs*, 3 (2), Winter, pp. 132–48.

Hadeneius, Axel (ed.) (1997) *Democracy's Victory and Crisis* (Cambridge: Cambridge University Press).

Haggard, Stephan and Robert B. Kaufman (1995) *The Political Economy of Democratic Transitions* (Princeton: Princeton University Press).

Hainsworth, Paul (1981) 'Northern Ireland: a European role?', *Journal of Common Market Studies*, 20 (1), September.

Hannan, D. F. and S. Ó Riain (1993) *Pathways to Adulthood in Ireland* (Dublin: Economic and Social Research Institute).

Hardiman, N. (1988) *Pay, Politics and Economic Performance in Ireland* (Oxford: Clarendon Press).

Hardiman, Niamh (1994) 'The State and Economic Interests: Ireland in Comparative Perspective' in J. H. Goldthorpe and C. T. Whelan (eds), *The Development of Industrial Society in Ireland* (Oxford: Oxford University Press) pp. 329–58.

Hardiman, Niamh and Christopher T. Whelan (1994a) 'Politics and democratic values' in Christopher T. Whelan (ed.) *Values and Social Change in Ireland* (Dublin: Gill and Macmillan) pp. 100–35.

Hardiman, Niamh and Christopher T. Whelan (1994b) 'Values and political partisanship' in Christopher Whelan (ed.) *Values and Social Change in Ireland* (Dublin: Gill and Macmillan).

Harkness, David (1996) *Ireland in the Twentieth Century: Divided Island* (London: Macmillan).

Harris. Rosemary (1972) *Prejudice and Tolerance in Ulster: A Study of Neighbors and 'Strangers' in a Border Community* (Oxford: Oxford University Press).

Hart, Peter (1996) 'The Protestant experience of revolution in southern Ireland' in Richard English and Graham Walker (eds) *Unionism in Modern Ireland: New Perspectives on Politics and Culture* (London: Macmillan).

Harvey, B. (1994) *Combating Exclusion: Lessons from the Third EU Poverty Programme in Ireland* (Dublin: Combat Poverty Agency).

Haughton, Jonathan (1995) 'The historical background' in J. W. O'Hagan (ed.) *The Economy of Ireland: Policy and Performance of a Small European Country* (London: Macmillan).

Hayes, Bernadette C. and Ian McAllister (1996) 'British and Irish public opinion towards the Northern Ireland problem', *Irish Political Studies*, 11, pp. 61–82.

Hechter, M. (1975) *Internal Colonialism: The Celtic Fringe in British National Development* (London: Routledge and Kegan Paul).

Heenan, Deirdre and Anne Marie Gray (1998) 'Women and nominated boards in Ireland' in Yvonne Galligan, Eilís Ward and Rick Wilford (eds) *Contesting Politics: Women in Ireland, North and South* (Boulder, Co: Westview Press).

Held, David (ed.) (1993) *Prospects for Democracy* (Cambridge: Polity Press).

Held, David (ed.) (1995) *Democracy and the Global Order* (Stanford: Stanford University Press).

Hinds, Bronagh (1998) 'Citizenship and constitutional change in Northern Ireland' in Yvonne Galligan, Eilís Ward and Rick Wilford (eds) *Contesting Politics: Women in Ireland, North and South* (Boulder, Co: Westview Press).

Hirst, P. and Thompson, G. (1992) 'The problem of globalisation: international economic relations, national economic management and the formation of trading blocks', *Economy and Society*, vol. 21, 4, November, pp. 357–96.

Hoppen, K. Theodore (1984) *Elections, Politics and Society in Ireland 1832–1885* (Oxford: Clarendon Press).

Hornsby-Smith, Michael P. and Christopher T. Whelan (1994) 'Religious and moral values' in Christopher T. Whelan (ed.) *Values and Social Change in Ireland* (Dublin: Gill and Macmillan) pp. 7–44.

Hornsby-Smith, Michael P. (1994) 'Social and religious transformation in Ireland: a case of secularisation? in J. H. Goldthorpe and C. T. Whelan (eds) *The Development of Industrial Society in Ireland* (Oxford: Oxford University Press) pp. 265–90.

House of Commons (1884) *Return for each county, city and borough in Ireland, of the names of the persons holding the commission of the peace* . . . (London: HMSO [*British parliamentary papers* 1884 (13) vol. 63]).

House of Commons (1910) *Return showing the names, addresses and occupations of the persons appointed to the commission of the peace in Ireland* . . . (London: HMSO [*British parliamentary papers* 1910 (182.) vol. 76]).

Hume, John (1996) *A New Ireland* (Boulder: Roberts Rinehart).

Hurley, Michael (ed.) (1970) *Irish Anglicanism, 1869–1969: Essays on the Role of Anglicanism in Irish life* (Dublin: Figgis).

Hussey, Gemima (1995) *Ireland Today* (London: Penguin Books).

Inglis, Brian (1962) *West Briton* (London: Faber and Faber).

Inglis, T. (1987) *Moral Monopoly: The Catholic Church in Modern Irish Society* (Dublin: Gill and Macmillan).

Inkeles, Alex (ed.) (1991) *On Measuring Democracy* (New Brunswick: Transaction Publishers).

Institute of Social Studies Advisory Service (1990) *Poverty in Figures: Europe in the Early 1980s* (Luxembourg: Office for Official Publications of the European Communities).

International Monetary Fund, Various issues (Washington DC: International Financial Statistics).

Ireland: Central Statistics Office (1995) *Statistical Abstract* (Dublin: Stationery Office).

Ireland: Central Statistics Office (1996) *National Income and Expenditure 1995* (Dublin: Stationery Office).

Ireland: Department of Finance (1997 and previous issues) *Economic Review and Outlook* (Dublin: Stationery Office).

Jackson, Harold (1971) *The Two Irelands: A Dual Study of Inter-group Tensions* (London: Minority Rights Group).

Jacobsen, J. K. (1994) *Chasing Progress in the Republic of Ireland: Ideology, Democracy, and Dependent Development* (Cambridge: Cambridge University Press).

Jardine, E. F. (1993/1994) 'Demographic structure in Northern Ireland and its implications for constitutional preference', *Journal of the Statistical and Social Inquiry Society of Ireland* XXVII, part I.

Jarman, Neil and Dominic Bryan (1996) *Parade and Protest* (Coleraine: Centre for the Study of Conflict, University of Ulster).

Jay, Richard and Rick Wilford (1991) 'Fair employment in Northern Ireland: A new initiative', *Irish Political Studies* 6, pp. 15–36.

Jennings, Anthony (ed.) (1990) *Justice Under Fire: The Abuse of Civil Liberties in Northern Ireland* (London: Pluto Press).

Keatinge, Patrick and Brigid Laffan (1993) 'Ireland in international affairs' in John Coakley and Michael Gallagher (eds) *Politics in the Republic of Ireland* (Dublin: Folens/PSAI Press) pp. 227–49.

Kellaghan, Thomas, Susan Weir, Séamus O'Huallacháin and Mark Morgan (1995) *Educational Disadvantage in Ireland* (Dublin: Department of Education and Combat Poverty Agency).

Kelleher, John V. (1957) 'Ireland: and where does she stand?' *Foreign Affairs* 35, pp. 485–95.

Kennedy, F. (1989) *Family, Economy and Government in Ireland* (Dublin: The Economic and Social Research Institute).

Kennedy, K., T. Giblin and D. McHugh (1988) *The Economic Development of Ireland in the Twentieth Century* (London: Routledge).

Kennedy, Kieran A. (1992) 'The context of economic development' in J. H. Goldthorpe and C. T. Whelan (eds), *The Development of Industrial Society in Ireland* (Oxford: Oxford University Press).

Kennedy, Liam (1994) *People and Population Change. A Comparative Study of Population Change in Northern Ireland and the Republic of Ireland* (Belfast and Dublin: Cooperation North).

Kennelly, Brendan and Eilís Ward (1993) 'The abortion referendums' in Michael Gallagher and Michael Laver (eds) *How Ireland Voted 1992* (Dublin: Folens and Limerick: PSAI Press).

Kenny, Mary (1997) *Goodbye to Catholic Ireland* (London: Sinclair-Stevenson).

Kenworthy, L. (1996) *In Search of National Economic Success: Balancing Competition and Cooperation* (London: Sage).

Keogh, Dermot (1996) 'The role of the Catholic Church in the Republic of Ireland 1922–1995' in *Building Trust in Ireland* (Belfast: Blackstaff Press) pp. 85–214.

Keogh, Dermot and Michael H. Haltzel (eds) (1994) *Northern Ireland and the Politics of Reconciliation* (Cambridge: Cambridge University Press).

Kiberd, D. (1995) *Inventing Ireland: The Literature of the Modern Nation* (Cambridge, MA: Harvard University Press).

Kirby, P. (1984) *Is Irish Catholicism Dying?* (Cork: Mercier Press).

Korpi, W. (1996) 'Eurosclerosis and the sclerosis of objectivity. On the role of values among economic policy experts', *The Economic Journal*, 106, pp. 1727–46.

Korpi, W., and J. Palme (forthcoming) 'The paradox of redistribution and strategies of inequality: welfare state institutions, inequality and poverty in the western countries', *American Sociological Review*.

Kramer, Gerald H. (1971) 'Short-term fluctuations in US voting behavior, 1896–1964', *American Political Science Review*, 65, pp. 131–43.

Krejci, Jaroslav and Vitezslav Velimsky (1981) *Ethnic and Political Nations in Europe* (London: Croom Helm).

Laffan, B., P. Keatinge and R. O'Donnell (1991) 'Weighing up the gains and losses', in P. Keatinge (ed.) *Ireland and EC Membership Evaluated* (London: Pinter).

Laver, Michael (1994) 'Are Irish Parties Peculiar?' in J. H. Goldthorpe and C. T. Whelan (eds) *The Development of Industrial Society in Ireland* (Oxford: Oxford University Press) pp. 359–82.

Lee, J. (1989) *Ireland 1912–1985: Politics and Society* (Cambridge: Cambridge University Press).

Lee, J. J. (1968) 'Capital in the Irish Economy' in L. M. Cullen (ed.) *The Formation of the Irish Economy* (Cork: Mercier Press).

Lee, Joseph (1989) *The Modernisation of Irish Society 1848–1918* (Dublin: Gill and Macmillan).

Lehmbruch, G. (1984) 'Concertation and the structure of corporatist networks', in J. H. Goldthorpe (ed.) *Order and Conflict in Contemporary Capitalism* (Oxford: Clarendon Press).

Lipset, Seymour Martin and E. Raab (1971) *The Politics of Unreason* (London: Heinemann).

Lyons, F. S. L. (1967) 'The minority problem in the twenty six counties' in Francis MacManus (ed.) *The Years of the Great Test* (Cork: Mercier).

Lynch, K. and S. Drudy (1993) *Schools and Society in Ireland* (Dublin: Gill and Macmillan).

McAllister, Ian (1975) 'Political opposition in Northern Ireland: The National Democratic Party, 1965–1970' *Economic and Social Review*, 6.3, pp. 353–66.

McArt, Pat, Colm McKenna and Dónal Campbell (eds) (1997*) Irish Almanac and Yearbook of Facts 1998* (Burt, Co. Donegal: Artcam Publishing).

McAuley, James W. (1994) *The Politics of Identity: A Loyalist Community in Belfast* (Aldershot: Avebury).

McConville, Michael (1986) *Ascendancy to Oblivion: the Story of the Anglo-Irish* (London: Quartet Books).

McDermott, R. P. and D. A. Webb (1945) *Irish Protestantism Today and Tomorrow: a Demographic Study* (Dublin: Association for Promoting Christian Knowledge).

McDowell, R. B. (1973) *The Church of Ireland 1869–1969* (London: Routledge & Kegan Paul).

McGarry, John and Brendan O'Leary (1996) *Explaining Northern Ireland* (Oxford: Blackwell).

McDowell, R. B. (1997) *Crisis and Decline: the Fate of the Southern Unionists* (Dublin: Lilliput Press).

McKeown, Michael (1986) *The Greening of a Nationalist* (Lucan, Co. Dublin: Murlough Press).

McLoughlin, Michael (1996) *Great Irish Speeches of the Twentieth Century* (Dublin: Poolbeg Press).

MacGréil, M. (1996) *Prejudice and Tolerance in Ireland Revisited* (Maynooth: Survey and Research Unit, St. Patrick's College).

McWilliams, Monica (1993) 'The church, the state and the women's movement in Northern Ireland' in Ailbhe Smyth (ed.) *Irish Women's Studies Reader* (Dublin: Attic Press).

McWilliams, Monica (1995), 'Struggling for peace and justice: reflections on women's activism in Northern Ireland', *Journal of Women's History*, 6: 4/7: 1, Winter/Spring 1995, pp. 13–39.

Mahon, E. and C. Conlon (1996) 'Legal abortions carried out in England on women normally resident in the Republic of Ireland', Appendix 21 in *Report of the Constitution Review Group* (Dublin: Stationery Office).

Mahon, Evelyn (1995) 'Ireland's policy machinery: the Ministry of State for Women's Affairs and Joint Oireachtas Committee for Women's Rights' in Amy Mazur and Dorothy McBride Stetson (eds) *Comparative State Feminism* (Thousand Oaks, Ca: Sage).

Mahon, Evelyn and Valerie Morgan (1998) 'State Feminism' in Yvonne Galligan, Eilís Ward and Rick Wilford (eds) *Contesting Politics: Women in Ireland, North and South* (Boulder, Co: Westview Press).

Mair, Peter (1993) 'The party system and party competition' in John Coakley and Michael Gallagher (eds) *Politics in the Republic of Ireland* (Dublin: Folens/PSAI Press) pp. 86–103.

Mankiw, N., D. Romer and D. Weil (1992) 'A contribution to the empirics of economic growth', *Quarterly Journal of Economics* 107(2).

Manning, Maurice (1978) 'Women in Irish national and local politics 1927–1977' in Margaret MacCurtain and Donnchadh Ó Corráin (eds), *Women in Irish Society: the Historical Dimension* (Dublin: Women's Press).

March, J. G. and J. P. Olsen (1984) 'The new institutionalism', *American Political Science Review* 78, pp. 734–49.

Marsh, D. and R. A. W. Rhodes (1992) *Policy Networks in British Government* (Oxford: Clarendon Press).

Marsh, M. (1991) 'Accident or design? Non-voting in Ireland', *Irish Political Studies*, 6, pp. 1–14.

Marsh, M. and R. Sinnott (1993) 'The voters: stability and change' in M. Gallagher and M. Laver (eds) *How Ireland Voted 1992* (Dublin: Folens/PSAI Press).

Maye, Brian (1993) *Fine Gael 1923–1987* (Dublin: Blackwater Press).

Mennell, Stephen (1997) 'A silent minority? Protestants as established and outsiders in the Republic' Lecture, Irish Psycho-Analytical Association, Newman House, Dublin, 5 December.

Milne, Kenneth (1966) *The Church of Ireland: a History* (Dublin: Association for the Promotion of Christian Knowledge).

Miller, Robert, Rick Wilford and Freda Donoghue (1996) *Women and Political Participation in Northern Ireland* (Aldershot: Avebury).

Mjoset, L. (1992) *The Irish Economy in a Comparative Institutional Perspective* Report No. 93. (Dublin: National Economic and Social Council).

Moxon-Browne, Edward (1986) 'Alienation: The case of Catholics in Northern Ireland', *Journal of Political Science*, 14, 1–2, pp. 74–88.

Munck, Ronnie (1993) *The Irish Economy: Results and Prospects* (London: Pluto Press).

Munger, Frank (1996) 'The legitimacy of opposition: the change of government in Ireland in 1932'. Paper prepared for delivery at the 1996 Annual Meeting of the American Political Science Association, New York City, September 6–10, 1996.

National Women's Council of Ireland (1997) *Beijing and Beyond: Achieving an effective platform for action – an independent report to the 4th UN World Conference on Women* (Dublin: NWCI).

Nelson, Sarah (1984) *Ulster's Uncertain Defenders: Loyalists and the Northern Ireland Conflict* (Belfast: Appletree).

NESC (1982) *A Review of Industrial Policy* NESC Report No. 64 (Dublin: National Economic and Social Council).

NESC (1986) *A Strategy for Development 1986–1990* NESC Report No. 83 (Dublin: National Economic and Social Council).

NESC (1989) *Ireland in the European Community: Performance, Prospects and Strategy*, Report No. 88 (Dublin: National Economic and Social Council).

NESC (1990) *A Strategy for the Nineties: Economic Stability and Structural Change*, Report No. 89 (Dublin: National Economic and Social Council).

NESC (1992) *The Impact of Reform of the Common Agricultural Policy*, Report No. 92 (Dublin: National Economic and Social Council).

NESC (1993) *A Strategy for Competitiveness, Growth and Employment*, Report No. 96 (Dublin: National Economic and Social Council).

NESC (1996) *Strategy into the 21st Century*, Report No. 99 (Dublin: National Economic and Social Council).

NESF (1996a) *Long-Term Unemployment Initiatives*, Forum Opinion No. 3. 1996 (Dublin: National Economic and Social Forum).

NESF (1996b) *Long-Term Unemployment*, Forum Report No. 5. 1996 (Dublin: National Economic and Social Forum).

NESF (1996c) *The National Anti-Poverty Strategy*, Forum Opinion No. 2. January 1996 (Dublin: National Economic and Social Forum).

NESF (1997a) *Early School Leavers and Youth Unemployment*, Forum Report No. 11. January 1997 (Dublin: National Economic and Social Forum).

NESF (1997b) *A Framework for Partnership: Enriching Strategic Consensus through Par-.ticipation*, Forum Report No. 16 (Dublin: National Economic and Social Forum).

Nolan, B. and T. Callan (eds) (1994) *Poverty and Policy in Ireland* (Dublin: Gill and Macmillan).

Nolan, B. and G. Hughes (1997) *Low Pay, the Earnings Distribution and Poverty in Ireland, 1987–1994* (Dublin: Economic and Social Research Institute).

Nolan B. and C. T. Whelan (1996) *Resources, Deprivation and Poverty* (Oxford: Clarendon Press).

Nolan, B., T. Callan, C. T. Whelan, and J. Williams (1994) *Poverty and Time: Perspectives on the Dynamics of Poverty*, Paper No. 166 (Dublin: Economic and Social Research Institute).

Northern Ireland (1997 and earlier) *Annual Abstract of Statistics* (Belfast: Department of Finance and Personnel).

Ó Broin, Leon (1985) *Protestant Nationalism in Revolutionary Ireland: the Stopford connection* (Dublin: Gill and Macmillan).

O' Connell, P. (forthcoming) 'Sick man or tigress?: The labour market in the Republic of Ireland', in R. Breen, A. Heath and C. T. Whelan (eds) *Ireland: North and South: Social Science Perspectives* (Oxford: Oxford University Press).

O' Connor, P. and S. Shortall (forthcoming) 'Does the border make the difference?: Variations in women's paid employment North and South', in R. Breen, A. Heath and C. T. Whelan (eds), *Ireland: North and South: Social Science Perspectives* (Oxford: Oxford University Press).

O'Brien, Brendan (1995) *The Long War: The IRA and Sinn Féin from Armed Struggle to Peace Talks* (Dublin: The O'Brien Press).

O'Brien, J. A. (1954) *The Vanishing Irish* (London: Allen and Unwin).

O'Clery, Conor (1996) *The Greening of the White House* (Dublin: Gill and Macmillan).

O'Clery, Conor (1997) *Daring Diplomacy: Clinton's Secret Search for Peace in Ireland* (Boulder: Roberts Rinehart).

O'Connell, P. and D. B. Rottman (1992) 'The Irish welfare state in comparative perspective' in J. H. Goldthorpe and C. T. Whelan (eds) *The Development of Industrial Society in Ireland* (Oxford: Oxford University Press).

O'Connor, Fionnuala (1993) *In Search of a State: Catholics in Northern Ireland* (Belfast: Blackstaff).

O'Danachar, Caoimhin (1962) 'The family in Irish tradition', *Christus Rex*, 16.

O'Donnell, R. (1991a) 'The Regional Issue', in R. O'Donnell (ed.) *Economic and Monetary Union* (Dublin: Institute of European Affairs).

O'Donnell, R. (1991b) 'The Internal Market', in P. Keatinge (ed.) *Ireland and EC Membership Evaluated* (London: Pinter).

O'Donnell, R. (1993), *Ireland and Europe: Challenges for a New Century* (Dublin: Economic and Social Research Institute).

O'Donnell, R. and C. O'Reardon (1996) 'Ireland's experiment in social partnership 1987–1996', Paper presented at COST A7 Workshop, Negotiated Economic and Social Governance and European Integration. Dublin. 24–25 May.

O'Donoghue, Freda and Paula Devine (1998) 'Is there a gender gap in political attitudes in Ireland?' in Yvonne Galligan, Eilís Ward and Rick Wilford (eds) *Contesting Politics: Women in Ireland, North and South* (Boulder, Co: Westview Press).

O'Donovan, Orla and Eilís Ward (1998) 'Networks of women's groups in the Republic of Ireland' in Yvonne Galligan, Eilís Ward and Rick Wilford (eds), *Contesting Politics: Women in Ireland, North and South* (Boulder, Co: Westview Press).

O'Farrell, P. N. (1980) 'Multinational enterprises and regional development: the Irish evidence', *Regional Studies*, 14, 2, pp. 141–50.

Ó Gráda, Cormac (1995) *Ireland: A New Economic History 1780–1939* (Oxford: Oxford University Press).

Ó Gráda, Cormac and Kevin O'Rourke (1995) 'Economic growth: performance and explanations' in J. W. O'Hagan (ed.) *The Economy of Ireland: Policy and Performance of a Small European Country* (London: Macmillan).

Ó Gráda, Cormac and Brendan Walsh (1995) 'Fertility and population in Ireland, North and South', *Population Studies* 49 (2), pp. 259–79.

O'Grady, T. (1992) 'Married to the state: A study of unmarried mother's allowance applicants'. Seminar paper presented to the Federation of Services to Unmarried Parents and their Children, Dublin, September 1992.

O'Hagan, J. W. (ed.) (1995) *The Economy of Ireland: Policy and Performance of a Small European Country* (London: Macmillan).

O'Halpin, E. (1993) 'Policy making', in J. Coakley and M. Gallagher (eds) *Politics in the Republic of Ireland* (Dublin: Folens and PSAI Press).

O'Hearn, D. (1989) 'The Irish case of dependency: an exception to the exceptions?' *American Sociological Review*, 54, pp. 578–96.

O'Leary, Brendan and John McGarry (1996) *The Politics of Antagonism: Understanding Northern Ireland* (second edn) (London: Athlone Press).

O'Mahony, P. (1997) *Mountjoy Prisoners: A Sociological and Criminological Profile* (Dublin: Department of Justice).

O'Malley, E. (1981) *Industrial Policy and Development: A Survey of the Literature from the Early 1960s* (Dublin: National Economic and Social Council).

O'Malley, E. (1989) *Industry and Economic Development: the Challenge for the Latecomer* (Dublin: Gill and Macmillan).

O'Malley, Eoin (1992) 'Problems of industrialization in Ireland', in J. H. Goldthorpe and C. T. Whelan (eds) *The Development of Industrial Society in Ireland* (Oxford: Oxford University Press) pp. 31–51.

O'Malley, Padraig (1997) *The Uncivil Wars: Ireland Today* (Boston: Beacon Press).

O'Sullivan, Dónal (1940) *The Irish Free State and its Senate: a Study in Contemporary Politics* (London, Faber and Faber).

O'Toole, F. (1993) 'Tax reform since the Commission on Taxation', paper to the SSISI, 9 December.

O'Toole, F. (1994) *Black Hole, Green Card: The Disappearance of Ireland* (Dublin: New Island Books).

O'Toole, F. (1995) *Meanwhile Back at the Ranch: the Politics of Irish Beef* (London: Vintage).

O'Toole, F. (1996) *The Ex-Isle of Erin* (Dublin: New Island Books).

O'Toole, F. (1997) *A Low-Income Perspective* (TCD/ Combat Poverty Agency).

O'Toole, F. (1998) 'EU provides a clearer context to define our old problems', *Irish Times*, 16 January.

OECD (1966) *Investment in Education. Report of the Survey Team Appointed by the Minister of Education in October 1966* (Dublin: Stationery Office).

OECD (1997) *Ireland 1997* (Paris: OECD Economic Surveys).

Offe, C. and V. Ronge (1982) 'Theses on the theory of the state', in A. Giddens and D. Held (eds) *Class, Power and Conflict* (London: Macmillan).

Osborne, R. D. and R. J. Cormack (1995) *Fair Shares? Employment, Unemployment and Economic Status* (Belfast: Fair Employment Commission).

Peace Watch Ireland (1997) *Looking Into the Abyss: Witnesses' Report from Garvaghy Road, Portadown, July 4–6, 1997* (Boston, MA: Peace Watch Ireland).

Plunkett, Horace (1904) *Ireland in the New Century* (London: John Murray).

Pollak, Andy (ed.) (1993) *A Citizens' Inquiry: The Opsahl Report on Northern Ireland* (Dublin: Lilliput).

Porter, Norman (1996) *Rethinking Unionism: An Alternative Vision for Northern Ireland* (Belfast: Blackstaff).

Przeworski, Adam (1991) *Democracy and the Market* (Cambridge: Cambridge University Press).

Przeworski, Adam (1993) *Capitalism and Social Democracy* (Cambridge: Cambridge University Press).

Przeworski, Adam (ed.) (1995) *Sustainable Democracy* (Cambridge: Cambridge University Press).

Putnam, Robert D. (1993) *Making Democracy Work* (Princeton: Princeton University Press).

Pyle, J. L. (1990) *The State and Women in the Economy: Lessons from Sex Discrimination in Ireland* (New York: State University of New York Press).

Randall, Vicky and Ailbhe Smyth (1987) 'Bishops and bailiwicks: obstacles to women's political participation in Ireland', *Economic and Social Review*, 18: 3, pp. 189–214.

Rees, Merlyn (1985) *Northern Ireland: A Personal Perspective* (London: Methuen).

Registrar General (1922–35) *Annual Reports of the Registrar General* (Dublin: Stationery Office).

Report of the Expert Commission on Integrating Tax and Social Welfare. June 1996 (Dublin: Stationery Office).

Report of the Task Force on Long-Term Unemployment (1995) Office of the Tanaiste (Dublin: Stationery Office).

Richey, Warren (1985) 'The NORAID Connection', *Christian Science Monitor* (international edition) 19–25 January.

Robinson, Lennox (1931) *Bryan Cooper* (London: Constable).

Robinson M. (1990) Inaugural Speech, Dublin Castle, 3 December.

Robinson M. (1995) 'Cherishing the Irish Diaspora', Address to the Houses of the Oireachtas, 2 February 1995.

Roche, W. K. (1997) 'Trade union membership in the Republic of Ireland' in T. V. Murphy and W. K. Roche (eds) *Irish Industrial Relations in Practice* (second edition) (Dublin: Oak Tree Press).

Rosaldo, R. (1989) *Culture and Truth: the Remaking of Social Analysis* (Boston: Beacon).

Rose, Richard (1971) *Governing Without Consent* (Boston, MA: Beacon Press).

Rowthorn, Bob and Naomi Wayne (1988) *Northern Ireland: The Political Economy of Conflict* (Cambridge: Polity Press).

Ruane, F. and F. O'Toole (1997) 'Taxation measures and policy', in J. W. O'Hagan (ed.) *The Economy of Ireland: Policy and Performance*, seventh (edn) (Dublin: IMI).

Ruane, Joseph and Jennifer Todd (1996) *The Dynamics of Conflict in Northern Ireland: Power, Conflict and Emancipation* (Cambridge: Cambridge University Press).

Ruane, Joseph and Jennifer Todd (1998) 'Irish nationalism and conflict in Northern Ireland' in David Miller (ed.) *Understanding Northern Ireland* (Harlow: Addison Wesley Longman).

Rumpf, Erhard (1977) *Nationalism and Socialism in Twentieth Century Ireland* (Liverpool: University Press).

Rutherford, Malcolm (1985) 'Dr FitzGerald and I', *Financial Times*, 22 February.

Sabel, Charles (1996) *Ireland: Local Partnerships and Social Innovation* (Paris: OECD).

Sacks, Paul M. (1970) 'Balliwicks, Locality, and Religion: Three Elements in an Irish Dáil Constituency Election', *Economic and Social Review*, 1, pp. 531–54.

Sacks, Paul (1976) *The Donegal Mafia: an Irish Political Machine* (New Haven: Yale University Press).

Sandford, C. (1993) *Successful Tax Reform* (Bath: Fiscal Publications).

Schmitt, David E. (1973) *The Irony of Irish Democracy: The Impact of Political Culture on Administrative and Democratic Political Development in Ireland* (Lexington, Mass: D. C. Heath).

Schultze, Kirsten E. (1997) 'The Northern Ireland Political Process: A Viable Approach to Conflict Resolution?', *Irish Political Studies*, 12, pp. 92–110.

Sexton, J. J. and P. J. O'Connell (eds) (1996) *Labour Market Studies: Ireland*. (Luxembourg: European Commission) December.

Sheehan, B. (1996) *Crisis, Strategic Revaluation and the Re-Emergence of Tripartism in Ireland* (Dublin: UCD Graduate School of Business, unpublished thesis).

Sheehy, Michael (1955) *Divided We Stand* (London: Faber).

Sinnott, R. (1995) *Irish Voters Decide: Voting Behaviour in Elections and Referendums Since 1918* (Manchester: Manchester University Press).

Sinnott, R. and B. Whelan (1992) 'Turnout in second order elections: the case of EP elections in Dublin 1984 and 1989', *Economic and Social Review*, 23, pp. 147–66.

Skocpol, T. (1985) 'Bringing the state back in: strategies of analysis in current research', in P. B. Evans, D. Rueschemeyer and T. Skocpol (eds) *Bringing the State Back In* (Cambridge: Cambridge University Press).

Smith, David J. (1987) *Equality and Inequality in Northern Ireland, part 3* (London: Policy Studies Institute).

Smith, Henry Stooks (1973) *The Parliaments of England* (new edition) (London: Harvester).

Smyth, Ailbhe, (1993) 'The women's movement in the Republic of Ireland 1970–1990' in Ailbhe Smyth (ed.) *Irish Women's Studies Reader* (Dublin: Attic Press).

Smyth, Emer (1997) 'Labour market structures and women's employment in the Republic of Ireland' in Anne Byrne and Madeleine Leonard (eds) *Women and Irish Society: a Sociological Reader* (Belfast: Beyond the Pale Publications).

Smyth, Michael (1993) 'The public sector and the economy', in P. Teague (ed.) *The Economy of Northern Ireland: Perspectives for Structural Change* (London: Lawrence and Wishart) pp. 121–40.

Soskice, D. (1990) 'Wage determination: the changing role of institutions in advanced industrialised countries', *Oxford Review of Economic Policy*, 6, 4, pp. 36–61.

Stanford, W. B. (1944) *A Recognised Church? The Church of Ireland in Eire* (Dublin: Association for Promoting Christian Knowledge).

Stephens, Meic (1976) *Linguistic Minorities in Western Europe* (Llandysul, Dyfed: Gomer Press).

Stigler, George J. (1973) 'General Economic Conditions and National Elections', *American Economic Review*, 63, pp. 160–67.

Sullivan, John L., James Pierson and George E. Marcus (1982) *Political Tolerance and American Democracy* (Chicago: University of Chicago Press).

Sundberg, Jan (1985) *Svenskhetens dilemma i Finland: Finlandssvenskarnas samling och splittring under 1900-tallet* (Helsingfors: Finska Vetenskaps-Societeten).

Sutton, Malcolm (1994) *An Idea of Deaths from the Conflict in Ireland 1969–1993* (Belfast: Beyond the Pale Publications).

Tánaiste, Office of the (1997) Report of the Task Force on Violence Against Women, Pn3831 (Dublin: Stationery Office).

Tannam, Etain (1996) 'The European Union and business cross-border co-operation: the case of Northern Ireland and the Republic of Ireland', *Irish Political Studies*, 11, pp. 103–29.

Taoiseach, Department of the (1997) *Sharing In Progress: National Anti-Poverty Strategy* (Dublin: Stationery Office).

Teague, Paul (ed.) (1993) *The Economy of Northern Ireland* (London: Lawrence and Wishart).

Todd, Jennifer (1987) 'Two traditions in Unionist political culture', *Irish Political Studies*, 2, pp. 1–26.

Todd, Jennifer (1995) 'Equality, plurality, democracy: justifications of proposed constitutional settlements of the Northern Ireland conflict', *Ethnic and Racial Studies*, vol. 18, no. 4, pp. 818–36.

Townsend P. (1979) *Poverty in the United Kingdom* (Harmondsworth: Penguin).

United Nations (1995) *World Population Prospects. The 1994 Revision* (New York: United Nations).

Viney, Michael (1962) *The Five Per Cent: a Survey of Protestants in the Republic* (Dublin: *Irish Times*).

von Rauch, Georg (1974) *The Baltic States: the years of independence. Estonia, Latvia, Lithuania 1917–1940* (London: C Hurst).

Walker, Brian M. (ed.) (1978) *Parliamentary Election Results in Ireland, 1801–1922* (Dublin, Royal Irish Academy).

Wallis R. and Bruce S. (1992) 'Secularisation: the Orthodox Model' in S. Bruce (ed.) *Religion and Modernisation* (Oxford: Oxford University Press).

Walsh, Brendan (1970) *Religion and Demographic Behaviour in Ireland* (Dublin, Economic and Social Research Institute).

Whelan, Christopher T. (1994) 'Work values' in Christopher T. Whelan (ed.) *Values and Social Change in Ireland* (Dublin: Gill and Macmillan).

Whelan C. T. (ed.) (1994) *Values and Social Change in Ireland* (Dublin: Gill and Macmillan).

Whelan C. T. (1996) 'Marginalization, deprivation and fatalism in the Republic of Ireland: class and underclass perspectives', *European Sociological Review*, 12, 1, pp. 33–51.

Whelan, Christopher T., Richard Breen and Brendan J. Whelan (1994) 'Industrialisation, Class Formation and Social Mobility in Ireland' in J. H. Goldthorpe and C. T. Whelan (eds) *The Development of Industrial Society in Ireland* (Oxford: Oxford University Press) pp. 105–28.

Whelan, Christopher T. and Tony Fahey (1994) 'Marriage and the family' in Christopher T. Whelan (ed.) *Values and Social Change in Ireland* (Dublin: Gill and Macmillan) pp. 45–81.

Whelan, C. T., D. F. Hannan and S. Creighton (1991) *Unemployment, Poverty and Psychological Distress* (Dublin: Economic and Social Research Institute).

White, Jack (1975) *Minority Report: the Protestant Community in the Irish Republic* (Dublin: Gill and Macmillan).

Whyte J. (1980) *Church and State in Modern Ireland, 1923–1979* (second edition) (Dublin: Gill and Macmillan).

Whyte, John (1991) *Interpreting Northern Ireland* (Oxford: Clarendon Press).

Wichert, Sabine (1991) *Northern Ireland Since 1945* (London: Longman).

Wilcox, Clyde (1991) 'Support for gender equality in West Europe: a longitudinal analysis', *European Journal of Political Research*, 20, pp. 127–47.

Wilford, Rick and Yvonne Galligan (1998) 'Gender and party politics in Northern Ireland' in Yvonne Galligan, Eilís Ward and Rick Wilford (eds) *Contesting Politics: Women in Ireland, North and South* (Boulder, Co: Westview Press).

Wilson, Andrew J. (1995) *Irish America and the Ulster Conflict, 1968–1995* (Washington: Catholic University of America Press).

Wilson, Robin (1997) *Continentally Challenged: Securing Northern Ireland's Place in the European Union* (Belfast: Democratic Dialogue).

Wright, Frank (1987) *Northern Ireland: A Comparative Analysis* (Dublin: Gill and Macmillan).

Young, Alwyn (1995) 'The Tyranny of Numbers: Confronting the statistical realities of the East Asian growth experience', *Quarterly Journal of Economics*, August, pp. 641–80.

Index